Through the Ranks on the Southern

A career in the Nationalised railway industry

by
Brian W. Aynsley

THE OAKWOOD PRESS

British Library Cataloguing in Publication Data
A Record for this book is available from the British Library
ISBN 0 85361 597 7

Typeset by Oakwood Graphics.
Repro by Ford Graphics, Ringwood, Hants.
Printed by Inkon Printers Ltd, Yateley, Hants.

This view looking down onto the Waterloo end of Surbiton station from Winthrop House shows, in the foreground, rebuilt 'West Country' class 4-6-2 No. 34013 *Okehampton*, in the background is an unrebuilt member of the same class, No. 34006 *Bude*.　　*Philip J. Gillmour*

Title page: A night time photograph of Guildford shed in 1956; amongst the locomotives visible are, *from left to right*, 'T9' class 4-4-0 No. 30338, 'Q1' class 0-6-0 No. 33018, 'U' class Nos. 31611 and 31622, 'Black Motor' '700' class No. 30325, 'U' class No. 31631 and 'Q1' class No. 33004.　　　　　　　　　　　　　　　　　　　　　　　*British Railways*

Front cover: Bulleid 'Q1' class 0-6-0 No. 33018 at Guildford on 21st June, 1964.
Rear cover, top: BR Standard class '5' 4-6-0 No. 73029, the last steam engine to be worked on by the author, at Waterloo on 6th August, 1965.
Rear cover, bottom: 4TC No. 8022 is seen leaving Southampton on 13th April, 1988.
　　　　　　　　　　　　　　　　　　　　　　　　　　　　　　　(All) B.J. Eagles

Published by The Oakwood Press (Usk), P.O. Box 13, Usk, Mon., NP15 1YS.
E-mail:　oakwood-press@dial.pipex.com
Website:　www.oakwood-press.dial.pipex.com

Contents

BR Standard class '4' 2-6-0 No. 76066 shunts a freight train as 4EPB electric multiple unit No. 5305 approaches Guildford with the 8.52 am Waterloo-Guildford service.

Gerald T. Robinson

Introduction

This book is based on my career with 'British Railways' from 1956 to 1995, a career spanning 39 years and moving through from Victorian steam locomotive technology to the age of computers. I apologise for any inaccuracies or discrepancies which may appear in the text, but it should be understood that much of the material for this book is drawn from memory and it may be that my impressions of events differ from that of other people involved. Nevertheless it is written in good faith and I believe it to be an accurate account.

My first contact with steam operated railways was in 1952 when I was sent to a convalescent school at Ventnor on the Isle Wight for health reasons. I stayed there from October 1952 until April 1953, part of the treatment was walking in the fresh air on the downs above the town. The line from Shanklin passed through a long tunnel under the downs, emerging shortly before Ventnor station which appeared to stand on a ledge cut into the side of the hill. I viewed the operations at the station with fascination from the hill above; my home village of Cobham in Surrey was on the electrified line between Surbiton and Guildford and I had never seen steam engines working before.

My interest in steam locomotives, inspired by the little tanks puffing about under the cliff at Ventnor, continued on my return home when I discovered that at Weybridge, about four miles distant, there was a main line frequently used by steam engines. I would cycle there and watch all day as the mainliners roared by, the 'Atlantic Coast Express' and the 'Bournemouth Belle' were two trains which caught my imagination, the latter consisted of all Pullman cars which appeared to be the ultimate in luxury.

About 1954 I discovered that there was a loco depot at Guildford and after that I spent many happy hours watching the operations in and around that station. I was invited onto the footplate of an engine standing at the station and I knew then that when I left school I wanted to work on steam locomotives, much to the consternation of my headmaster who had me labelled for an office job. When I left school after the summer term in 1956 I attended an interview at Guildford loco; my parents thought that it was a passing fancy on my part but thought that it was best to let me work it out of my system. Perhaps I might then settle down to work at the Vickers Armstrong aircraft factory with my father.

The author driving a 'Crompton' (later class '33') in 1967.
Author's Collection

Chapter One

Cleaner and Passed Cleaner:
1956 to 1959

I attended the interview in August 1956 in the shedmaster's office at Guildford. Mr George Stovold was the shedmaster at that time, he conducted a simple test in the three Rs, explained the duties which I would be required to perform, the footplate line of promotion and career prospects; he then said that he considered me to be suitable and if I wanted the job I could start on 3rd September. I agreed to this and was instructed to report to the general office at 9.00 am on that date. I presented myself at the appointed time and was issued with a lot of books and pamphlets which I was told to study carefully, especially the British Railways Rule Book, on which I would have to pass an examination before being allowed out on the track.

I was then taken to the stores where I was issued with a set of overalls and a shiny-topped cap. The next stop was the cleaners 'cabin' where I was introduced to Mr Foan, the chargehand cleaner, who showed me around the depot and instructed me in safety requirements. He then handed me a bucket of paraffin and some cloths and assigned me to a gang of cleaners, the oldest lad being given the job of looking after me. I was lucky to have this boy as a guardian on my first day; it transpired that he was held in high esteem by the other cleaners and I was spared the usual initiation ceremony which consisted of debagging the luckless initiate and smearing him with thick superheater oil, a most uncomfortable experience it must have been.

I must have stood out like a sore thumb in my new overalls, I was picked on by all and sundry to carry out joke errands, some of which I fell for. The stores clerk spent a lot of time pretending to look for the key to wind up the turntable when I was sent to ask for it. After my clothing had been washed a few times the colour faded and I became less conspicuous, and I myself became one of those who played pranks on newcomers.

We cleaned the engines with paraffin which was spread about with gusto, wiping it off with a dry cloth; we would unofficially add a little lubricating oil to the paraffin which made the black livery shine like new. The junior lads always got the dirtiest jobs, such as cleaning the motion on engines with Stephenson link motion between the frames, or the wheels of any engine. Sometimes we would clean the dirtiest parts with the 'Weaver' plant, a strange machine which fired a jet of high pressure steam and caustic soda to loosen thick accumulations of oily dirt. In charge of the 'Weaver' was a man called Jack who told us that he had a silver bolt in his leg because of a war wound. If he became upset by our persistent pranks he would hold his knee and moan 'Oh me bolt', but instead of the sympathy which this display was supposed to invoke it just made us laugh. We led poor Jack a dog's life, playing all sorts of tricks on him hoping to provoke him to perform his 'Oh me bolt' routine.

Mr Foan was a nice old man, he always referred to us tender youngsters as 'Bloody yips', I think it must have been a term of endearment. As I became established I was allowed to help out with other jobs in the shed, such as fire lighting and steam raising. To light a fire you had to spread coal over the grate,

Engine cleaners at Guildford loco in 1956. The author *(left)* with George Michie.

Author's Collection

leaving a space in the centre, into this space were placed large pieces of dry wood and cloths soaked in paraffin. A lighted cloth was then thrown in and when the wood was well alight large pieces of coal were placed on top. It was then a matter of waiting as it would be several hours before enough steam was produced to work the blower to give draught to the fire and make it really hot. I would also assist the fitters or the boiler washers at times, it was all valuable experience, giving me a good idea of the functions of the various parts of the engines.

Another job I was frequently given was that of 'Call boy', this involved walking for miles in the Guildford area delivering notices of late alterations to drivers' and firemen's duties. Sometimes I would have to call up the fitters belonging to the breakdown gang if they were required in emergency. Not many of the staff were on the telephone in those days and I sometimes spent most of the day walking about. It was very frustrating to arrive after a long walk only to find nobody in or a man standing at his front door and telling me that he was not in, not an infrequent happening. After a few fruitless trips I got wise, I brought my bicycle to work with me which made it a lot easier. I came to know the Guildford area intimately and found some lovely places where I could relax in the spare time created by the use of my bike.

Once I got to know the people working around the shed and was accepted by them, I found the loco depot a happy place to work, it was also very interesting as I learned more about the different types of engine and their history. In fact , Guildford loco in 1956 was like a working museum with some of the engines dating back to the 1880s and 90s. The shed was built as a half-roundhouse but No. 1 to 7 roads had been extended and this section was known as the new shed, the remaining section was of course known as the old shed. Each road in the new shed held about three tender engines, those in the old shed held either one tender engine or two tank engines. Generally, the new shed was used as a running shed and the old section for repairs and washouts, etc.

The wide variety of motive power at the depot was due to the development of railways in the area where three different companies jockeyed for position. First, of course, was the London & South Western Railway (LSWR) which arrived in Guildford in 1845 from Woking, then the South Eastern Railway (SER) built the line from Reigate to Shalford Junction and from Ash Junction to Reading in 1849, finally came the London Brighton & South Coast Railway (LBSCR) which built a branch from Horsham to Guildford in 1865. Although when I started work these companies had been dead for many years, the three divisions of the Southern Region still kept the locomotives built by their constituent companies. Although the 'U' and 'N' classes were ubiquitous most of the older engines tended to stay on 'their patch'. The fact that Guildford was connected to all three companies made it a unique place for engines and men. The engine crews there worked on the old SER and LBSCR engines as well as LSWR veterans. Men from the Central and Eastern divisions sometimes referred to South Western men as 'Drummond Men'. They did not get on well with engines built by that great engineer so the term was probably meant to be derogatory, however, the South Western men were fond of his engines.

I hope that the preceding text will help the reader to understand the environment which this 15-year-old lad had entered into. Over the years I had

Engine cleaners at Guilford in 1956. *From left to right*: Bill Symons, Sammy Rowe, George Michie, the author, John Ashby and David Bryant.   *Author's Collection*

The author stands on the running plate of 'M7' class 'Motor Tank' No. 30124 in 1957.
Author's Collection

many trials and tribulations and had it not been for the interest and the solid feeling of belonging then perhaps my resolve would have weakened and I would have given the job up, I came close to it several times.

In early 1957 I attended a course of instruction in the duties of a fireman, this included rules and regulations, the principles of steam traction, methods of firing to locomotives and preparation and disposal duties. The course was held in the 'Ambulance hut' at Guildford and lasted for three weeks. In retrospect it was amazing that so much could be absorbed in so short a time, but to my delight I passed the exam at the end of it, four out of the 12 attending the course failed. I was now qualified to act as a fireman and I had a new title, 'Passed cleaner', which placed me above the common or garden cleaner. My pride was soon to take a knock, but that was a little later, for the time being I was qualified as a fireman and whilst carrying out my normal duties I waited eagerly for my first firing turn. Normally a newly qualified fireman would be booked on various duties as 'Third man' to gain experience but due to a shortage of staff at the time I did not benefit from this arrangement.

Until now I had worked from 8.00 am to 4.00 pm on Monday to Friday and 8.00 am to 12 noon on Saturday, but in my new position I worked three shifts, 12.01 to 8.00 am, 8.00 am to 4.00 pm and 2.00 to 10.00 pm, with a rest day once a fortnight. I was available for firing duties at any time of the day unlike the firemen who were shown on the roster, they came under the conditions agreed by the trade unions and could only be moved two hours either way of their rostered time. The only condition which applied to passed cleaners was that they must have 12 hours rest between firing duties, the same as all other train crew personnel. Even this condition was exploited to the full by the List clerk; I would sometimes start the week at 10.00 pm and work back with 12 hour rest periods, finishing the week at two of three o'clock in the morning.

My first outing came a week or so after passing out. I was on the 8.00 am cleaning shift when the running foreman sent for me. A Redhill driver had travelled to Guildford to work a train back to Redhill but his fireman had not turned up and I was to replace him. I told the driver that this was my first time out on the track and he was very good about it and told me not to worry as he would make sure that I did the right things. We left the shed with a 'Q' class engine and set off for the down goods yard to pick up the train, this consisted of about 20 wagons of general freight for intermediate stations to Redhill. I was really excited as we left the yard, it was the first time I had been through the tunnel on an engine. We turned off at Shalford Junction which was just beyond the tunnel and called at Shalford yard to put off and pick up, then on to Chilworth and then Gomshall where we spent some time shunting and waiting for another train to pass us by, then over the hill and down to Dorking Town. To my dismay the missing fireman was waiting on the platform there and that was the end of my first trip. I travelled back to Guildford unable to tell my friends that I had been to Redhill; we had all heard about the place from the firemen and we all hoped to be the first in our group to go there.

One of the most important duties for a fireman was preparing the engine before leaving the shed, it could be the difference between a good trip and a bad one. The first job was to spread the fire evenly over the firebox and turn the

An aerial view of Guildford station and engine shed.

blower on a little to give a gentle draught to the fire. While the fire was warming up we would collect all the required tools and equipment, all these items were supposed to be locked in the tool boxes on the engine but invariably they were missing. The only way to collect a full set of tools was to rob the other engines in the shed. Having gathered all the equipment we would then go to the stores to pick up the ration of lubricating oil and superheater oil, the former being to oil all the bearings on the engine and the latter for lubricating the cylinders. It was the driver's job to 'oil' the engine.

The next task at Guildford loco was to collect a bucket of pebbles, which were spread over the fire before it was built up. This was because the depot stood under a tall cliff and on top of which were houses, and we were not allowed to make smoke in this location, so the depot was supplied with 'Soft Welsh' steam coal which gave off very little smoke. The trouble was that it contained a lot of iron and the clinker formed would melt and run between the fire bars so inhibiting free burning. Once there it was very difficult to dislodge but the pebbles had the effect of weakening the clinker formation making it easier to break and remove. Having spent some time on these various tasks the fire would be even and bright, and ready to be built up prior to leaving. The type of fire to be made depended on the shape of the firebox and the duties to be performed.

Another important job was disposal at the end of the duty. On the Southern Region it was the fireman's job to take the clinker out of the fire when disposing of the engine, he also had to clean the ash from the smokebox and ashpan. The method of cleaning the fire was, with a long 'clinker' shovel, to move the good fire to one side of the box leaving the clinker exposed on the other side. This was then broken up with a heavy dart and removed with the clinker shovel, then the fire was moved to the clean side and the operation repeated. This was extremely hot work in the summer. Disposal was always referred to as 'Squaring up' and one of the worst engines to square up was the 'Lord Nelson' class, the firebox on these engines was about 11 feet long and it dropped away steeply at the front making it very difficult to get the clinker out. The clinker shovel was about 12 feet long and if it got too hot it would buckle and the fireman would have to do a bit of blacksmithery to get it straight again. Another hard disposal was the 'Q1' class, mainly due to the restricted space on the footplate. Strangely, the 'West Country' class had a trapdoor in the centre of the grate through which the clinker was passed to hoppers at the side of the engine and onto the ground, whilst the 'Merchant Navy' class with a larger grate area had no such arrangement; the fire had to be cleaned as on more conventional types, but at least they had a short firebox.

It was a real treat at that time to get an engine fitted with a 'drop grate' as on the BR Standard classes and the converted 'West Country' and 'Merchant Navy' classes. I thought that it was the best invention ever, you could either release one catch and just rock the grate to break up the clinker or release both catches, the grate section then turned vertical, dropping the clinker and/or fire into the pit, a real fireman's friend.

My worst experience of this period came in the summer of 1957, shortly after I had passed out. It was a steaming hot day and the duty involved relieving a freight train from Feltham at Woking, putting off in the yard then working a

'U' class 2-6-0 No. 31638 leaves Guildford's platform 5 with the 10.04 am departure for Redhill on 26th April, 1962. A Maunsell 'S15' class 4-6-0 blows off, while standing in platform 1 with a ballast train.   *R.S. Greenwood*

An 'N' class 2-6-0 arrives at Guildford with the 5.31 pm Redhill-Reading train on 26th July, 1963.
          G.D. King

general goods train to Guildford, calling at Worplesdon yard *en route*. On arrival at Guildford depot we had to 'square up' the 'Q1' class that we had brought in and then dispose of five more engines, a 'Jumbo' ('0395' class), a 'Black Motor' ('700' class), a 'Monty' ('U' class), a 'Vulcan' ('C2X' class) and another 'Charlie' ('Q1' class). Being rather inexperienced I made hard work of it and when I had finished one locomotive the next one was waiting for me. My driver had disappeared after checking the first engine over and I had no idea where he had gone to. I worked all day continuously in the searing heat and as I started work on the last one I began to feel faint; having moved the good fire to one side in readiness for removing the clinker I was unable to pull the clinker shovel out of the firebox.

I laboriously climbed down from the footplate and staggered slowly from the coal stage where I had been working to the loco office. I practically collapsed on the running foreman's desk as I tried to explain what I had been doing. The foreman sent me to the drivers' cabin and asked another fireman to make me some tea. As I drank the tea and ate my sandwiches I began to feel a little better and gradually my strength returned. When the foreman found my driver he really read him the riot act and told him in no uncertain terms that he considered him to be the most stupid and inconsiderate person he had met in a long time. I agreed with him but said nothing. After I had recovered I went back to the engine and finished the disposal, never again did I allow myself to work so long and hard without rest and refreshment.

A few days later I was booked to work a proper running duty. I was warned by several firemen that the driver I was to work with was a bit of a tyrant who liked everything to be in apple pie order and did not like to hear his engine 'blowing off' as he considered it a waste of fuel. I decided that I would come to work early that day so as to have things tidy before my driver arrived, this would create a good impression. I arrived half an hour early and set to work, I cleaned the boiler front and swept up all the dust on the footplate after preparing the engine (an 'M7' tank). When I was satisfied I went to have a wash and pick up some things from the stores.

On my return I found the steam gauge reading rather high and not wanting any blowing off I closed the damper. From under the engine came a stream of choice expletives and my driver climbed out of the pit his previously spotless overalls covered in oil and dirt. He was furious. Apparently he had arrived during my absence and gone under the engine to oil the axle. To make it easier for himself he had sat on the damper flap, of course when I closed the flap he fell straight into the pit. He hardly spoke to me for the rest of the day, so much for my efforts at creating a good impression. Still I have had many a good laugh about it since.

I did not do much cleaning after that and when I was booked cleaning I usually helped the shed staff with various jobs. We passed cleaners did not work many Guildford duties but were booked 'on loan' to other depots to cover their shortages. It was excellent experience and for the next year or so I travelled over most of the South Western division and parts of others, I also worked a little on the Western Region. The depots I went on loan to were Nine Elms, Stewarts Lane, Feltham, Reading (Southern), Redhill, Basingstoke, Fratton, Eastleigh and once to Horsham.

BR Standard class '5' 4-6-0s are being prepared for duty at Nine Elms depot on 28th June, 1966.
M.S. Stokes

The last days of steam at Nine Elms with 'Merchant Navy' class Pacifics Nos. 35028 *Clan Line* and 35008 *Orient Line* standing outside the shed in July 1967.   *Leslie Sandler*

Nine Elms, Lambeth, London

At Nine Elms I was employed mainly on preparation and disposal (P&D) duties. It was hard work but I gained experience on the larger types of engine which did not normally work in the Guildford area. The largest engines to come to my home depot were the three of class 'H15' which were rebuilt from the Drummond 'F13' class. They could not turn on the table at Guildford due to their size and had to be taken around the triangle at Addlestone Junction to turn. They were based at Salisbury and worked the stone trains up to Woking and back, for some reason they were known as the 'City' breed. At Nine Elms I worked on 'Lord Nelsons' , 'King Arthurs, 'Merchant Navy' and 'West Country' class locomotives.

The shed at Nine Elms was enormous, there were about 25 sidings there, each siding could hold about 10 engines although they were not all under cover. There was a steep gradient down from the main line at 'Loco Junction' to the coal hopper and drivers had to take great care when entering the depot; in the other direction it was sometimes extremely difficult to climb the gradient when leaving the depot, especially if it was raining. I used to detest going to Nine Elms as it was a dirty old place and I was only given the lowest type of work.

One night however, my luck changed. I had gone to Nine Elms for a P&D job but when I arrived the foreman told me that a Guildford driver was there to work a special but his fireman was absent, so I was to take his place. I found driver Jack Cook and he informed me that we were to work the 2.55 am special train to Salisbury. I was delighted as I had never been to Salisbury before and to work an express train on my first trip was really something special. We were booked a 'Merchant Navy' class and as we walked across the shed, Jack asked, 'Have you worked on these big engines before'? 'Yes', I replied with confidence, well I had prepared and disposed them many times. 'Good', said he, 'Because I have never been on one before'. My confidence disappeared like a bucket of steam but having stuck my neck out there was no going back, this was going to be a real baptism by fire. My delight turned to dread of what was in store for me.

I told the driver that I had not been to Salisbury before and he said, 'Don't worry son, you just keep her steaming and I will tell you when to stop firing'. After preparing the engine we left for Waterloo. I had mixed feelings about the trip, on the one hand I was excited about working an express for the first time but on the other hand I was afraid that due to my inexperience I would make a hash of it. What a combination, a driver who said he had never worked on a 'Merchant Navy' before and a 16-year-old boy who had hardly done anything before and had no idea where our destination was, geographically. I need not have worried, I fired for all I was worth and the engine responded by steaming at full pressure all the time.

We left Waterloo with 10 coaches and a luggage van and I have never in my life, before or since, been so exhilarated and terrified all at the same time. We really thundered along and as the night was pitch dark I had no idea where we were or how far we had to go. The driver called out: 'Andover coming up, you can stop firing now'. I looked out but could see nothing because I had been looking at the fire; as my eyes became accustomed to the dark I could see lights in the distance and we passed through Andover at a terrific speed. The driver said that it was about 100 mph but that may have been an exaggeration on his part. When we arrived at Salisbury I was feeling very satisfied with myself and my driver said that I had done a good job, then I opened the fire hole door and we saw a veritable mountain of white hot fire. 'What are we going to do with that lot?' said the driver, I didn't know so I said nothing. I uncoupled the engine from the train and we ran into the loco depot. While we were wondering what to do with all that fire a fireman came up to us and said, 'The foreman asked if you would put her right for a trip for Wilton'. My driver readily agreed, phew!, what a let off. We went home on the cushions (as passengers), both well satisfied with the night's work.

An interesting point about this trip was that it was the only time that I worked on an unconverted 'Merchant Navy' class outside the shed. At other depots I performed a wide variety of local running duties and worked over many small branch lines which unfortunately no longer exist.

Fratton, Portsmouth

In the summer some of the firemen from Fratton would go on loan to the Isle of Wight and the passed cleaners from Guildford would perform their duties at Fratton. I worked a lot of 'Brighton' engines there which was a change to those I normally worked on. Most of these locomotives were fitted with Westinghouse air brakes, the compressed air being supplied by a steam driven 'donkey pump'. These pumps were apt to stop without warning and there was a special procedure to restart them;, you hit the side of the pump with a big hammer. I don't think that it did the pump much good but it inevitably worked.

The 'Terrier' tanks ('A1X' class) were quite common at Fratton and I spent a lot of time on them. They were a very small engine and as I was six feet tall, I could only stand up properly in the middle of the footplate. It was very difficult to take coal from the bunker and turn with the shovel to the firehole door, luckily they had a correspondingly small firebox so it was not necessary to throw the coal very hard. I worked a 'Terrier' on the Hayling Island branch one day. My driver was generally known by his nickname, 'Lofty', and for good reason as he was about six foot six tall, you can imagine the problems we had. We overcame them with a simple shift system: when I was firing he would stand outside the cab and vice versa when he had to use the controls. I stood outside as we passed over Langston bridge, this was a rickety, wooden trestle bridge which crossed Langston harbour onto the island. It had a swinging section in the middle to allow larger boats to pass through, it was an unnerving experience and one that I would not want to repeat. I never worked on that line again so the situation never arose.

The shed at Fratton was a true roundhouse with a turntable in the middle of the building although the building was actually square, but that is splitting hairs. Behind the shed was a concrete installation which had formerly held the large fuel tanks when some of the Southern engines had been converted to oil burners in about 1947 (a short-lived experiment).

I also worked on the Fareham to Gosport branch and up the Meon Valley line as far as Droxford. The middle section of this line between Droxford and Farringdon had been closed and lifted some years before but goods trains still ran to Droxford with coal and sugar beet traffic and from Alton to Farringdon with coal and grain traffic. All these local jobs were worked with 'Vulcans' ('C2X' class engines).

I had a nasty experience one day when working a sugar beet train from Lavant on the Chichester to Midhurst branch. The line was closed from Lavant to Midhurst, only the section at the Chichester end was still used. On this section there was a very steep gradient towards the junction with the main line. We had stopped at the top of the bank and I went back to pin down the brake levers on the 10 wagons which our train consisted of, we had no 'fitted' stock on the train. As we descended the incline towards the junction the driver found that he was unable to hold the train back, we were out of control. At the junction was a set of catch points and it looked as if we would be derailed, the driver was sounding a series of short blasts on the whistle PIP-PIP-PIP-PIP. It was a relief as we approached the catch points to see them move over to the closed position, it was a near thing.

I worked several trains from Portsmouth to Salisbury during this period. That was a lovely trip with eight coaches hauled by a 'Monty' ('U' class), my favourite type of engine. It was an interesting route to work with many ups and downs and curves, it passed through some lovely countryside and also some dense urban areas especially around the Southampton area.

A 1940s view in the roundhouse at Fratton with, *from left to right,* 'Q1' class 0-6-0 No. C10, 'A1X' class 0-6-0T No. 2640, 'M7' class 0-4-4T No. 54 and 'S11' class 4-4-0 No. 402.

R.S. McNaught

A general view of Feltham shed in pre-Nationalisation days.

Maunsell 'S15' class 4-6-0 at Feltham, with a Bulleid 'Q1' class 0-6-0 lurking in the background, in May 1955.   *Brian Morrison*

One day on arrival at Fratton the foreman told me, 'You are on the bug', meaning the shunting engine on the yard. The engine was a little 'Terrier' and when I arrived the driver was already there. I climbed onto the footplate and said 'Good morning driver'. He made no reply, he was an old man and I thought that he may be a little deaf so I spoke a little louder, 'GOOD MORNING DRIVER', still no reply. For more than an hour I worked in silence until the driver turned to me and said, 'What is the highest number in Commercial Road?' 'I don't know', I replied, at which he burst into laughter and said, 'It is the twelve on the Guildhall clock'. He thought that was really funny and after that he talked all day. I did meet some strange people in my travels.

Feltham

Feltham was another interesting depot to work at, the work there was all freight and many of the turns which I worked were on transfer services from Feltham marshalling yard to other similar establishments on other Regions. I went to Neasden on the old Great Central line out of Marylebone, Willesden on the LNWR main line out of Euston, Brent on the Midland line out of St Pancras (mainly coal traffic there), Hither Green on the South Eastern division of the Southern Region; on one occasion I went to Temple Mills on the Eastern Region. The yard there was gigantic and to me in my teens a completely baffling place.

The big 'H16' 4-6-2 tanks were often used on these services as well as 'S15' and 'Q1' classes. The 'H16' engines were known as 'Green Tanks' and I believe that they were painted green at one time although when I worked on them they were painted black. The routes to West and North London were mostly uphill from Feltham which was lucky as many of the trains in that direction were empty, those in the opposite direction were generally loaded more heavily. On the outward trip we would struggle up the bank to Acton Wells Junction and on the return trip it was a struggle to keep control on the descent.

I also worked many of the local freight services in the Feltham area and came to know the suburban routes quite well. Although I still did my share of P&D work it was not as hard as the Nine Elms duties but it was still heavy work. The shed at Feltham was a long straight building with six roads. It was possible to leave the shed at either end, each road held about eight large tender engines and there was a tall 'coal hopper' on the service roads outside the shed. The engines there were mainly 'S15s', both 500 and 800 types, 'Q1s', 'H16' and 'G16' eight-coupled 'humping tanks' for use in the marshalling yard, although these were being replaced at that time by 350 hp diesel shunters. There were also some smaller tender engines such as '700' class ('Black Motors') and '0395' class ('Jumbos') plus a few odd small tanks.

Feltham yard covered a large area and it was about a mile long, stretching from Hounslow Junction in the east to Feltham station in the west. There were two sections in the marshalling yard, 'Up' and 'Down' and each section was in two parts, 'Arrival' and 'Departure'. Trains arriving in the Up Arrival section were pushed over the hump and sorted into the various sidings in the Up Departure section, The same applied for the down side. There was a large wagon repair shop in the yard, this was probably needed as there were no mechanical retarders between the humps and the departure sections, the only control over descending wagons was by means of men known as 'Brake chasers'. These men carried a 'brake stick' which was something like a square baseball bat; if the wagons were required to be stopped short of other vehicles in the siding the brake chaser would run beside them down the slope holding the brake lever down with the stick. Sometimes they could not run fast enough or were not quick enough applying the brake, whatever the reason, the resulting collision was sometimes quite violent, a fact attested to by the amount of coal lying on the ground in the yard. (After the yard was closed many years later, people could be seen with shovels and wheelbarrows clearing away the coal which had resulted from nearly 50 years of rough shunting.)

There was one more section in Feltham yard and this was known as the 'West End'. I don't know what traffic it was used for but it was always full up. In this section there was also a workshop for maintaining the 'Matisa' tamping machines which were in service at that time. These machines were crude in comparison with the later developments of 'on track' maintenance machines which performed a variety of maintenance functions all at the same time.

I had my first accident at work when I was at Feltham. I was on the shed shunting duty, the driver's and fireman's job was to place all the engines in the correct position in the shed for their next working or for servicing/repair. Engines for washout or repairs had to be moved with another engine as their fires had been thrown out, also engines coming off repairs or washout were often unable to move under their own steam. This day in particular we were using an 800 type 'S15' 4-6-0 as a shunting engine and we picked up three more locomotives from Nos. 5 and 6 roads and pulled them up over the top points by the turntable. We were now standing on a curve and the driver told me to uncouple the last engine, another 800, then give him the tip that I was ready. I was to ride on this last engine whilst he pushed it into No. 3 road in the shed where I was to stop it with the handbrake.

Because of the curve on which our string of engines was standing, I was unable to see my driver and after uncoupling the last engine I walked across three sidings until he could see me. I gave him the tip to push into the shed and ran back to the last engine, unfortunately tripping over the rails as I ran and falling heavily to the ground. Before I could get up the driver started pushing the engines into the shed, I watched in horror as he stopped pushing and the last engine kept on going. When he saw me sitting on the ground he yelled, 'Who is on that 800?' 'Nobody', I replied, the remainder of the conversation is unfit to print but anyway it made no difference to the 800 which continued on its merry way through the shed. Luckily No. 3 road was empty and the engine clattered right through the shed and out of the other end, eventually coming to a stop after colliding with the stop block. Luckily there was little damage to the engine or the stop block, but my self confidence was a little dented.

Reading (SR)

Reading was one of my favourite depots to visit, it was originally a South Eastern Railway depot and in 1957 trains still ran from there to London Bridge via Guildford and Redhill at certain times of the day; I believe it was the 7.27 am from Reading to London Bridge and the 5.25 pm return from London Bridge to Reading. It always seemed ridiculous to me that the Great Western Railway (GWR) main line ran 36 miles from Reading to Paddington, the LSWR line via Ascot was 43 miles but going via Redhill was about 65 miles; this was a result of the original railway companies vying for traffic in the same areas.

There was very little P&D work there as most of the crews were booked to prepare and dispose their own engines as part of the day's work. Many of the duties at Reading Southern depot worked over the GWR lines in the area, usually freight trips from Reading to Moreton Cutting yard at Didcot. These trains were transfer traffic to and from the Southern Region and started and terminated at 'Reading Spur', sidings between Reading Spur Junction on the Southern and a junction on the Western line just to the east of Reading General station. It consisted of about four sidings, two in each direction.

The working on one of the duties was to run light engine to Didcot with an 800, then round the triangle to turn and then on to Moreton Cutting which was on the up side about a mile to the east of Didcot station. It was not quite as simple as that as the curve from the up Swindon line to Didcot North on the Oxford line was always blocked with engines waiting to turn or trains waiting for a pathway in the Oxford direction. It would sometimes take an hour or more to get away from Didcot. From Didcot North to the up main line there were about five different routes you could take; when the signal was cleared, different combinations of letters appeared in a box under the signal denoting which route was to be taken. I can't remember them all now but one which was often used was UPAL which stood for 'Up Avoiding Line'. I had never seen such signals on the Southern and I don't believe that they ever had them; there appeared to be hundreds of signals in that section and nearly as many water columns.

After picking up the train from Moreton we would work up to the 'Spur', uncouple, then go round the triangle at Reading West and then go back to Didcot for a repeat performance. It sometimes took so long to do the first trip that there was not time for a second. Freight trains apparently had no priority on the Western and they appeared to run at the signalman's pleasure. The Southern men would joke that Western goods drivers were issued with a calendar instead of a timetable. There was light-hearted rivalry between Southern and Western men and when they got together there was always a lot of banter between them.

Western men would say that GWR stood for 'God's Wonderful Railway' whilst Southern men would say that it stood for 'Go When Ready'. We called the Western men 'Blower Kings' due to the fact that their engines had a very powerful blowers and for some reason they always had them turned on when stationary, probably because the firemen did not clean their fires on the Western. But for all the digs that we had at the others most Southern men admired the Western engines, they had a distinctive appearance which made them instantly recognisable. Even the larger classes looked neat, compact and uniform, they had a certain aura about them which was probably why the engine crews had such a high opinion of themselves. In comparison the motley collection of engines on the Southern looked a bit 'tatty'.

Between Didcot and Reading there were water pick-up troughs, there were none on the Southern so they were a novelty to me. One day we happened to be over these troughs when an express was passing the other way. I had never seen a pick-up before and leaned out of the cab to get a better view. The water from the trough went everywhere and I was saturated, much to the amusement of my driver; he knew what might happen but decided to let me find out the hard way.

The signals at Reading General station were all Great Western style semaphore types and completely baffled me, I was glad that I was not a driver with responsibility for reading them. The Western engines were fitted with Automatic Train Control (ATC) which must have been of great assistance to their drivers, there were no such aids on Southern engines. One driver had me worried when we stopped at a large gantry of signals, one signal was lowered and he said: 'Let's take that one before somebody else does'. I hoped he was joking and was greatly relieved when he burst into laughter.

The Southern station at Reading stood beside the Western establishment and was very small and tatty in comparison, there being four short platforms with a tiny concourse across the platform ends, even so there was a fair amount of passenger traffic passing through. There were also two goods yards on the Southern, which again were tiny in comparison with the vast yards on the Western side. The loco depot stood between the embankments of the two lines and was a rather insignificant building, having only three roads holding about two engines each. There were no mechanical coaling facilities there and the coalman had to unload the wagons with a shovel onto a small platform then shovel it up onto the tenders. This was extremely difficult on the 'Q1' class because of their high-sided tenders. I always felt sorry for the old coalman but was unable to help as I could not throw it up there either. This was the only depot I knew where this system existed although I understand that it was not uncommon in years gone by.

One feature of Reading which I remember vividly is the smells; as you approached from the Guildford direction the first smell to 'hit' you was the gas works. This was a horrible smell and always woke me up if I was asleep as a passenger. The second smell was more pleasant and came from the Huntley & Palmer biscuit factory. I think I could have identified the approach to Reading even if I was blindfolded.

The engines to be found at Reading Southern were mainly the ubiquitous 'U' and 'N' classes although there were some 500s and 800s and 'Q1s 'which were mainly used on freight trips to and from Feltham. 'T9s' and 'Black Motors' also worked in the area but the Reading men did not like them because they were 'Drummond' engines and they were true 'South Eastern' men. That depot must have been like the last outpost to the drivers in Kent and Sussex. A 'Q' class also worked to Reading once a day, it came on a freight from Norwood Junction near Croydon. This train called at every siding *en route* and was commonly known as 'The Creep', the engine worked a passenger train back to Redhill in the evening. The usual engine was No. 30549 which differed from the rest of that class in having a single blast pipe and a stove pipe chimney. The others had been modified by Bulleid to wide chimneys and multiple blast pipes, the same as the 'Q1' class.

Although everything on the Southern at Reading was small in comparison with its neighbour, one feature which stood out was the excellent turntable. This was very large so that even the Pacific 'West Country' class could be turned. There was no mechanical drive at all and the only power was that of the driver and fireman pushing on a bar at either end. However, when an engine was balanced nicely on the table it was no trouble to push it round, in fact the main problem was stopping it at the right place once you had started it. I remember turning a 'Schools' class one day, there was a gale blowing and the wind kept catching the engine as it turned, it went round three times before we managed to get it under control. I think that must have been the best turntable that I ever used.

I will not describe all the other depots that I went to but suffice it to say that each depot had its own atmosphere, its own engines and its own characters. All these things together made going on loan an interesting and informative occupation. It was also remunerative: as a cleaner my wages were about £3 a week, as a fireman they were about £7, but when on loan I had to sign on and off at Guildford and was paid for time spent travelling to and from the on loan-depot. Sometimes I would earn about £20 a week which seemed a lot at the time.

Maunsell 'S15' class 4-6-0 No. 30834 on shed at Reading on 7th July, 1964.   *Alan L. Bailey*

In the middle of 1958 I was appointed as a fireman and placed on the roster in the holiday relief link, but before I had a chance to do much work in this link somebody decided that it was against the law for boys under the age of 18 to work nights. This meant that I was not allowed to start work before six in the morning and not work after ten at night, this ruled out half the turns at the depot which I might have been booked to cover, so I was rather restricted for the next six months or so.

Because of this restriction I found myself booked to work with shed drivers quite often. These were drivers who due to ill health were not allowed out on the main line and were employed moving the engines about the depot or from the coal stage to the depot. The coal stage at Guildford consisted of a large shed open on one side, about 20 feet wide by 80 feet long and about 30 feet high. There were two electric cranes there and the coal was unloaded from wagons placed in the shed into 10 cwt skips which were then hoisted onto the engines standing at the open side of the shed. One of the jobs of the coal stage fireman was to place the skips in the correct position and pull the handle to allow the coal to fall out, he then had to crack up the larger lumps and stack it all neatly on the tender. I became an expert coal stacker.

A strange situation came to my notice due to my restriction, this was the 'Ash Gang', although this was nothing to do with ashes. When the old South Eastern depot at Ash was closed, three drivers were transferred to Guildford, but instead of being integrated within the depot they had their own three turns which they worked in rotation. They had no regular firemen in the gang so the few lads who were on the roster and were under 18 would work with these drivers, all three duties came within the limits of day work. I worked these duties many times, the early turn started off with the 7.20 am empties to Gomshall (tender first with a 'T9'), run round and work as a passenger train back to Guildford where we were relieved, the train went on as the 8.24 am to Reading. These drivers being South Eastern men did not think much of the 'T9' and were very pleased when the train was extended to Dorking and the 'T9' replaced by a 'U' class. The middle turn was a shunting duty and local goods at Aldershot and the Government sidings there. The late turn was shunting at Farnham and a freight train up to Woking. The three drivers in the Ash gang continued to work these duties until their retirement.

Before the ban on night work was imposed I had a nasty experience which shattered my ego for some time, the loss of my pride which I mentioned earlier. I was booked a turn for the week which involved working the 'Angerstein' goods from Woking to Redhill, which was always a heavy train with a full load (= 65) with a 'Q1' class engine. The Redhill road was a steeply graded road and you needed all the power you could get to climb the banks. In all the turns I had worked at various depots I had never once stopped short of steam, it was a proud boast of mine. However, this particular week with 'Q1' class 0-6-0 No. 33019, we stopped three times on the Redhill road, once on Shere Heath bank, once just short of the summit of Dorking bank and once between Betchworth and Reigate. I was ribbed unmercifully by some of the other firemen which was a painful experience for me, but at least it brought me down to earth. It wasn't the last time I stopped either, not by a long chalk. I was 18 on 18th April, 1959 and was then able to take up my normal duties in the holiday relief link, a short stay in that link as you will see later.

Chapter Two

The Engines

At the Grouping in 1923, the engines were given new numbers, those of LSWR origin had three figure numbers, those of the South Eastern & Chatham Railway (SECR) had a '1' added and those of the LBSCR had a '2' added to the front. When the railways were Nationalised in 1948 a prefix '3' was added, '30' in the case of LSWR engines, thus:

Class 'S15' No. 508 became 30508
Class 'U' No. 1790 became 31790
Class 'E4' No. 2505 became 32505

The three constituent companies were very different in the type of service they operated and of course their engines differed accordingly, the 'Brighton' was only a short line with a lot of suburban traffic, therefore it had mainly smaller types of engines. The 'South Eastern' was longer but had severe weight restrictions on some of its routes so its engines tended to be light, fast types. The 'South Western' was the longest route of the three and had many larger types, although it also had a large suburban network and had smaller types for this work. All had small country branch lines and had a range of tank engines for these services.

When looked at as a whole the engines inherited by the Southern Railway were a motley selection of all types and sizes dating back to the 1880s. This chapter describes the engines which I came into contact with during my 11 years on the steam footplate; some classes I worked on frequently and some I only saw working, many were based at Guildford or worked in the area, others I came across when on loan to other depots. The views expressed are entirely my own based on my experience, other people may have had different views based on their own experiences.

I have sorted them into sections according to the company of origin and the date of original introduction as follows: London & South Western Railway, South Eastern & Chatham Railway, London Brighton & South Coast Railway, Southern Railway, British Railways and other Regions' engines.

The engines were rarely referred to by their full numbers, but by the last figures after the prefix '3' and excluding noughts.

No. 30086 was referred to as '86'
No. 30124 became '124'
No. 31722 became '1722'
No. 32505 became '2505'

'Q1' class engines were always known as 'C' plus the last two figures of the number, thus No. 33019 was known as C19 and so on. This relates to the Continental numbering system used when the engines were introduced wherein the number was prefixed by the letter 'C'. 'Merchant Navy', 'West Country' and BR Standard classes were known by their full numbers.

Some types were known by a nickname the origin of which is sometimes obscure and sometimes not known at all. The following is a list of those classes which had unofficial names as used at Guildford.

Class	Nickname	Reason if known.
0395	Jumbo	
700	Black Motor	
G6	Adams tank	Designed by Adams
M7	Motor Tank	Fitted for push/pull (Motor) working
U	Monty or Golloper	The original types used a lot of coal
N	Woolie or Woolworth	Some were built at Woolwich Arsenal
C2X	Vulcan	Built at Vulcan foundry, Newton le Willows
B4	Little Jim	This was the name always given to the Guildford loco shunting engine
E4	Brighton Tank	Built for the LBSCR
S15	500 or Chonker	Numerical series Sound made when coasting
S15	800	Numerical series
30331/2/3	City Breed or Cathedral	Due to high cab roof?
Q1	Charlie	Original prefix C to number
G16	Green tank	Originally painted green
H16	Hump tank	Built for use in hump marshalling yards
A1x	Terrier tank	A small busy engine
T9	Greyhound	A long-legged fast engine
H15	King Arthur	Class named after Knights of the Round Table
MN	Channel Packet	Name of the first engine in class, No. 35001
C	Eastern 'C'	Built for the South Eastern Railway
D	Coppertop	Copper cover on dome
L	German	Some of class built in Berlin
L1	Glasshouse	Similar to 'L' but with side windows

BR Standard classes were referred to by the first two figures of their numbers, thus: 73000 ('73 Standard'), 75000 ('75 Standard'), 76000 ('76 Standard'), 92000 ('92 Standard'), 82000 ('82 tank'), 80000 ('80 thousand tank').

LSWR Engines

William Adams

Class	0395 (Jumbo)	Steam pressure	150 lb.
Type	0-6-0 tender	Driving wheels	5 ft 1 in.
Designer	W. Adams	Cylinders	17½ in. x 26 in. (2)
Introduced	1881	Tractive effort	15,353 lb.
Weight	38 tons 14 cwt		

These were the oldest engines in regular use at Guildford and were originally built in 1881, they were commonly known as 'Jumbos'. There were two of this class at Guildford when I started firing in 1957, mainly used on shunting duties

Note: Where the weights of tender engines are given, this is for the locomotive only.

at Woking and short trips to other local sidings such as Byfleet or Brookwood and sometimes at Godalming.

Designed by W. Adams and built by Neilson & Co. they were once a very widely used goods engine on the LSWR; during World War I many were sent to either Palestine or Mesopotamia for military service. Of the 70 original engines only three survived into the period covered by this book, the last one in service, No. 30575, was shedded at Feltham and used for the West End shunting duty. They had a strange cab layout: the steam/vacuum combination brake was in two separate parts, the vacuum ejector was on the left of the cab whilst the steam brake lever was on the right, the reversing lever was on the left and the regulator lever could be easily reached from either side. Depending on which side the shunting signals were being received the fireman would have to assist the driver by operating either the steam brake or the reverser. The vacuum brake was not often used when shunting, especially if it was foggy and operations were being controlled by audible signals: the steam from the vacuum ejector was exhausted through the chimney and although it did not make a loud noise it was of a pitch which made it difficult to listen for the sound of a whistle. The sound of the vacuum ejector was a fault on all vacuum-braked shunting engines and could make life very difficult at times, at such times a 'Jumbo' was a good engine for shunting because the steam brake was silent and the vacuum exhauster could be turned off.

Class	G6 (Adams tank)	Steam pressure	160 lb.
Type	0-6-0 tank	Cylinders	17½ in. x 24 in. (2)
Designer	W. Adams	Driving wheels	4 ft 10 in.
Introduced	1894	Tractive effort	17,235 lb.
Weight	47 tons 13 cwt		

The other two Adams engines at Guildford that I worked on were the 'G6' and the 'B4' tanks. There were two of these engines based at Guildford. They spent most of their time in 'mothballs' at the back of the shed and were only 'lit up' at Christmas time for the extra shunting duties around the station due to the special traffic. They were unusual in that there were no powered brakes on the engine and when running light had to be stopped with the hand brake, but they had vacuum brake equipment for operating the train brakes.

Class	B4 (Little Jim)	Steam pressure	140 lb.
Type	0-4-0 tank	Cylinders	16 in. x 22 in. (2)
Designer	W. Adams	Driving wheels	3 ft 9¾ in.
Introduced	1891	Tractive effort	14,650 lb.
Weight	33 tons 9 cwt		

The 'B4' was a tiny four-wheeled shunting tank designed for working in Southampton docks, there was one based at Guildford, No. 33086, and there was another at Winchester, No. 33089. These two were changed over for some reason and 33089 became 'Little Jim'; it was always in steam and ready for use except when the boiler was being washed out. When this engine was withdrawn and replaced by a 'USA' tank, the name stuck and right to the end of steam the Guildford Shed shunting engine was known by this name.

Adams 'G6' class 0-6-0 No. 30270 of 1896 vintage at Guildford on 3rd September, 1949. The locomotive remained in service until January 1959.   *H.C. Casserley*

Adams 'B4' 0-4-0T No. 30089 on shed at Guildford on 1st October, 1961.   *P.H. Wells*

The 'B4' was surprisingly strong for its size and would easily move three large tender engines together. I once fired to 'Little Jim' as a light engine outside the shed; we were going to Farnborough North to release the engines arriving there with special trains for the Farnborough Air Show, there being no run-round facilities there. This was the only time that I worked one out on the track and I must say it was a very uncomfortable experience; having only four wheels the little engine rocked lengthways at every rail joint. To my knowledge these three types were the only Adams engines left on the Southern and were all withdrawn by about 1960.

Dugald Drummond

Drummond was the locomotive superintendent of the LSWR from 1895 to 1912 and in this period produced some outstanding engines, many of which had passed from existence before my entry onto the scene, although they were talked about constantly by the older men at the depot. However, there were three Drummond classes which I worked on regularly, these were the '700', 'T9' and 'M7' classes.

Class	700 (Black Motor)	Steam pressure	180 lb.
Type	0-6-0 tender	Cylinders	19 in. x 26 in. (2)
Designer	D. Drummond	Driving wheels	5 ft 1 in.
Introduced	1897	Tractive effort	23,540 lb.
Weight	46 tons 14 cwt		

The '700' class was a goods engine built in 1897 by Dübs & Co. of Glasgow, there were about 10 of this class based at Guildford in 1957 and they were employed on local freight work all over the 'South Western'. Considering their age they were in superb condition and were sometimes out on the road for 18 or 20 hours a day and continued to do so until their withdrawal in 1962, after 65 years of sterling service during which time they worked from end to end of the old LSWR.

For some reason they were known as 'Black Motors' and were well liked by all who used them. For their size they were a strong engine and on the heavily graded lines in the Guildford area they could be seen hauling really heavy loads. They would shake and rattle and the sparks would shoot out of the chimney, but personally I had no trouble at all with them and thought that they were a good little engine. The main problem that I found with the 'Black Motors' was that they had a rather open footplate and a low tender which made them very cold to work on in the winter, especially when running tender first as was frequently the case on Guildford duties.

Class	T9 (Greyhound)	Steam pressure	175 lb.
Type	4-4-0 tender	Cylinders	19 in. x 26 in. (2)
Designer	D. Drummond	Driving wheels	6 ft 7 in.
Introduced	1899	Tractive effort	17,675 lb.
Weight	51 tons 0 cwt		

The 'T9' was probably Drummond's finest design, it was also one of the best looking engines ever to run on the Southern lines. They were known as

A '700' class 'Black Motor' 0-6-0 on the turntable at Guildford Shed.   *Author's Collection*

'T9' class 4-4-0 No. 30313 arrives at Guildford with the 12.05 pm Reading to Redhill train on 5th September, 1953. The stock consists of a main line corridor coach, an ex-SECR 3-set and an ex-GWR six-wheel van or horse box.   *John Faulkner*

'Greyhounds', a very suitable name for such a long-legged and elegant machine, they would fairly leap along the track and had superb suspension which gave a comfortable ride. Introduced between 1899 and 1901, some were built at Nine Elms and some came from Dübs & Co. - they were numbered in three groups:

Group A:	30117, 30120 and 30287-30289
Group B:	30702-30732
Group C:	30300-30338

Groups A and B had coupling rod splashers fitted beside the wheel splashers. Group C had a wider cab and wheel splashers but no coupling rod splashers. Apart from this and a few minor details all the types were of the same appearance.

Although they were originally an express passenger engine, in the period that I worked on them they were used for anything and everything. Of course they were best at what they were designed for and I had some memorable trips on them. On stopping trains they tended to slip a lot when starting due to the large 6 ft 7 in. driving wheels. The wheels and coupling rods on the 'T9' had a distinctive ringing sound when running freely which made them instantly recognisable even when out of sight. I always thought they sounded like a travelling church, they went 'ding dong, clang clong' as they coasted along, very musical if you like that sort of thing. I did and that sound is one of my abiding memories of the period.

Class	M7 (Motor Tank)	*Weight*	60 tons 0 cwt
Type	0-4-4 tank	*Steam pressure*	175 lb.
Designer	D. Drummond	*Cylinders*	18½ in. x 26 in. (2)
Introduced	1897-1903	*Driving wheels*	5 ft 7 in.
	(1925 for push-pull type)	*Tractive effort*	19,775 lb.

The 'M7' was built for LSWR suburban services, in which capacity they performed until electrification of those lines between 1915 and 1925. They were also used on country branch lines and some were fitted for push-pull working. The only line I saw them working in this capacity was the Guildford to Horsham line, but I never worked such a train.

They were a lovely little engine to work on and were smooth riding, especially when running bunker first with the bogie leading. Like the 'T9' they were used for all manner of work and were to be found from one end of the South Western division of the Southern Region to the other. Some were even working on certain parts of the Central Division; both Brighton and Horsham had some 'M7s' allocated, mainly the push and pull types which were used from Brighton to Horsham via Steyning and from Horsham to Guildford via Cranleigh.

There were three types making up the class, the original type of 1897, the 'X14' of 1903 with a steam reverser in place of the large pole lever of the earlier type, and the 'X14' of 1925, fitted for push-pull working. All were lumped together in the 'M7' class and all three types were to be found at Guildford. They were known as 'Motor Tanks' due to the ability of some of them to work in a push-pull formation (or motor trains). Whatever type they belonged to they were all 'Motor Tanks'.

Drummond 'M7' class 0-4-4T No. 30132, of 1903 vintage, shunts carriages at Clapham Junction on 14th March, 1952. Withdrawal finally came for this locomotive in October 1962.

R.E. Vincent

A Urie 'H15' class 4-6-0, No. 30477, passes Raynes Park with an up train on 4th October, 1958. These locomotives had detail differences with the 'H15s' rebuilt from Drummond 'F13s' by Maunsell in 1924, on which the author worked.

K.L. Cook

Class	H15 (F13) (City breed)	Steam pressure	175 lb.
Type	4-6-0 tender	Cylinders	21 in. x 28 in. (2)
Designer	D. Drummond		(Originally 4)
Introduced	1905 (Modified by	Driving wheels	6 ft 0 in.
	Maunsell in 1924)	Tractive effort	25,510 lb.
Weight	80 tons 0 cwt		

The only other Drummond engines that I worked on were the class 'H15s' which were originally built in 1905 as a four-cylinder 4-6-0, class 'F13'. They were rebuilt by Maunsell in 1924 as a two-cylinder type. I imagine the great man had giants in mind when he designed the footplate of these locomotives. I was over 6 ft tall and I could only just reach the steam valves for the injectors, some of my shorter colleagues had to climb on the seat to reach them. There was usually a short end of sleeper on the footplate to enable those drivers of shorter stature to see where they were going and be able to reach the controls more easily.

There were only three of this type in service when I was firing, Nos. 30331, 332 and 333, they were usually known as the 'City Breed' but they were also called 'Cathedrals' by some, perhaps because of the height of the cab roof. They were included in class 'H15' but were noticeably larger that the other members of that class. They always worked the same duties when I saw them, namely the stone trains up from Meldon Quarry to Woking, after which they would go round the triangle at Addlestone Junction to turn as they were too big for the turntable at Guildford.

I was never very happy when working on them and was never very successful at keeping the steam pressure up, although to be fair I never stopped short of steam on one. But then they had a maximum pressure of 175 lb. of steam and could work quite happily with 100 lb. Another advantage was that as the boiler was so large, a full boiler of water would last for many miles before it needed topping up, probably because the boiler was designed to supply four cylinders and now only supplied two.

They were a difficult engine to fire, the firebox was about 11 ft in length and level all the way, the brick arch was very low and if any large lumps of coal should land in the centre of the grate it was not possible to throw any more coal to the front of the fire. It was then necessary to get the long pricker down from the tender to clear the obstruction. This tool was probably 12 ft long and it could be very tricky lifting it from the tender and turning it to the firehole door; the footplate being only about 8 ft wide you had to be careful not to hit any lineside structures or passing trains.

On the Drummond engines the firehole door was very small, it was rectangular and approximately 12 in. x 18 in. The door itself was a flap which lifted inside the firebox and was operated by a lever and ratchet beside the firehole. In the open position this flap acted as a baffle plate, there was also a smaller flap on the outside which, when lifted, covered half the aperture, this was known as the half-door for obvious reasons. An expert fireman could crack up the coal into small pieces and fire over the half-door. By the time that I got the hang of that trick all the Drummond engines had been withdrawn so I never performed it with any success.

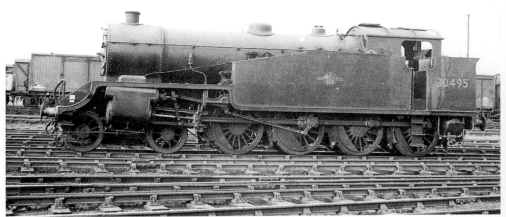

Urie 'G16' class 4-8-0T No. 30495 at Feltham on 5th November, 1960.   *J.C. Haydon*

Urie 'H16' class 4-6-2T No. 30519 with an empty stock working at Clapham Junction in August 1952.   *P. Ransome-Wallis*

Robert Urie

After the demise of the great Dugald Drummond came Robert Urie; considering that he had spent many years working under Drummond he did not seem to be influenced by his predecessor, he was a completely different engineer with his own ideas. Whereas the former designed engines with fine lines and an elegance which was pleasing to the eye (at least to my eye), Urie built his locomotives to be purely practical and I don't think any of them were particularly good to look at, although all were good reliable machines.

Class	G16 (Hump tank)	Steam pressure	180 lb.
Type	4-8-0 tank	Cylinders	22 in. x 28 in. (2)
Designer	R. Urie	Driving wheels	5 ft 1 in.
Introduced	1921	Tractive effort	33,990 lb.
Weight	95 tons 0 cwt		

There is not much to say about the 'G16'; they were an eight-coupled tank designed to operate on the 'Hump' marshalling yards at Feltham, in which capacity they performed until their withdrawal. My only contact with them was occasionally in the shed when I was required to prepare or dispose of them. They were apparently quite suitable for the job they were designed for but were no match for the 350 hp English Electric diesel shunters which replaced them on those duties.

Class	H16 (Green tank)	Steam pressure	180 lb.
Type	4-6-2 tank	Cylinders	21 in. x 28 in. (2)
Designer	R. Urie	Driving wheels	5 ft 7 in.
Introduced	1921	Tractive effort	28,200 lb.
Weight	96 tons 0 cwt		

The 'H16' was a large tank engine and was designed for heavy freight work, mainly used on inter-regional workings in the London area; they were a good strong engine, always up to the task in hand. I worked many trips from Feltham to other London yards, I also worked them on coal and general goods trains round to Surbiton and Wimbledon via Chertsey. They were also to be found at times on empty stock workings in the London area, especially at peak holiday times. They were commonly known as 'Green tanks' as they were apparently painted in that colour at one time. When I worked on them they were painted black.

Class	S15	Steam pressure	180 lb.
Type	4-6-0 tender	Cylinders	21 in. x 28 in. (2)
Designer	R. Urie	Driving wheels	5 ft 7 in.
Introduced	1920	Tractive effort	28,200 lb.
Weight	80 tons 0 cwt		

The 'S15' was the most numerous class of Urie engine and many were based at Feltham where they were utilised for heavy long-distance freight. These engines were numbered 30490 to 30515 and were generally known as '500s' but

Urie 'S15' class 4-6-0 No. 30505 passes Farnborough with the 2.47 pm Feltham-Southampton goods in September 1952.   *J.M. Davenport*

Wainwright 'C' class 0-6-0 No. 31267 stands in Clapham Junction station with a permanent way train on 4th March, 1962.   *Leslie Sandler*

we at Guildford referred to them as 'Chonkers', due to the fact that when running with steam shut off, they would rattle and shake and make a strange sound which went like this, 'Chonka-chonka-chonk, chonka-chonka-chonk'. The crews at Feltham thought that they were a good engine but at Guildford we more often worked on the later addition to the class, built by Maunsell in 1927. These were far superior to the earlier type and were much more free running, they also lacked the knocks and bangs so noticeable on the '500s'.

The later type were numbered from 30823 to 30847 and were duly known as '800s', they were based mainly at Salisbury, although there were also a few at Feltham and Exmouth Junction. The '800s' which I worked on most were based at Redhill and they were a superb engine for the steeply graded route from Redhill to Reading. To compare the two types of 'S15' is probably unfair to Mr Urie as Maunsell had the advantage of a well proven locomotive to improve on, but the drivers at Guildford would say that with a 'chonker' you did not need brakes, closing the regulator was sufficient to cause the engine to stop.

To sum up the Urie engines, they were generally a capable and reliable machine but I would not say that any of them were outstanding. Urie engines always had the same appearance and could be identified at a glance, all were large cumbersome machines which lacked the elegance and aesthetic qualities of the Drummond types. Perhaps it was because old 'Drum' was of the old school of Victorian engineers whilst Urie was a 20th century man in his ideas.

I have not mentioned the class 'N15' 'King Arthurs' here, because the original Urie 'Arthurs' were all gone by the time I came to work the main line and the only type that I came into contact with were those built by Maunsell, although they were based on the same design as the Uries and had the appearance of a Urie engine. I have been told that when both types were running, the engine crews preferred the later type by Maunsell to the earlier type.

The foregoing were all old LSWR engines and I performed much of my work as a fireman on these classes; however, as previously stated we also had 'Central' and 'South Eastern' engines at Guildford, the next group of engines described are all of SECR origin.

SECR Engines

H.S. Wainwright

Class	C	Steam pressure	160 lb.
Type	0-6-0 tender	Cylinders	18½ in. x 26 in. (2)
Designer	H.S. Wainwright	Driving wheels	5 ft 2 in.
Introduced	1900	Tractive effort	19,520 lb.
Weight	43 tons 16 cwt		

These engines were known at Guildford by the self-explanatory title 'Eastern C', they were a general goods engine and at one time they were the mainstay of freight operations on the old SECR. The two examples based at Guildford were Nos. 31722 and 31723, both were fitted with equipment for scraping ice from conductor rails which was probably the reason for their being allocated to the depot,

Wainwright 'D' class 4-4-0 No. 31496 approaches Guildford with a Reading-Redhill train *c.*1955
Michael E. Ware

Wainwright 'H' class 0-4-4T No. 31309 at Redhill in April 1954. *F.J. Saunders*

although to my knowledge they were never used for that purpose. They were used for local freight work in the area and in that capacity they performed very well. They had an excellent steam reverser which was fitted to many of the South Eastern engines, operated by two separate levers, one for forward and reverse movement and the other to lock the reverser in the required position. This was the best type of steam reverser in use on the Southern and was superior to both the Drummond and the Bulleid types which were both unreliable and erratic.

These two engines often worked on the Ascot branch which has gradients of 1 in 60, or local goods trains on the Portsmouth line which has gradients of 1 in 80. They always seemed to perform better when being driven hard and they were usually driven in such a manner, much to the annoyance of the Forestry Commission and lineside farmers. I did not find them as good as the 'Black Motors', but they were much better riding and had less knocks and bangs than experienced on these Drummond types.

Class	D	Steam pressure	175 lb.
Type	4-4-0 tender	Cylinders	19 in. x 26 in. (2)
Designer	H.S. Wainwright	Driving wheels	6 ft 8 in.
Introduced	1901	Tractive effort	17,450 lb.
Weight	50 tons 0 cwt		

Another of Wainwright's engines, they were good looking and apparently they were good steamers and fast runners. We always called them 'Coppertops', this was an inaccurate name as the dome cover from which the name derived was made of brass not copper. There were a couple of this class at Guildford when I started work and I was once assigned the task of scraping the black paint from the dome of one of them in preparation for a special train to 'Woburn'. The engine carried a special headboard with the title 'Woburn special', I don't know if it referred to Woburn Abbey or not. Both of these engines had left Guildford before I started firing so I never had any experience with them. Most of the 'Ds' were rebuilt in 1925 and took on a completely different appearance with a Belpaire firebox; these were classified as class 'D1' and I did work on these types when on loan to Stewarts Lane depot.

Class	H	Steam pressure	160 lb.
Type	0-4-4 tank	Cylinders	18 in. x 26 in. (2)
Designer	H.S. Wainwright	Driving wheels	5 ft 6 in.
Introduced	1904	Tractive effort	17,360 lb.
Weight	54 tons 0 cwt		

The 'H' class tanks were numerous on the South Eastern division. I worked on them several times when on loan to Stewarts Lane, mainly on shunting duties but I once recall working an empty train from Stewarts Lane to Cannon Street. Unfortunately I had no idea of the geography of the division so I am unable to comment as to the performance of the engine, it seemed all right to me. One thing which sticks in my mind is that the cab roof overhung at each side, which was very nice when it was raining, especially on shunting duties.

'L' class 4-4-0 No. 31773 on the turntable at Redhill on 10th April, 1954.   *A.R. Carpenter*

A portrait of Maunsell 'L1' class 4-4-0 No. 31786.

Class	L (German)	Steam pressure	160 lb.
Type	4-4-0 tender	Cylinders	20½ in. x 26 in. (2)
Designer	H.S. Wainwright	Driving wheels	6 ft 8 in.
Introduced	1914	Tractive effort	18,575 lb.
Weight	57 tons 9 cwt		

These 4-4-0s were designed by Wainwright but were built in the time of Maunsell; as some of the class were built by a company in Berlin engines of this class were known as 'Germans'. They were a strong and fast engine and excellent steamers but the firebox was very deep with a flat grate which made it difficult to clear out the clinker. I worked on these engines several times at Stewarts Lane, one of them was always booked to 'double head' the 'Night Ferry' to Dover. It always looked strange, this old fashioned-looking engine coupled to the front of a 'West Country' class with the blue 'Wagon Lits' coaches trailing behind.

Richard Maunsell

Class	L1 (Glasshouse)	Steam pressure	180 lb.
Type	4-4-0 tender	Cylinders	19½ in. x 26 in. (2)
Designer	Maunsell	Driving wheels	6 ft 8 in.
Introduced	1926	Tractive effort	18,910 lb.
Weight	57 tons 16 cwt		

The 'L1' was Maunsell's improved version of the 'L' and was of completely different appearance, being more like the 'E' or 'E1' class to look at with their stepped-up framing and flat-topped firebox. Because they had glass windows in the cab side they were generally known as 'Glasshouses'. I could not tell the difference between the 'L' and the 'L1' but I believe that some of the 'Ls' had been modified with the improved valves and cylinders as fitted on the later types, so perhaps that was why they seemed so alike to me.

All these preceding engines had the same excellent steam reverser as described on the 'C' class and all were recognisable as 'South Eastern' engines. I find it difficult to pinpoint any particular feature of their appearance which marked them as such but as with other great engineers, Wainwright had his own ideas as to what an engine should look like.

The SECR had many weight and loading gauge restrictions so perhaps that had some influence on the appearance of the engines, it certainly resulted in the finest 4-4-0 ever to run on rails, namely the 'V' or 'Schools' class of which more later. The 'N' and 'U' class and other Maunsell types are shown in the section headed 'Southern Railway', this is to avoid duplication and is fitting as Richard Maunsell of the SECR became the first CME of the new Southern Railway company.

'A1X' class 'Terrier' 0-6-0T No. 32640 at Fratton on 15th June, 1951.   *A.W. Martin*

An 'E4' class 0-6-2T on the turntable at Horsham on 4th July, 1959.   *J.H. Scrace*

Brighton Engines

William Stroudley

Class	A1X (Terrier tank)	*Steam pressure*	150 lb.
Type	0-6-0 tank	*Cylinders*	12 in. x 20 in. (2)
Designer	Stroudley	*Driving wheels*	4 ft 0 in.
Introduced	1872 (rebuilt 1911)	*Tractive effort*	7,650 lb.
Weight	28 tons 0 cwt		

Originally built in 1872, the 'Terrier' tanks started life on the London suburban services. They were rebuilt in 1911 by Marsh and were found all over the 'Brighton' section on shunting and short branch line workings. I only worked on them at Fratton and I found them awkward to work on due to their miniature size (it could have been me that was awkward I suppose). I think Stroudley must have had midgets in mind when he designed them, however, they were quite sufficient for the duties required of them. They shunted at Fratton yard and at Portsmouth town station, they worked trips to HM dockyard and also operated the passenger service from Havant to Hayling Island. When shunting on the yard at Fratton they were known as the 'Bug', a good name for them, I thought.

R.J. Billinton

Class	E4 (Brighton tank)	*Steam pressure*	170 lb.
Type	0-6-2 tank	*Cylinders*	17½ in. x 26 in. (2)
Designer	R.J. Billinton	*Driving wheels*	5 ft 0 in.
Introduced	1897	*Tractive effort*	19,175 lb.
Weight	57 tons 10 cwt		

Commonly known at Guildford as 'Brighton tanks', this class was very common on the Central division. Introduced by R.J. Billinton in 1897 they were a development of an earlier type, the 'E3' of 1894 which itself was developed from a Stroudley design of 1891. There were two of these engines at Guildford, Nos. 32505 and 32506, and used for many varied duties, although the regular duty for one of them was the early morning fish vans to Petersfield. They were a capable little engine but personally I preferred the 'Motor Tanks'.

D. Earle Marsh

Class	C2X (Vulcan)	*Weight*	45 tons 0 cwt
Type	0-6-0 tender	*Steam pressure*	170 lb.
Designer	Marsh (Rebuild of	*Cylinders*	17½ in. x 26 in. (2)
	Billinton 'C2')	*Driving wheels*	5 ft 0 in.
Introduced	1908	*Tractive effort*	19,175 lb.

This 0-6-0 goods engine was originally built by R.J. Billinton between 1893 and 1902, and was rebuilt by Earle Marsh from 1908 onwards; some of them

'C2X' class 0-6-0 No. 32529 at Redhill in October 1964.   *Brian Morrison*

'King Arthur' class 4-6-0 No. 30449 *Sir Torre* approaches Surbiton with a down express in the summer of 1954.   *R. Russell*

were fitted with two domes. They were generally knows as 'Vulcans' due to the fact that they carried a plate on the framing proclaiming that they were built at the Vulcan Foundry. Those with the second dome were known as 'Double Humpers' but were sometimes called 'Dromedaries', an inaccurate name as the camel of that name has only one hump, but I heard them referred to in some quarters as 'Old Camels' so perhaps the name was fitting after all.

Personally I never had any trouble with them and I considered them to be a good engine, they used to work into Guildford from Norwood Junction with a local freight via Epsom. I also worked on them many times at Fratton where they were used on many local goods turns and also on passenger trains from Portsmouth to Fareham, where the coaches were attached to the rear of cross-country trains from Brighton to the West Country.

The only other Brighton engines that I came into contact with was the 'K' class Mogul, although I never worked on the main line with them so I do not know much about them. They were unusual in that although they had outside cylinders the motion was between the frames. They also had a cab door which opened outward and was hinged to the tender, an unusual feature which I have never seen on another engine.

All these Brighton engines were fitted with Westinghouse air brakes, and also had vacuum equipment in the cab for use when working vacuum-fitted stock but the vacuum did not work the brakes on the engine. As with the 'South Eastern' engines the 'Brighton' types had a distinctive appearance and any Southern engineman could identify at a glance the division of origin of most Southern locomotives.

Southern Railway Engines

With the formation of the Southern Railway in 1923, Urie of the LSWR and Billinton of the LBSCR both retired and R.E.L. Maunsell of the SECR took over as chief mechanical engineer of the new company. He had been locomotive superintendent on the SECR for the past nine years and during that time had produced two rebuilds, namely the 'D1' and 'E1', and two new locomotives, the 'N' class 2-6-0 tender and the 'K' class tank which were later converted to tender engines when they proved unstable as built. (Both these types were identical mechanically.)

In his new post he proceeded to design and build a superb fleet of engines which I doubt had an equal at that time as far as variety of types was concerned. They ranged from the 0-6-0 goods engine of class 'Q' to the impressive 'Lord Nelson' class. The first job taken in hand by the new CME was the provision of a large express engine to replace the ageing assortment of locomotives which made up the stock of the new company. Some of Drummond's 'G14' 4-6-0s were rebuilt from four cylinders to two and the Urie 'N15s' were also modified in various ways. These engines were named after Knights of the Round Table and were know as the 'King Arthur' class, always called simply an 'Arthur' by the crews.

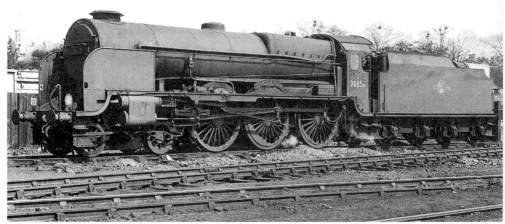

'Lord Nelson' class 4-6-0 No. 30856 *Lord St. Vincent* at Basingstoke on 25th April, 1962.

R.S. Greenwood

Maunsell 'S15' class 4-6-0 No. 30835 on an up freight near Reigate on 25th September, 1954.

S.C. Nash

Richard Maunsell

Class	N15 (King Arthur)	Steam pressure	200 lb.
Type	4-6-0 tender	Cylinders	20½ in x 28 in. (2)
Designer	Maunsell	Driving wheels	6 ft 7 in.
Introduced	1925	Tractive effort	25,320 lb.
Weight	80 tons 0 cwt		

In 1925 30 new engines were ordered and were built by the North British Locomotive Co., these became known as the 'Scotch Arthurs'. They were slightly different from the earlier types, the cab roofs being shaped so as to permit them to run on the Kent coast lines which had loading gauge restrictions. Although the 'Arthurs' all had the look of a Urie engine, they certainly did not perform like a Urie. They were a superb locomotive in every way and well liked by all who worked on them, being fast, free running and free steaming and were still performing main line duties when I was a fireman.

There followed in successive years, three new classes and three extensions to existing classes, these were as follows:

1926	'Lord Nelson'	New class
1927	'S15' '800' type	New engines. Improvement to Urie 'S15'
1928	'U' class '1600' type	New engines similar to existing 'River' class tanks
1929	'Z' class tanks	New class
1930	'V' class ('Schools')	New class
1931	'W' class tanks'	New engine based on the 'N1' tender engines

Class	Lord Nelson	Steam pressure	220 lb.
Type	4-6-0 tender	Cylinders	16½ in. x 26 in. (4)
Designer	Maunsell	Driving wheels	6 ft 7 in.
Introduced	1926		(6 ft 3 in. on No. 30859)
Weight	84 tons 0 cwt	Tractive effort	33,510 lb.

These engines were a departure from anything that Maunsell had done before, having four cylinders, they were giants of their time. Everybody who worked on them praised their ability, unfortunately due to my youth I never worked them on the main line. My experience on the 'Nelsons' was restricted to empty stock trips between Waterloo and Clapham yard or light engine to and from Nine Elms depot, where I spent a fair amount of time preparing and disposing them. They were sometimes referred to as 'Whispering Giants' due to the fact that they had eight exhaust beats to the turn of a wheel and when running the exhaust note was nearly a continuous hiss. They were an impressive looking engine and were probably the best 4-6-0 to run on Southern metals, especially after Bulleid had applied his genius to them in 1937 when new cylinders were fitted and a wide chimney and multiple blast pipe.

Class	S15 (800) 4-6-0	Steam pressure	200 lb.
Type	4-6-0 tender	Cylinders	20½ in. x 28 in. (2)
Designer	Maunsell	Driving wheels	5 ft 7 in.
Introduced	1927 and 1936	Tractive effort	29,855 lb.
Weight	80 tons 0 cwt		

The Maunsell 'S15s' were an extension to the earlier class by Urie, like the 'Arthurs' they had the Urie look about them, and like the 'Arthurs' the new type was far superior to the former. Generally known as '800s' they were a terrific freight engine and I was always impressed with their performance. I should think that the engineer must have been well pleased with his latest creation. There were two types of '800s', those built in 1927 (Nos. 30823-37) and those of 1936 (Nos. 30838-47), the differences were slight, the later type being 1½ tons lighter. Those engines numbered from 30833-37 had six-wheeled tenders and were intended for the Central Division.

Probably the most ubiquitous engines on the Southern were the 'U' and 'N' classes. In their various forms they were to be seen working all manner of trains all over the Region. In my early years as a fireman the most common type of 'Mogul' I worked on was the 31600 numbered group. This type was built between 1928 and 1931 and had 6 ft driving wheels as did the ex-'River' class, also a common type on the South Western Division. For a reason unknown to me the group numbered from 31610 to 31639 was known as 'Montys' and the ex-'Rivers' numbered from 31790 to 31809 were known as 'Gollopers'. Nine Elms men always called any 'U' class a 'Montgolloper'.

There were five types of engine built to basically the same design, these were the 'N' class, the original type and also the most numerous. The 'N1' class was a three-cylinder version of the 'N', only six of these were built; the 'U' class with two cylinders and the 'U1' with three cylinders; the 'W' class was a tank version of the 'N1'. All had the same excellent boiler and were an easy engine to fire, the method was to build the fire up under the firehole door and have it sloping towards the front of the grate. The grate itself sloped towards the front, so once the fire was built up it was only necessary to place the coal just inside the door and it would roll to the front on its own.

Class	U (Monty or Golloper)	Steam pressure	200 lb.
Type	2-6-0 tender	Cylinders	19 in. x 28 in. (2)
Designer	Maunsell	Driving wheels	6 ft 0 in.
Introduced	1917 and 1928	Tractive effort	23,865 lb.
Weight	63 tons 0 cwt		

The 'Us' which were based at Guildford were very well maintained, they were a smooth riding engine, very free steaming and generally a pleasure to work on. They were used for all types of work and were equally at home on freight or passenger duties on the main or branch lines. There were two types of 'U', those numbered 31790 to 31809 were originally built between 1917 and 1926 and started life as 'K' class 2-6-4 tanks; they were named after rivers and carried the numbers 790 to 809. After an accident at Sevenoaks in 1927 they were declared unstable and in 1928 they were all converted to 2-6-0 tender engines, at the same time a start was made on building 30 new engines which were eventually numbered 31610 to 31639.

The converted engines were slightly different from the new ones, the framing or running plates of the former type were the same height as the 'N' class and larger splashers were fitted to accommodate the 6 ft driving wheels. On the new engines the framing was placed higher up. The ex-'Rivers' had cab front windows identical to the 'Ns', one round and one oval on each side, the new engines had only one inverted 'L' shaped window on each side and the cab was slightly narrower.

In the cab the ex-'Rivers' had the remains of the side tanks as seats for the crew whilst the others had wooden flaps hinged to the cab sides. These differences were probably not very noticeable to the casual observer, but to anyone with close knowledge of the engines the two types were instantly recognisable.

Class	N (Woolie or Woolworth)	Steam pressure	200 lb.
Type	2-6-0 tender	Cylinders	19 in. x 28 in. (2)
Designer	Maunsell	Driving wheels	5 ft 6 in.
Introduced	1917	Tractive effort	23,035 lb.
Weight	61 tons 0 cwt		

To start with I did not work on the 'N' class very much, they were mostly allocated to the South Eastern and Central divisions or the West Country. When the South Eastern was electrified in about 1960 many of the 'U' class based at Guildford were transferred to the West Country and replaced by 'Ns'. The new arrivals had not been looked after very well, they were filthy dirty and were full of knocks and bangs and leaks. After they had been there for a while they began to improve a little but never reached the standard of those they replaced. The 'N' class had 5 ft 6 in. driving wheels and was more suitable for freight work than the 'U' class but apart from that and the lower framing they were almost the same.

Class	N1	Steam pressure	200 lb.
Type	2-6-0 tender	Cylinders	16 in. x 28 in. (3)
Designer	Maunsell	Driving wheels	5 ft 6 in.
Introduced	1922	Tractive effort	27,695 lb.
Weight	64 tons 0 cwt		

I never worked on an 'N1' but was told that it was an excellent engine. They were all based at Hither Green on the South Eastern. They were used mainly on transfer freights between London marshalling yards, this was very heavy work, made easier by the free steaming qualities of the Maunsell boiler and the smooth traction produced by the three cylinders.

Class	U1	Steam pressure	200 lb.
Type	2-6-0 tender	Cylinders	16 in. x 28 in. (3)
Designer	Maunsell	Driving wheels	6 ft 0 in.
Introduced	1928	Tractive effort	25,385 lb.
Weight	65 tons 0 cwt		

The 'U1' was a rare engine in the Guildford area and I rarely worked on them, although I saw many at work in the Redhill area. They were all based on the Central and South Eastern divisions, and were basically the same as the 'N1' except for the larger driving wheels. Again, they were considered superb engines and were well liked by all who worked on them.

'U' class 2-6-0 No. 31618 at Dorking Town on the 9.45 am Reading-Redhill train on 15th December, 1962.   *L. Sandler*

'N' class 2-6-0 No. 31405 passes Guildford Shed with the 9.43 am ex-Redhill on 28th November, 1964.   *John Faulkner*

'N1' class 2-6-0 No. 31877 at Tonbridge. *J. Davenport*

'U1' class 2-6-0 No. 31908 climbs Dorking bank with the 10.18 am Redhill-Reading service on 22nd September, 1962. *D.B. Clark*

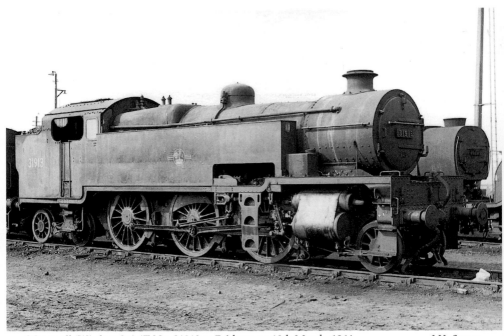

Maunsell 'W' class 2-6-4T No. 31913 at Feltham on 10th March, 1964.   *J.H. Scrace*

'Z' class 0-8-0 No. 30952 at Eastleigh in October 1964.   *F.R. Sherlock*

Class	W		Steam pressure	200 lb.
Type	2-6-4 tank		Cylinders	16½ in. x 28 in. (3)
Designer	Maunsell		Driving wheels	5 ft 6 in.
Introduced	1931		Tractive effort	29,450 lb.
Weight	90 tons 0 cwt			

Now the 'W' tanks I did work on and found them to be a superb locomotive, they were almost the same as the 'N1' apart from the fact that being a tank they had a bogie under the cab. All the motion parts were interchangeable with the 'U1' and 'N1' classes and the extra cylinder gave them that smooth traction so noticeable on their tendered sisters, but the bogie under the cab gave an even smoother ride. Several times I worked a full load of freight out of Feltham yard to Basingstoke or Eastleigh and each trip is remembered for the beautiful performance of the engine. The only drawback was the 2,000 gallon capacity of the water tanks, but personally I thought that the inconvenience of stopping for water was more than compensated for by the extra smooth riding of the tank form and the cosiness of the fully enclosed footplate.

All of these Maunsell types were right-hand-drive for some reason which made them rather awkward on a stopping train as most of the platforms were on the left. However, there were some 'N' class locomotives which were modified for left-hand-drive, they were numbered from 31407 to 31414 and some of them were allocated to Guildford while I was there. They were the last 'Ns' to be built (1932-1933) and were generally in better condition than the earlier ones of 1920-25.

The 'N' class were known as 'Woolies' or 'Woolworths' due to the fact that some of them were built at Woolwich Arsenal to provide work at the ordnance factory after World War I, those fitted for left-hand-drive were known as 'left-handers'. All these engines were fitted with 'Davies & Metcalfe' combination brakes which provided steam power for the engine brakes and vacuum operation of the tender and train brakes. It was an excellent system which allowed the driver to maintain a full brake application on the tender and train whilst being able to ease the engine brake to prevent the driving wheels from locking. The 'W' tanks, of course, had no tender brake, the whole system being operated by steam. This included brake equipment fitted to the trailing bogie which, when added to that of the driving wheels, gave a high brake power for a tank engine, very useful as they were used mainly on heavy freight duties.

Class	Z		Steam pressure	180 lb.
Type	0-8-0 tank		Cylinders	16 in. x 28 in. (3)
Designer	Maunsell		Driving wheels	4 ft 8 in.
Introduced	1929		Tractive effort	29,375 lb.
Weight	71 tons 10 cwt			

The 'Z' tank was an eight-coupled shunting engine introduced in 1929. I only came into contact with them once, but that is a story on its own and is related later in the book.

'Schools' class 4-4-0 No. 30926 *Repton* at Stewarts Lane Shed on 6th June, 1962.   *J.H. Scrace*

'Q' class 0-6-0 No. 30540 passing Shalford East Lane crossing with a Guildford-Redhill pick-up goods *c*.1956.   *Michael E. Ware*

Class	V (Schools)	Steam pressure	220 lb.
Type	4-4-0 tender	Cylinders	16½ in. x 26½ in. (3)
Designer	Maunsell	Driving wheels	6 ft 7 in.
Introduced	1930	Tractive effort	25,135 lb.
Weight	67 tons 0 cwt		

This class, in my opinion, was one of the best engines of all the Maunsell types and, as a 4-4-0, was unusual in 1930 as that wheel arrangements had been considered virtually obsolete years before. Named after famous schools, these locomotives can only be described as superb; I have seen them described as the finest 4-4-0 ever built. In my experience they certainly lived up to that reputation, they were free running, free steaming and extremely powerful. The tractive effort was high for a four-coupled engine and was more likely to be found on a six-coupled type. But with three cylinders and perfectly balanced cranks the power was smoothly transferred from the boiler to the wheels and little of the wheel slipping normally associated with this wheel arrangement occurred.

There were three of this class at Guildford whilst I was there, namely Nos. 30903 *Charterhouse*, 30906 *Sherborne* and 30909 *St Paul's*. No. 30909 had been modified by Bulleid and fitted with a multiple blast pipe and wide chimney. If my memory serves me correctly they came there in about 1960 when our best '1600' 'Us' were transferred away. Although they were used mainly on stopping services on the Reading to Redhill route, they also worked the 'Conty' over that route and sometimes on specials on other lines. Unfortunately I never had the chance to work one on an express duty. I would have loved to see one in full flight with a heavy train over a long distance, the nearest I came to such a trip was to work a relief to the 'Conty' one Saturday. The trip was spoiled by frequent signal checks so I did not see the engine doing all she could. The only fault I found with the 'Schools' was that to enable them to run on the Hastings line, the cab roof was tapered in at the top and I often bumped my head on the side of the roof when I stood up without thinking.

To explain, the 'Conty' was a cross-country train which ran from Birkenhead to Dover. I believe that the train divided at Redhill and went to several destinations, it usually consisted of 10 or 11 coaches which was heavy over the Redhill road. The name was an abbreviation of 'Continental' which of course referred to the onward connections from Dover. The 'Conty' ran in both directions daily from Monday to Saturday and in the summer there were often several relief trains on a Saturday as well.

Class	Q	Steam pressure	200 lb.
Type	0-6-0 tender	Cylinders	19 in. x 26 in. (2)
Designer	Maunsell	Driving wheels	5 ft 1 in.
Introduced	1938	Tractive effort	26,160 lb.
Weight	49 tons 10 cwt		

This was Maunsell's last design and when considered against his other designs, was old fashioned, having Stephenson link motion between the frames. I never found them very special, even though Bulleid had fiddled with them they were never more than adequate. The only thing unique about them was that they were the only Maunsell Southern Railway-type fitted with a steam reverser; not a very good one either, which is surprising from the former locomotive engineer of the SECR who had many years' experience with the excellent steam reversers fitted to the engines under his charge.

O.V.S. Bulleid

When Maunsell retired in 1937, Oliver Bulleid took over as CME. He was arguably the most controversial locomotive engineer ever to hold such a post in Britain and I have heard him described variously as 'a man of vision', 'a genius', 'a man before his time', 'the last giant of steam', 'a man out of his depth', 'a man of many ideas but not much idea as to the practicalities of producing his ideas commercially'. Whatever his attributes or faults, he was to produce some of the finest steam engines ever to run in this country. They were not perfect by any means, but then what is! He did not arrive at a good time with World War II in the offing, the Southern was not in a position to spend vast amounts of money on new and untried designs, nevertheless Bulleid managed to produce them.

Apart from modifying existing engines, which he did with some success, he introduced only four new designs, namely the 'Q1', the 'Merchant Navy', 'West Country' and the 'Leader' classes. The 'Leader' was the most controversial of his designs and was a departure from all traditional ideas. Unfortunately, or fortunately, depending on your point of view, they were not in service when I was firing so my information is only second-hand. Although he had trained under Sir Nigel Gresley he did not bring much of Gresley to the Southern with him; he had his own ideas which were amply displayed in his first full production, the 'Merchant Navy' class.

Class	MN (Merchant Navy)	*Steam pressure*	250 lb.
Type	4-6-2 tender		(280 lb. originally)
Designer	Bulleid	*Cylinders*	18 in. x 24 in. (3)
Introduced	1941	*Driving wheels*	6 ft 2 in.
Weight	94 tons 15 cwt	*Tractive effort*	33,495 lb.

With this class Bulleid employed his inventiveness to the full, the result was an extremely powerful locomotive, even if its appearance was a little strange. Some unkind people called them 'Spam cans'. They had three cylinders and the valve gear for all three was operated by a large chain which was driven from the middle axle. The chain drive was enclosed in an oil bath and the only parts of the works visible were the outside cylinders plus the connecting and coupling rods. The whole locomotive was enclosed in a casing for the purpose of streamlining, but unlike his tutor, Gresley, he did not design a sleek and elegant engine but more of a box on wheels. It always fascinates me, the way that different designers came up with completely different ideas in trying to solve the same problem. But to be fair the Bulleid pacific types were not described as 'streamlined', they were 'air smoothed'; there is a subtle difference there somewhere.

The 'MNs' had a large footplate but because of the wide boiler casing the front windows of the cab were very narrow which gave a restricted lookout. They were set at an oblique angle to give a larger area of glass that the aperture permitted, but it was not much help as steam from the chimney would roll back along the casing to obscure the driver's view. They had a steam reverser which was very unreliable and would 'creep' when it was supposed to be locked. If you set the cut-off at 25 per cent you would sometimes find after a few minutes that the pointer had worked its way into mid-gear or even past mid and into reverse.

They were an extremely smooth riding engine and it was sometimes possible to hear the sound of the wheels passing over the rail joints, an unusual sound on a steam engine. The absence of any exposed valve gear made them an easy engine for the driver to oil, there being only five corks on each side. Also there were electric lights all around the engine, driven by a small steam generator mounted under the cab. This saved the fireman the chore of trimming and filling the normal paraffin lamps. All the bearings on the engine were lubricated from three trays of trimmings, two on the footplate and one near the smokebox, the engines had been designed with ease of servicing in mind.

The firebox was the short wide type and was fitted with Nicholson thermic siphons which were of great assistance in producing steam. These siphons took the form of two curved tubes of about six inches in diameter which passed through the firebox from the tube plate to the crown plate. They also acted as a support for the brick arch. Their effect was to cause the cooler water in the lower part of the boiler to be heated rapidly in the siphon tubes, causing it to rise up the tubes, being replaced by cooler water, thus circulation was set up ensuring even heating of all the water. The boilers were excellent steamers and, having a short firebox, the fireman did not have far to move the coal, which was just as well because these engines were heavy on coal.

They were fitted with 'Ajax' patent steam-operated firehole doors which were a wonderful invention if you like that sort of thing, or a nuisance, it depends on your point of view. Personally I did not get on well with them and when I was

Unrebuilt 'Merchant Navy' class 4-6-2 No. 35013 *Blue Funnel* on the down fast line entering Vauxhall.   *R. Russell*

Unrebuilt 'Battle of Britain' class 4-6-2 No. 34066 *Spitfire* passes Railway Staff Halt, Wimbledon with an up train on 2nd July, 1964.　　　　　*R. Fisher*

'Merchant Navy' class 4-6-2 No. 35030 *Elder-Dempster Lines* at Surbiton, with the stock for the Surbiton to Okehampton car-carrying train in 1965.　　　　　*Author's Collection*

driving at Nine Elms the firemen there rarely used them, although I have been told that Salisbury and Exeter crews were keen on them. There was a pedal on the floor which, when pressed, caused the butterfly type doors to fly open, when the pedal was released they would drop into the closed position with a bang. If you let go of the pedal too soon, the doors would drop and trap the firing shovel before you could get it out.

All the isolating valves were ranged above the boiler face inside the cab which made it extremely hot in the summer but cosy in the winter. All three classes of Bulleid engines that I worked on had this arrangement and I always thought it was bad and preferred the BR Standard types where all these valves were outside and were operated by rods from inside. Dirt from the chimney rolled back along the flat top of the boiler and entered the cab through the ventilator in the roof, this was another defect which existed on all three classes.

From 1945 to 1948 his 'Light Pacifics' were introduced, these were the 'West Country' and 'Battle of Britain' classes, and were really scaled down versions of the 'Merchant Navy' class, the dimensions were as follows:

Class	WC/BB (West Country/ Battle of Britain)	*Steam pressure*	250 lb. (280 lb. originally)
Type	4-6-2 tender	*Cylinders*	16⅜ in. x 24 in. (3)
Designer	Bulleid	*Driving wheels*	6 ft 2 in.
Introduced	1945-1948	*Tractive effort*	27,715 lb.
Weight	86 tons 0 cwt		

One improvement on the smaller class was the provision of a drop section in the grate which saved the fireman having to throw the clinker out of the side of the cab; he just had to drop it through the trapdoor whence it fell through the ashpan and onto the ground.

The 'Merchant Navy' class was always known as 'Channel Packets' after the first of that class, No. 35001, which was so named; this was further abbreviated in later years to 'Packet'. The name 'Battle of Britain' was rarely used and the smaller type were all known as 'West Countries', there was no difference anyway, apart from the name. From 1956 onwards, all the 'Merchant Navies' and the majority of the 'West Countries' were modified to a more conventional pattern. The chain drive was removed and replaced by three sets of Walschaerts valve gear and the steam reverser was replaced by a screw type with a rolling drum indicator. The air smoothing casing was also removed and the engine took on a more traditional appearance. Personally I thought that the new form looked much better that the original and whilst having most of the attributes of the original, many of the snags were removed.

The 'Converteds', as they were known were a superb engine although not as smooth riding as the 'Unconverteds'. Because the casing had been removed the driver now had a better look out although the steam still came down from the chimney to obscure his view, but the dirt no longer rolled back along the boiler. Another big improvement was the provision of proper dampers which gave the fireman much more control of the boiler. The steam equipment was removed from the fire doors leaving just the manual operating lever. These and other small modifications gave the footplate a much neater appearance, they now

Rebuilt 'Battle of Britain' class 4-6-2 No. 34056 *Croydon* passes Surbiton with a Waterloo to Salisbury train on 12th August, 1966.   *J.H. Scrace*

looked similar to the large BR Standard types although the isolating valves remained in the same place. The firebox was fitted with a proper rocking/drop grate which again was to the fireman's benefit. On the debit side, from the driver's point of view, it was now necessary to go under the engine to oil the inside motion.

I thought that the 'Converteds' now looked like a real steam engine but any true Bulleid fan would tell you that when his finest engines were modified they were 'Butchered' and were a bastard engine not fit to carry the Bulleid name. That is a matter of opinion and I always felt that the advantages outweighed the disadvantages. The boilers of all these engines were excellent steam producers and they never seemed short of power. I worked some heavy 'boat trains' up the bank from Southampton with both types and although the climb is not particularly steep it is nearly 20 miles long. It is very satisfying for the crew to watch their steed haul 400 tons up a bank like that without a sign of any shortage of power and the boiler producing full pressure continually.

All the Bulleid Pacifics were fitted with a hot bearing detector on the middle big end. When the bearing became overheated a smell of either garlic or aniseed was given off. I never noticed either of these smells when working on them so either I never had a hot bearing or the detector did not work, it was probably the former as the engines were oiled every three to four hours. The details of the 'Converteds' were as follows.

Class	Merchant Navy	*Class*	West Country/Battle of Britain
Type	4-6-2 tender	*Type*	4-6-2 tender
Designer	Bulleid	*Designer*	Bulleid
Introduced	1956	*Introduced*	1957
Weight	97 tons 18 cwt	*Weight*	90 tons 1 cwt
Steam pressure	250 lb.	*Steam pressure*	250 lb. (280 lb. originally)
Cylinders	18 in. x 24 in. (3)	*Cylinders*	16⅜ in. x 24 in. (3)
Driving wheels	6 ft 2 in.	*Driving wheels*	6 ft 2 in.
Tractive effort	33,495 lb.	*Tractive effort*	27,715 lb.

Class	Q1 (Charlie or Coffee pot)	*Steam pressure*	230 lb.
Type	0-6-0 tender	*Cylinders*	19 in. x 26 in. (2)
Designer	Bulleid	*Driving wheels*	5 ft 1 in.
Introduced	1942	*Tractive effort*	30,080 lb.
Weight	51 tons 10 cwt		

With the war in progress there was a need for extra freight engines and to meet this need Bulleid produced the 'Q1' class. This class must rank as one of the strangest looking ever to run. It had no external framing or splashers at all and when new had the continental type numbers which were prefixed by the letter 'C'. The numbers were changed to BR standard types after 1948 and the 'Q1s' became Nos. 33001 to 33040. However, although the 'C' was gone from the cab side it remained right up to the last in the language of the motive power men. A 'Q1' was always called a 'Charlie' and the full number was never stated, they were referred to by the letter 'C' and the last two figures of the number, thus No. 33019 was C19.

Apart from their odd appearance which prompted the nickname 'Coffee pot' and allegedly prompted William Stanier to ask Bulleid, 'Where do you put the key in to wind it up?', the mechanical side was quite ordinary, there being two inside cylinders with normal Stephenson link motion between the frames. They were a strong engine for an 0-6-0 but the boiler was not easy to manage and if you got short of steam it was very difficult to recover without stopping. With a full head of steam they would pull a house down, but when low on pressure they did not perform very well at all. As with the 'MN' and 'WC' classes all the valves for isolating various pieces of equipment were arranged above the boiler face in the cab, a fully enclosed cab again making it very hot in the summer.

The boiler was quite large but the injectors were slow to fill it and when the engine was being worked hard it was necessary to have one injector working most of the time. This was all right all the time the boiler was steaming freely, but if the pressure fell the injector had to be turned off in order to create more steam. Then of course the water level fell and when the extra steam had been created both injectors were needed to restore the water level, which of course made the steam pressure drop again.

This was where the route knowledge of the crew came into play, the driver would know where he could shut off steam without stopping or losing time and the fireman would know where he could safely allow the water level to fall in order to maintain steam pressure. At a certain point he would be able to use both injectors to refill the boiler whilst not having to worry too much about the steam pressure.

Personally I did not like the 'Charlies', I found them dirty to work on as smoke and ash from the chimney would roll back along the flat top of the boiler and came in through the roof ventilator. There was also restricted space on the footplate due to the fully enclosed cab and having a long firebox made them difficult to square up. They were officially described as an 'Austerity' engine, that they certainly were; on one engine the flap in the side casing giving access to the steam reverser had an advert for 'Swan Vestas' matches on the back. Again, the steam reverser was erratic and unreliable and tended to creep one way or the other when it was supposed to be locked. This was a fault with all Bulleid steam reversers and was probably not helped by lack of maintenance.

With the formation of British Railways (BR) in 1948, Bulleid retired from the scene and no more 'Southern' engines were built, all the new engines after that time were of the BR Standard classes.

A 'Charlie' 'Q1' class 0-6-0 shunts at Surbiton in 1965.   *Bill Trigg*

BR Standard class '3' 2-6-2T No. 82018 arrives at Clapham Junction with empty stock from Waterloo on 8th December, 1962.   *J.C. Haydon*

British Railways Standard Classes

The 'Standards' as they were known were supposed to encompass the best in British locomotive design and in many ways this aim was achieved, but considering that the committee had a hundred years of experience to draw on, some of the results of their efforts were disappointing. On the South Western division we used six of the standard types, those that I worked on were as follows.

Type	Wheels	Number series
BR5	4-6-0	73000
BR4	4-6-0	75000
BR4	4-6-0	76000
BR4	2-6-4 Tank	80000
BR3	2-6-2 Tank	82000
BR9F	2-10-0	92000

All the standard engines had similar footplate fittings, some of the common features included on these locomotives were:

1. High framing giving easy access to the working parts.
2. Roller bearings for free running.
3. Steam operated cylinder cocks.
4. Mechanical lubricators.
5. Steam/vacuum combination brakes with steam operating the brakes on both engine and tender.
6. Steam isolating valves outside the cab operated by rods from inside, this made the footplate competitively cool, in fact in the winter time they were quite cold but with the large sliding side windows closed the cab offered good protection from the elements.
7. Screw operated dampers for fine control of the boiler.
8. Screw reverser with indicator drum for fine control of the valve cut-off.
9. Rocker/drop grate for easy fire cleaning, hopper ashpan, again for easy cleaning.
10. Regulator valve on the side of the boiler operated by a rod connected to a lever in the cab which was pulled towards the driver to open and pushed shut.
11. Proper seats for both enginemen, the driver's seat was padded.
12. Self-cleaning smokebox, cutting down disposal time.

All the 'Standards' looked like 'Midland' engines and I suspect that the committee must have been greatly influenced by the work of Fowler, Ivatt and Stanier in their choice of designs for the new locomotives.

Classification	BR3 (82000)	Steam pressure	200 lb.
Type	2-6-2 tank	Cylinders	17½ in. x 26 in. (2)
Designed	Swindon	Driving wheels	5 ft 3 in.
Introduced	1952	Tractive effort	21,490 lb.
Weight	73 tons 10 cwt		

These little tanks were based mainly on the Southern and in my area they replaced the 'Great Western' pannier tanks which had taken over from the 'Motor Tanks' on the Waterloo stock workings. They were a strong little engine

BR Standard class '4' 2-6-4T No. 80087 blasts away from Guildford with the 6.16 pm to Dorking Town on 26th July, 1963. *G.D. King*

BR Standard class 4' 2-6-0 No. 76044 passes Clapham Junction with a Waterloo-Basingstoke train on 15th May, 1964. *Brian Stephenson*

and in their limited role, very capable. They often hauled 12 or 13 coaches between Waterloo and Clapham yard and were much better to work on than the older types; of course, with all the standard features they were much easier to prepare and dispose.

Classification	BR4 (80000)	*Steam pressure*	225 lb.
Type	2-6-4 tank	*Cylinders*	18 in. x 28 in. (2)
Designed	Brighton	*Driving wheels*	5 ft 8 in.
Introduced	1951	*Tractive effort*	25,100 lb.
Weight	88 tons 10 cwt		

This was a much larger type than the '82000', they were an outstanding engine and were basically a 'tank' version of the '75000' type tender engines but had only a single blast pipe in place of the double type fitted to the tender engines. The boilers were extremely free steaming and the engine very smooth riding and free running. I used them on all types of duty from semi-fast passenger trains in connection with the Farnborough air show to coal trains to and from the National Coal Board depot at Tolworth. They easily handled all the loads I worked with them and I found them a very pleasant engine to work on.

Classification	BR4 (76000)	*Steam pressure*	225 lb.
Type	2-6-0 tender	*Cylinders*	17½ in. x 26 in. (2)
Designed	Doncaster	*Driving wheels*	5 ft 3 in.
Introduced	1953	*Tractive effort*	24,170 lb.
Weight	59 tons 2 cwt		

The '76000' Standards were one of the least successful types and in my opinion many of the older 2-6-0s were far superior to the new locomotives. Of course the Standards' features made them an easy engine to work, but their performance was never more than adequate and they tended to rattle a lot and often gave a rough ride when running fast. Personally I preferred to have an old 'Monty' than a '76'.

Classification	BR4 (75000)	*Weight*	69 tons 0 cwt
Type	4-6-0 tender	*Steam pressure*	225 lb.
Designed	Brighton	*Cylinders*	18 in. x 26 in. (2)
Introduced	1951 (1957 type with	*Driving wheels*	5 ft 8 in.
	double chimney)	*Tractive effort*	25,100 lb.

This type was a much better engine. Those that I worked on were the 1957 introductions with a double blast pipe and chimney. They tended to be noisy especially when starting, they used to make a terrific din when they were banking trains out of Waterloo, made louder by the large enclosed area of the station. Some drivers would work them harder than usual just to hear their lovely 'bark'.

BR Standard class '4' 4-6-0 No. 75074 at Nine Elms in June 1967.   *Leslie Sandler*

A line up of BR Standard class '5' 4-6-0s. From left to right, Nos. 73119, 73118 and 73020 are seen on Basingstoke Shed on 10th September, 1966.   *E. Wilmshurst*

Classification	BR5 (73000)	Steam pressure	225 lb.
Type	4-6-0 tender	Cylinders	19 in. x 28 in. (2)
Designed	Doncaster	Driving wheels	6 ft 2 in.
Introduced	1951 and 1956	Tractive effort	26,120 lb.
Weight	76 tons 0 cwt		

This 4-6-0 was larger than the '75000' type and the difference was noticeable, they seemed much more powerful and faster than that type although they were not that much bigger. Although they were all the same, it seemed that those in certain groups in the number range were better than others; those in the '80s' seemed to perform much better than those in the lower numbers and those numbered from about 100 to 120 were better than those in the '90s'. The engines built in 1956 were fitted with Caprotti valve gear which apparently made them even more free running. I don't think that there were any of this later type on the Southern, if there were I certainly never saw them.

The Western Region '73s' were fitted with the old GWR automatic train control and some were painted green. In fact the last steam engine that I worked on was a green Western '73', No. 73029, which was a pity because it was one of the weakest engines I ever came across and had a job to pull itself along, never mind a train.

Classification	BR9F (92000)	Steam pressure	250 lb.
Type	2-10-0 tender	Cylinders	20 in. x 28 in. (2)
Designed	Brighton	Driving wheels	5 ft 0 in.
Introduced	1954	Tractive effort	26,120 lb.
Weight	86 tons 14 cwt		

This heavy freight engine was probably the best of all the Standards and was an improvement on the old 'WD' class of 1948, the only other British 2-10-0 to be built. I never worked on the 'WDs' but many of my older colleagues did and they told me that they were real old clatter carts. The '92s' were not seen much on the Southern but some were based at Eastleigh and used on heavy oil trains from Fawley to the Midlands.

BR Standard '9F' class 2-10-0 No. 92220 *Evening Star* passes Surbiton with a special.

Bill Trigg

Ex-GWR 0-6-0PT No. 4672 with empty stock from Waterloo at Clapham on 14th October, 1959.
J.H. Scrace

An unidentified Ivatt 2-6-2T on the down road between Waterloo and Vauxhall on 19th October, 1963. Millbank Tower can be seen in the background.   *Colin P. Walker*

Later some were shedded at Feltham where I worked on them, although to be honest the trains out of Feltham yard were not heavy enough to warrant such a giant engine. They sometimes appeared on passenger trains and surprisingly for an engine with such small wheels they were extremely fast and smooth riding. They had a wide firebox which was also very shallow and the first time I worked on one I nearly let the fire go out, but luckily I was able to get it going again. The centre driving wheels had no flanges to enable them to negotiate the sharper curves, but they were not allowed into Waterloo because of the tight reverse curves there.

Other Regions' Engines

Class	5700	*Steam pressure*	200 lb.
Type	0-6-0 pannier tank	*Cylinders*	17½ in. x 24 in. (2)
Designer	Collett (GWR)	*Driving wheels*	4 ft 7½ in.
Introduced	1929 to 1948	*Tractive effort*	22,515 lb.
Weight	47½ to 50 tons		

These Great Western pannier tanks were built by Collett originally in 1929 and some were transferred to Nine Elms when the 'M7' tanks were withdrawn. They were used for empty stock working between Clapham Yard and Waterloo and were superb locomotives for that job. They would start out of Waterloo with 13 bogies and with never a sign of slipping, which was a change from the four-coupled Drummond tanks which had much larger wheels. Apart from being very strong engines they were the most awkward machine to work on that I have ever seen.

The footplate was not level but had a well in the middle, either that or both sides were raised, whichever it was I found out the hard way. The first time I stepped on one I entered on the driver's side and went to walk to the fireman's side; there was a drop of about four inches into the well and down I went. I tripped and finished up halfway out of the cab on the fireman's side. They also had a large pole reverser which got in the way and I found the firing space in the well very restricted.

Class	Midland type 2	*Steam pressure*	200 lb.
Type	2-6-2 tank	*Cylinders*	16 in. x 24 in. (2)
Designer	Ivatt (LMS)	*Driving wheels*	5 ft 0 in.
Introduced	1946	*Tractive effort*	17,410 lb.
Weight	63 tons 0 cwt		

Another foreign engine to make an appearance on the Southern was what were known as 'Teddy Bear' tanks. They came from the 'Midland' and were numbered in the '41000' range. They were a well liked little engine and not dissimilar from the small standard tanks. I saw them working around Stewarts Lane when I was on loan there and they sometimes appeared on the branch between Horsham and Guildford so they were probably based at either Horsham or Brighton. I never fired on them but had to wait until I was driving at Nine Elms to sample them myself. I found them a pleasant little engine and quite capable of all that was required. The only memorable experience I can recall was a nasty incident with the stock for the 'Royal Wessex' which I shall tell of later.

I once worked a Midland 'Black Five' when I was at Nine Elms but the trip was not anything out of the ordinary and the 'Five' was not worked hard at all. I came into contact with the Great Western 'Hall' class at Guildford, Basingstoke and Fratton, but my only experience on them was squaring them up and the less said about that the better.

The reader will gather from this chapter that the engines I worked on or saw working were many and varied. They were conceived in the minds of many different men from many different generations and for many different purposes, so it is not surprising that classes were so different from each other. However, each engineer had stamped his personality on his engines; it was not always noticeable to the casual observer but to anyone having close contact the engines of a particular designer were instantly recognisable. Enginemen had a close affinity with the engineer even though he may have been dead for many years; they would defend his work and argue the merits of his engines against those of a rival engineer from another company. South Western crews were 'Drummond' men and proud of it.

Having said that, it is also true that no two engines ever performed the same, one of a class would need different handling to another and that was part of the driver's and fireman's skill as a team. When a regular pair of men worked together for a long time they came to know how the other would react to particular circumstances and it was not necessary for either to say anything to the other, it was all done by understanding.

It may be difficult for anyone without personal experience to understand, but with a steam engine the power was not on tap as with diesel or electric traction; the fireman had to make it and the driver had to use it to best advantage. The crew both worked by instinct born of experience and it was the feel of the engine rather than any set rules which motivated their actions. When the driver, the fireman and the engine were all in tune there was a terrific feeling of satisfaction. Perhaps this was one of the main attractions of the job, it certainly sustained me at times when the unsociable hours and personal problems got on top of me and I felt ready to look for a more normal job. I could never think of another job which could give me that sort of satisfaction.

An ex-LMS Stanier 'Black Five' No. 45349 heads the 3.35 pm Waterloo-Bournemouth train at Weybridge on 23rd June, 1966.   *M. Stokes*

Chapter Three

Fireman: 1959 to 1964

I was 18 in April 1959 and looked forward to taking up my proper position in No. 6 link (the holiday relief gang) and working my proper turns; also, I was to have a regular mate which I looked forward to immensely. Ken Parker was to be my driver which pleased me as I knew him well and found him to be a pleasant person. He was a youngish driver in his mid-thirties. I had worked with him a lot in the past and we always got on well together. Unfortunately, after only six weeks I was promoted to No. 5 link and during that time I had only worked with him for two weeks so I never really had time to settle down.

In those days, the work allocated to a depot was segregated into 'links' according to type. No. 1 link was the 'Top Link' and had the best work, mostly passenger trains, the senior drivers and firemen were in this link. The work was scaled down through the links so that the junior men were in the highest numbered link and performed the lowest type of work. Seniority dictated their progression through the links and at Guildford there were six links of 12 pairs of men, plus the 'old man's gang', the 'ash gang' and the 'turning gang', these last three were not progressive. The 'old man's gang' was a special link which any driver over the age of 60 could volunteer for; the work was light and they did not work such unsociable hours as other drivers. It was intended for those men who felt unable to perform their normal duties and wanted a quiet life for the last five years of work. They performed shunting duties at Guildford and Woking and worked local goods trains up the 'New Line' to Epsom and Surbiton.

The 'ash gang' has been described in Chapter One. The 'turning gang' was composed mainly of men who because of ill health or defective eyesight were unable to perform 'track' work. They worked three shifts and there were two pairs of men on each shift, one pair in the shed and one at the coal stage. The men at the coal stage moved the engines into position for coaling and made sure that the coal was stacked properly. They then took the engines down to the turntable and left them for the shed crew to deal with, they also performed any shunting duties required at the coal stage. The shed crew moved engines into and out of the shed and filled tenders with water as required, they performed any shunting duties at the shed end.

The progressive links started with the holiday relief link and worked up from there. The name of this link speaks for itself and the drivers and firemen were rostered spare most of the time, but during the holiday period were booked to cover particular men during their annual leave. The driver and fireman rarely covered the same duty so unless they were 'spare' they did not often work together.

No. 5 link was next and Eddie Greavesherd was my mate, the work in this link was mainly local freight work and Nine Elms men always referred to it as 'Short road goods'. We usually started from Woking yard with a load of coal and general goods which had arrived during the night from Feltham or Nine

Elms. We used to go down the Alton line, across the Ascot branch and down the Portsmouth 'direct', stopping at nearly every station *en route*. Most stations, even the tiny ones, had a siding of some sort in those days and we went into them all to put off and pick up. I used to enjoy this work, we would meet all sorts of people on these trips and there were some real characters about.

We had a turn to Redhill which I always used to enjoy, it was a night duty which started by relieving a pair of Reading men when they arrived at Guildford with a general freight. We would then go into the down yard to sort the train and pick up the wagons which were being dispatched from Guildford. We left at about midnight for Redhill, the train was not usually very heavy and the '800' 'S15' made light work of it. We were relieved by Redhill men who worked the train forward to an unknown destination (unknown to me that is). We then walked to the loco depot and after having a cup of tea and a sandwich we prepared an 'N' class and left the shed for the up yard to pick up our second train.

This train was much heavier and consisted of six 'Presflo' bulk cement wagons and 32 box wagons, loaded with hundredweight bags of cement, and a brake van. The train started from Snodland in Kent and because of this the duty was always known as the 'Snodland', its destination was somewhere in South Wales. We always carried the same load on the 'Snodland', 38=60. At that time the way a load was calculated was in units of 10 tons. Depending upon what was being carried the wagon was said to weigh so many units, the guard would tally them up and tell the driver that his load was so many wagons equal to so many units; therefore, 38=60 meant that we had 38 wagons (not counting the guard's van), which was equal to 60 units or 600 tons. This was not a very accurate method and judging by the trouble we had with the 'Snodland' it was way out.

On leaving Redhill yard there was a sharp right-hand bend for ¼ mile and a gradient of 1 in 100 for two miles up to Reigate. This was a hard climb from a standing start but we always reckoned that if we could get up to Reigate then we could get up Dorking Bank which was the next obstacle.

From Reigate it was all downhill to Deepdene and this section was used to prepare the engine for the climb of 1 in 96 up to Welcome Bridge which was four miles distant. We would come down though Deepdene like a bat out of hell with the train stretched out and all the couplings tight ready for the assault on Dorking. As soon as we spotted the distant signal for Dorking Town signal box showing green, the driver would apply more power to start the climb. By the time we were halfway up the bank, we were down to about 15 mph and with full regulator the reverser was progressively moved forward until it was in full gear at 75 per cent cut off. It was then a matter of keeping the boiler at full pressure and hoping that the wheels did not slip. Every beat from the exhaust was accompanied by a kick from one side or the other alternately as the crank passed either back or front dead centre and took power again.

It is one of my abiding memories of this period, working the 'Snodland' up Dorking Bank on a cold frosty morning with the sounds of the engine flogging on full power being echoed from the hills all around. Right at the top of the bank was a deep cutting, this was crossed by a high bridge which was formed by two cast-iron frames with a wooden deck and a picket fence as a parapet. The frames were decorative and had heart shapes about six feet high all across, when approaching the summit from either side the frames were silhouetted against the night sky. This was 'Welcome Bridge', so named for obvious reasons and on trips such as I have described it really was welcome.

It was downhill nearly all the way from Welcome Bridge to Guildford, so if the ascent went all right you were on the home stretch, at least the fireman was. The driver still had the problem of controlling the train on the steep descent to Gomshall and from Shere Heath to Chilworth. We had a frightening experience on the 'Snodland' one morning when my driver was unable to stop the engine wheels from locking when he applied the steam brakes, the vacuum brakes on the tender and the 'Presflo' wagons were working and the guard had his hand brake on, but the wheels on the engine would not grip the rail. All the time we were getting nearer to Chilworth and the distant signal was at caution, eventually he managed to get the wheels to stay down but it was too late by then and we passed the home signal at danger. I was popping the whistle to warn the signalman of our approach, the level crossing gates at Chilworth were not operated from the signal box but had to be pushed open by hand. The signalman ran out and pushed the gates open as we neared the opposite end of the station, which was a good thing because when we stopped we were about 50 yards past the gates.

On arrival at Guildford we were relieved by another pair of Guildford men, after taking water they worked the train on to Reading where the Western Region took over. At least that was the idea, but a particular driver who took over from us often failed to coax the train round the sharp curve and up the 1 in 100 gradient out of Guildford. That would have been all right but on his reports he always tried to blame me for his failure, he would say that I had too much water in the boiler or the fire wasn't right or I hadn't filled the sandboxes. My driver always supported me and said that the other driver wasn't trying, he called him 'Old lion heart', and said that if we could get up Reigate and Dorking banks, then he should be able to get up 'Pinks Hill', which was the name of the bank out of Guildford on the Reading line.

About six months after my entering No. 5 link, Eddie took up a position in the dual link, this was a voluntary move as the dual link was not progressive. He would be trained on electric traction and would be rostered both steam and electric duties as and when required. My new driver was John Hartfree who had transferred from Fratton on a promotion move. I got on well with him and he had a wide route knowledge which made us available for many duties which other crews were unable to work.

One of the rostered duties in No. 5 link was the 'No. 2 ballast turn'. The term ballast turn referred to any duty associated with engineering work, such as track relaying, bridge rebuilding, cable laying, fencing and a host of other activities; a ballast train was any train connected with such work. When on relaying jobs the No. 1 ballast crew would push the relaying machine backwards and forwards picking up track sections and replacing them; the No. 2 crew were on the material train which was a much easier job and was not required to move very often.

There was a pre-assembly depot (PAD) at Woking and the relaying gang were out most nights of the week and many weekends. We went all over the place on these jobs, they were well paid jobs as we usually worked the complete duty without relief and this often meant 11 or 12 hours a night; in later years relief was sent out by taxi to the site of work. These duties were very hard but also very interesting and I watched many aspects of civil engineering in operation which gave me an good insight into the problems faced by the engineers. It also provided me with a deep appreciation of the original railway builders and I am still amazed at the enormous task they faced and the fantastic results of their labours when considered in relation to the available tools.

Many of the engines had now been fitted with the new British Railways Automatic Warning System (AWS), which was different from the old GWR system which had been in use for many years, the new system being operated by magnets fitted to the track. At that time on the South Western only the main line was fitted with the track equipment so, although most of the engines carried locomotive equipment, it was not often used except that at the exit from every depot there was a permanent magnet to test the equipment.

Even some of the older engines had been fitted, one in particular stands out in my mind; she was one of the push-pull 'Motor Tanks'. With the battery boxes and control levers for the push-pull equipment in the cab, together with the AWS equipment, space on the footplate was restricted to say the least. This engine was also fitted with the water softening plant which was being introduced at the time. The tanks or tenders had a container with small holes in it inserted, into these containers were placed brown briquettes to soften the water and loosen the scale in the boiler; the boilers were fitted with blow-down valves so that the resulting sludge could be cleaned out while the boiler was still in steam. This equipment increased the period between boiler washouts from two to four weeks. The briquettes were sometimes known as 'Beeching's Pills', an allusion to Dr Beeching who was Chairman of BR at that time and had previously been with ICI chemicals. On some of the larger types the softened water tended to cause priming and a special white milky substance was added to the water to prevent this. In addition to the brown water pills, there were green pills of the same size (about the size of a tin of baby food) which were placed on the fire in order to clean the tube plate and smoke tubes.

I imagine it must have been the chemical company background of the famous doctor that influenced the BR Board to employ so many chemical substances. In addition to the foregoing there were also weed killer pills which saved a lot of permanent way work. The little wooden inserts used when bolts were screwed though the track chairs to hold them down were replaced by a new type which was man made (Nylon or plastic). I am sure that there were many more examples of this sort of thing which I did not know about. Although they obviously saved money in the long run, their introduction must have' cost a small fortune and many of these items were not in use long enough to recoup the original investment.

Back to No. 5, we had many interesting duties in this link, unfortunately most of them started very early in the morning which rather took the shine off of them. The Ascot turn was one such duty, we signed on at 3.45 am and prepared the engine, an 'Eastern C'; we then ran tender first to Woking down yard to pick up our train which was mainly coal but with some general goods. We went down the main line to Sturt Lane Junction where we turned right onto the Ascot branch at Frimley Junction. There was a three-way junction at Frimley: an up and down curve to the main line at Farnborough, an up and down curve to the main line at the Woking end of Sturt Lane and a single line under the main line which joined the Alton line at Ash Vale. The Ascot branch was electrified and the Woking end curve was electrified, as were the up and down local lines between Brookwood and Sturt Lane and the single line to Ash Vale.

Frimley station was about a mile away from the junction and was our first call, the siding there was small and we left our train on the running line while we went into the yard to pick up and put off. Camberley was the next stop, the yard there was larger and we took the train in with us, stayed there for some time, sorting the yard, then set off for Bagshot after the first passenger train. This came from Woking and was one of the few electric services to use the section from Pirbright Junction to Frimley Junction.

There was a 1 in 60 climb for about 1½ miles from Camberley to the tunnel at the summit and a 1 in 60 descent from there to Bagshot where we called briefly. There was another steep climb out of Bagshot then it was down hill all the way to Ascot, where we shunted the yard, turned the engine and took water. The turntable there was quite large but it was rather stiff and it took a fair amount of effort to push it round. We were relieved at Ascot and went home as passengers to Guildford, the new crew worked a trip to Ascot gas works and then went to Bracknell and back. Later they worked across to Bagshot and Camberley where they in turn were relieved, the late turn shunted at Camberley and later worked the goods back to Woking.

There was only one other steam duty over this line, known as the 'Ascot fish', this duty was in No. 3 link and started by relieving a freight up from Fratton which was worked on to Feltham where the engine was disposed. The crew walked to Feltham station and relieved on the fish train which had left Waterloo at about 4.00 am, calling at all stations to Camberley, unloading parcel traffic as well as fish; from Camberley the train ran empty to Woking.

The Alton turn was similar, 3.45 am was the signing-on time again, then tender first to Woking where fish vans were attached. We left Woking at 5.25 am and ran fast to Aldershot where the fish was unloaded, then on to Farnham where we changed engines with the crew who had worked the 5.00 am goods from Woking. It seemed rather a strange arrangement as we both had a 'Black Motor' and we all signed on at the same time. However, they stayed at Farnham with our engine and we took theirs and their train and went on to Alton where we sorted the yard out before making short trips to various destinations depending on what day it was. We either went down the (now preserved) 'Mid-Hants' to Medstead and Ropley or down the former Meon Valley line to Farringdon which was where that line ended. The section between there and Droxford had been closed in about 1955. On the days that we went to Farringdon we also went to the siding at Treloars hospital; this siding which was at Butts Junction was originally the start of the line to Basingstoke which had been closed many years before in the 1930s. The Mid-Hants was always known as 'The Alps' and was a very steeply graded line.

Those old 'Black Motors' hauled a full load of goods up the bank to Foxhill tunnel between Pirbright Junction and Ash Vale and they were out on this duty until about 10.00 pm. When they were worked hard they tended to throw large sparks out of the chimney which were known as 'rockets'. When they were worked in full gear and full regulator white hot pieces of coal were emitted at a terrific speed; in the dark they looked like lines in the sky and were known as 'stair rods'. It always surprised me to see a sign halfway up the bank from Alton to Medstead advising drivers that there was a fire risk in that area and to avoid making sparks, in that situation it was almost impossible.

When we returned to Alton we were relieved and made our way back to Guildford, our relief worked up to Farnham and then down the Bordon branch, calling at Bentley on the way. This was only a short branch with one intermediate halt and the passenger service had ceased in the late 1950s. The goods still ran and at times it was fairly well loaded, much of the traffic was for transfer to the Longmoor Military Railway which ran from Bordon to Liss, and was connected to the BR lines at both ends. After leaving Bordon they ran to Aldershot where they turned the engine, took water and were themselves relieved. The late turn men shunted at Aldershot and worked to Farnham again before taking a parcel train up to Woking and then returning to depot.

The turntable at Aldershot was small and when turning a 'Monty', which was the largest engine that could turn there, you had to have the boiler half-full and the tender full up. The engine was then placed on the table with the wheel flanges just clear of the fixed rails at either end, then the injector was turned on and you waited until the table balanced as the boiler filled. You could then push it round quite easily but if this procedure was not carried out the table would not budge.

I got on well with John Hartfree and we had many a good laugh together as we shared the same sense of humour, much to the annoyance of some people who tended to look on black side of everything. One amusing incident happened very early one morning, the duty we were booked for the week started by preparing a 'Black Motor' and going light engine to Woking at about 2.00 am (engine first for a change). After performing some shunting in the up yard we assembled the train before being relieved by Feltham men who worked the train to Feltham at about 3.30 am. On the trip to Woking, another pair of Guildford men were booked to ride with us and the other driver always sat on my seat so that I had to stand up, he did not even ask.

I was annoyed about this but did not want to cause a fuss, but my annoyance must have showed because John asked me about it. When I told him my feelings he said, 'Don't worry, I will show you how to deal with him tomorrow night'. The next morning after we had prepared the engine and were ready to leave, John got the can of superheater oil and placed a large blob on my seat, then we waited for the other driver to arrive: the same man, incidentally, who had left me to work on my own that day when I nearly passed out, so I was going to get double satisfaction this night. We heard him approaching and waited for him to climb onto the footplate and sit on my seat. To our horror it was not the offending driver who appeared, but a motive power inspector, George Bollom, before we could stop him he sat right on the blob of oil. He was wearing a fawn raincoat over his uniform and when he got off at Woking he had a large black mark on his coat. We didn't dare to say anything but I expect that Mr Bollom was annoyed when he found it, I never played that trick again.

On that same duty at a later date, after we had assembled the train, the guard came into the shunters' cabin and said, 'There is a cow lying down in the first wagon, I will not take the train until they are all standing up'. There were always a few cattle wagons on the front of this train. We took the first wagon up the yard and placed it in the cattle dock; when the shunters opened the door the cow which was lying down was the first one out, closely followed by all the others. Of course, nobody had thought to close the gate of the cattle pen and the cows all ran down the slope and out into the road with the shunters in hot pursuit. It was some time before they were all captured and returned to the wagon.

The next night the same guard said the same thing and one of the shunters said, 'I will soon get him up', and so saying left the cabin with shunting pole in hand. A few minutes later he returned, covered in cow dung; he had pushed the pointed end of his shunting pole into the wagon and prodded the cow to make it stand up, unfortunately he prodded the wrong end. A few days later the same problem arose, but this time the shunter was wiser and did not stand on the ground to prod the cow. Instead he climbed up the side of the wagon and was about to poke the cow from above when one of the standing cows moved its head, knocking the man's hand from the rail that he was holding. He fell to the ground and lay there winded. He swore that in future if any cows laid down, they could b . . . . . well stay there as far as he was concerned. Not being involved, we thought it was all very funny and whenever we met that particular shunter we would make wisecracks about cows or dung, all of which he found extremely unfunny and made this known to us in the strongest terms, of course this made us laugh even more.

This period was one of the happiest in my working life, I had no personal problems and work was a pleasure, even when things went wrong we managed to laugh about it. We laughed at our own misfortunes and even more so at other people's; in retrospect I think that some people must have thought that we were a pair of rotters, but they were only the people who lacked a sense of humour.

There was a serious incident at the depot one day which was not funny at all at the time, but when the facts behind it were known we could see the funny side of it. A pair of Redhill men had brought a 'Z' tank to Guildford which was on its way to the West Country but was to berth at Guildford over the weekend. There was no space in the shed so the running foreman ordered it to be berthed in the coal siding at the coal stage, the fire was withdrawn and was not lit again until the day it was to continue its journey.

The 'Z' class were not normal visitors to Guildford and I had never seen one before, nor had the firelighter had ever seen one either. Before lighting the fire he would check that all steam valves on the engine were in the closed position, when he got on the 'Z' he found the regulator wide open, at least he thought it was open so he closed it and lit the fire. On this type of engine the regulator was different, instead of lifting the lever to open it you had to pull it down, so in fact he had opened it fully.

When a driver went to get the engine from the coal road, as soon as he released the brake the engine started to move and he was unable to stop it again. It went towards the shed and luckily the turntable was in the correct position, it went straight across the table and crashed into three other locomotives which were standing in No. 1 road. It bounced back and then crashed into them again, eventually stopping halfway in the pit of No. 1 road after causing considerable damage. As I have said, it was not funny at the time, but the sequence of events which culminated in the crash do have a certain comic inevitability about them, or perhaps I have a warped sense of humour.

Another incident with the same comic sequence happened when I was shunting the ballast yard at Woking early one morning. Some of the drivers, instead of bringing sandwiches to work, would bring rashers of bacon and eggs which they cooked by placing them on the firing shovel just inside the firehole door. The recipe was something like this,

1. Wash the firing shovel with the pet pipe.
2. Place the rashers on the shovel and hold over the fire, allowing the bacon to cook in its own fat.
3. When the bacon is cooked, remove from shovel and cook the eggs in the bacon fat.

This may sound a bit gruesome but believe me the result was really delicious. This particular day, the shunting was taking longer than usual and I had made a can of tea to drink while we were working. My driver was getting really fed up and said, 'If we go on much longer I shall have my rashers for dinner instead of breakfast'.

There was no sign that the work was nearing completion and eventually the driver asked me if I would drive the engine while he cooked his breakfast, I readily agreed and we changed sides. He started to prepare the shovel while I looked out for the shunter. We had a 'T9' on this day, not the best of engines for heavy shunting duties, but I managed quite well, at least I thought I did. We picked up a long string of 'Grampus' wagons which were loaded with new sleepers and started to pull them up the yard, the bacon was cooked and smelled really delicious, then just as the eggs were ready, the wheels slipped and the blast from the chimney sucked the eggs right off the shovel and into the fire.

I will not tell you what the driver said, but it was not complimentary and when I offered him one of my sandwiches by way of compensation he said a rude word and suggested that I put it where the squirrel puts his nuts. I felt sorry for him, having lost half his breakfast, but when he told the shunters about his stupid fireman, instead of sympathising with him, they fell about laughing and I found it very difficult to keep a straight face and had to leave the room before I disgraced myself.

In early 1961 I was moved up to No. 3 link, for some reason I missed No. 4. My driver was now Bert Heath, he had been one of the two drivers based at Bordon when that depot existed and had been transferred to Guildford on its closure. Number 3 link was similar to No. 5 but we tended to go further afield. We had turns to Havant, Portsmouth, Reading, Redhill, Feltham, Nine Elms and Horsham. The two turns to Horsham were a goods train in the morning and an evening commuter train. The goods duty was my favourite, we left Guildford at about eight in the morning with a small train of mixed goods. Our first stop was Peasmarsh Junction to unload sacks of coal when required for the signal box. We picked up the single line staff there which authorised our passage to Bramley and Wonersh, the first station on the branch, where we went into the siding to pick up and put off then waited for a train to pass before continuing.

The next station was Cranleigh where we spent some time shunting the yard, Cranleigh was the most important station on the line and the village was large enough to have a gas works and a cinema. Some of the other villages on the route were barely large enough to support a pub and some stations were far away from the villages.

Baynards was our next call then though the tunnel to Rudgewick, where there was an unusual layout which is worth a mention. The single line came round a curve into the station and straight ahead was the shunting neck, the single line slued over to the right and ran alongside the neck; when running from the station towards Horsham we would jokingly call it 'going out on the through'. From the shunting neck a single siding ran behind the station and terminated at a small turntable; from here, two sidings sloped towards stop blocks. When putting wagons into the sidings we pushed them one at a time onto the table, then the porter/shunter turned them and left them to gravitate down the sidings. When they were empty they were pulled up to the table by the coal merchant's lorry and gravitated to the siding behind the station to await picking up. Originally the wagons were pulled up by a capstan.

On leaving Rudgewick we ran fast to Horsham, missing Slinfold. At Horsham the train was sorted and made ready for the return trip, we then retired to the canteen to enjoy a lovely dinner which was always available there in those days. Unfortunately most of the canteens disappeared in the 1960s and are now only a memory. On the return trip we stopped at Slinfold for a short while to attend to the coal siding and the ladder factory, then giving Rudgewick a miss we went up the bank to Baynards again where we sorted the sidings and waited while a tractor pushed the wagons out from Fullers Earth siding. We waited for a train to pass before proceeding to Cranleigh for the second time, we then ran fast to Guildford.

The line was single track all the way from Peasmarsh Junction on the Portsmouth Direct line to Christ's Hospital on the Mid-Sussex line, with passing loops at Bramley, Cranleigh and Baynards. From Peasmarsh to Bramley, Bramley to Cranleigh and Cranleigh to Baynards, the passage of trains was controlled by train staff equipment. The section between Baynards and Christ's Hospital was operated under train staff and ticket regulations, the only place I ever saw this system in operation.

The passenger turn was the 6.05 pm from Guildford which connected with a fast train from London, there was a popular song at the time called '6-5 Special', so of course this train was known by that name. We called at all stations to Horsham; at Bramley and Baynards where the station exit was at the Horsham end the passengers would tip their bowler hats and say 'Goodnight driver' and the driver would reply likewise, it was a pleasant atmosphere.

'M7' class 0-4-4T No. 30108 with an ex-LBSCR two-car push-pull set on the 9.30 am from Horsham after arrival at Guildford on 2nd April, 1955.   *John Faulkner*

An 'E4' class 0-6-2T with the stock for the 1.04 pm to Cranleigh in the North sidings at Guildford on 6th September, 1958.   *John Faulkner*

The goods turn was usually powered by a 'Motor Tank', but when the '350' shunting engine at Horsham was low on fuel, the duty would be worked by a '350' with the engines being changed at Horsham. A road tanker visited the coal stage at Guildford when the '350' needed fuel as there was never any oil storage facility there. The 6.05 pm was always hauled by a 'Charlie', the largest engine allowed over that route because of the small tunnel at Baynards. All engines ran engine first to Horsham and tender or bunker first to Guildford, because there was a steep gradient from Rudgewick through the little tunnel to Baynards. If the chimney was leading when climbing the bank all the smoke and steam came back into the cab and would nearly choke the crew.

The Horsham branch was my favourite piece of railway, it was a true country branch and had a relaxed atmosphere about it, everybody knew what his job was and no orders were needed. Some people had several different jobs depending on the time of day. At Baynards, one of the staff lived on the station, I think it was the signalman, he was a keen gardener and grew beautiful dahlias all over the station; it looked absolutely fantastic when they were in full bloom. He used to sell them to us for 6d. a bunch and when the time was right the men at the loco would ask the crew of the Horsham goods to buy them a bunch. At such times we would arrive at the depot with our cab full of flowers.

There were four turns on the 'Pompey' road. The first started at Woking and ran to Guildford where wagons for intermediate stations to Haslemere were detached, then fast to Haslemere where more wagons were put off for later sorting. The train then called at Liphook and Liss on the way to Petersfield, more wagons were left here whilst the train went on to Rowlands Castle and then to Havant; here the engine ran round the train before returning to Petersfield where the crew were relieved.

The new crew shunted at Petersfield for a long time before proceeding to Liss where the yard was sorted, the same went for Liphook and finally Haslemere where considerable time was spent, after which the train ran fast to Guildford. The 'Rowlands Castle', as the duty was called was a heavy train on the down trip and usually carried a full load, on the up trip most of the wagons were empty.

The second turn was the Haslemere goods, this started at Guildford and carried traffic for Milford, Witley and Haslemere. The first call was Witley to put off and pick up, then on to Haslemere where the two yards were sorted, the train calling at Milford on the return trip to Guildford.

The third duty was the Godalming goods, this was part of a larger duty and only conveyed traffic for Godalming goods yard which was nearer to Farncombe than Godalming and was the original terminus of the old LSWR line before the Portsmouth Direct line was built in 1859. On the return trip the train called at both Arlington 'deep freeze' siding and Peasmarsh siding, from where a coal merchant operated.

The fourth turn was the Petersfield fish train, which did not carry much fish in those days and was mainly loaded with heavy parcels and general traffic too big to be handled as ordinary parcels. This train called at all stations between Godalming and Petersfield where the wagons were placed in the goods shed, the engine then went back to Guildford where it was used for carriage shunting duties.

The 'Rowlands Castle' was usually worked by a 'Charlie' although a 'Monty' was sometimes used. The Haslemere goods was hauled by either an 'Eastern C' or a 'Black Motor'. The Godalming goods had a 'Monty' as motive power in later years but it was a 'Jumbo' job previously. The Petersfield fish was worked by a 'Brighton tank' but this was later changed to a 'Motor Tank'. The 'Pompey direct' was a heavy route to work on and the wide variety of engines we used made the work more interesting. Each type needed different handling to get the best out of them and on the long climb from Farncombe to Haslemere an inexperienced crew could soon come to grief.

When recalling this period, the work which stands out in my mind most is the 'ballast' turns, probably because they were rather unpleasant as they were nearly all night work and usually involved overtime. I remember one night in particular. We left Woking with a 'Monty' hauling a heavy train of assorted equipment; we had two steam cranes, two mess vans, long bogies stacked with prefabricated track sections, two empty bogies, several 'hoppers' of ballast stone and a guard's van at each end.

We were going to Bagshot and when the guard came up to give Bert the load, he also told him that it was the first time he had worked a loose-fitted train over this route. Bert gave him strict instructions about using his handbrake, he said: 'When we pass through Camberley and climb the bank to the tunnel, keep your eyes on the yellow street lamp which you will see in front of you, when you lose sight of it screw your brake on hard and keep it on'. After the struggle up the 1 in 60 gradient to the tunnel we started the equally steep descent to Bagshot; as we emerged from the tunnel the wheels picked up on the engine and Bert was having trouble in keeping the train under control. After a lot of effort between us we gradually gained control of the situation and Bert had the train moving very slowly down the bank.

About halfway down, the train suddenly surged into the engine causing the wheels to pick up again and all our efforts made no difference at all. We gathered speed and Bert was helpless, even when he got the wheels down he could not stop the train. As we came onto the straight approaching Bagshot we could see a cluster of Tilley lamps all across the line ahead, I was sounding the alarm on the whistle and Bert was trying to control the train as best he could. The lamps scattered in all directions as we went right through the station and out the other side, eventually stopping some two or three hundred yards past the station. Bert scrambled down from the engine and ran back along the train to see the guard. When he asked him what he was up to, he replied, 'You were going so slow that I thought I was stopping you, so I took the brake off'. Bert's reply is unfit to print.

Another awful experience was when we were on a job in the middle of Queen Elizabeth Forest between Petersfield and Rowlands Castle. It was a bitterly cold night, all the fir trees in the forest were glittering in the moonlight which is very nice on a Christmas card, but not much fun when you are out in the open. The cab on our 'Monty' did not offer full protection and we frequently had to lean out to watch for hand signals. When the job was finished we went down to Havant to run-round the train, I suggested to Bert that we should take the engine down to Fratton to turn so that we would be warm on the trip up to

Woking, but he said that he didn't want to be late getting home, so we went tender first as booked. Even with the storm sheet up the footplate of that 'Monty' was like an ice box and by the time we arrived at Woking I was frozen to the marrow.

With those sort of conditions to endure it is surprising that enginemen did not suffer serious ill health. But it never seemed to affect anyone for long. Considering my own weakness and poor health at the age of 11, it is even more surprising that I was in the peak of fitness, I sometimes played football after being out all night. There was one driver at Guildford who never wore a vest or a shirt, he only wore an overall jacket in summer and an overall jacket and 'serge' jacket in winter, his chest was always bare and when it was really cold it would be bright red, I could never understand how he endured it but it did not seem to do him any harm.

I met this driver, Charlie Boskett was his name, just as he arrived at work early one morning. He had ridden his motorbike from his home at Ash, and walked into the roster room wearing a long railway mackintosh, a pair of leather gauntlets and his driver's hat pulled firmly on his head. He took off the gauntlets and rubbed his hands together, 'It's a cold one this morning' he said, we all agreed, then he took off his mac. All he had on under his mac was an overall jacket, his chest was glowing red and he had said that his hands· were cold. He was in his late fifties then but I saw him one day many years later, after he had retired, working in the churchyard at Ash and he still had no shirt on.

It was while I was with Bert Heath that I had the worst trip of all my career on the steam. It was the Thursday before Good Friday in 1962 when we signed on and prepared No. C19; we ran light engine to Fratton, turned on the triangle and berthed the engine outside the shed while we went to the drivers' cabin to have some tea and food. We were to work a train of condemned wagons up to Feltham, which was probably why we were doing it early on a bank holiday. These wagons were known as 'cripples' and as such they were not very free running and quite likely to suffer from 'hot boxes'.

Whilst our engine was unattended, some kind person decided to do us a favour and filled the tender with coal. Actually they filled it with 'eggs' which were small oval briquettes made from compressed coal dust. When I returned to build the fire up in readiness for our departure I had to use these eggs as I was unable to reach the ordinary coal. We went out into the yard and picked up our train, 42 cripples and a brake van. We left Fratton and ran on the level to Havant where we turned onto the 'Pompey Direct' line and began the long twisting climb up to Buriton tunnel.

As soon as Bert started to work the engine hard the steam pressure fell and I used the dart and the pricker in an attempt to liven the fire up. The only effect this had was to break the eggs into dust and the fire took on the appearance of red hot sand. The further we climbed up the bank the worse it got and by the time we reached Ditcham at the start of the Queen Elizabeth Forest, the pressure was down to 100 lb. The surprising thing was that the vacuum level remained sufficient to keep the brakes off, usually on a 'Charlie' they would go on if the pressure dropped below 120 lb.

We reached the top of the bank at walking pace with only 80 lb. of steam in the boiler and breathed a sigh of relief, we had a downhill run to Petersfield and would be able to recover our position. We passed Petersfield with a full head of steam and a full pot of water, I thought our troubles were over; not so, as we commenced the long climb up to Haslemere the pressure fell rapidly and it was obvious that we would soon be in trouble again. We were. Before we reached the summit of Liss Bank the pressure was below 100 lb. again and on the fairly level section from there to Hammer Bottom, about four miles away, I was unable to coax any increase in boiler pressure. As we approached the station at Haslemere the pressure was down to 60 lb. and the engine breathed her last sigh and stopped with the regulator still open. We were only 400 yards short of a 14 mile free run into Guildford.

I picked up the shovel intending to put some coal on the fire, but was overcome with fatigue and for the second time in my career I was completely unable to continue. Bert told me to go to the signal box, have a drink of water and tell the signalman why we had stopped and that we would be on the move shortly. As it turned out he was being optimistic and when I returned to the engine 10 minutes later the pressure had still not risen above 80 lb. despite all Bert's efforts.

Eventually I managed to raise 100 lb. on the gauge, which proved enough to lift us the last ¼ mile uphill and on to the long descent to Guildford. When we arrived at Guildford the gauge still showed 100 lb. and I expected my mate to call for a fresh engine from the depot, but he said, 'Put the pipe in the tender then I will see to it while you take some clinker out of the fire'. I was annoyed at this, but he was the driver and it was his decision whether to carry on or not. I managed to extract only four pieces of very thin clinker from the fire and then proceeded to rebuild the fire. Luckily, nearly all the eggs were gone and I could use some good 'Welsh' steam coal again, although I did not have a good base to build on, it still looked like a load of red hot sand. However, the pressure soon started to rise and by the time we left we had a full head of steam and a boiler full of water.

As we climbed Stouton Bank out of Guildford the engine was blowing off and we had an excellent trip as far as Staines, but between there and Feltham the pressure continually dropped and nothing I did would make it rise again. We eventually came to a stand halfway into Feltham yard and stayed there for five minutes before we could move the last few hundred yards to clear the main line. After turning the engine and having a cup of tea we set off light engine for Guildford. We departed with 100 lb. on the steam gauge and I never managed to raise more than 120 lb. all the way, was I glad to go home that morning. I worked on No. C19 many times after that and she never performed as badly as that again, so I think it must have been the 'eggs' that caused the trouble.

One of our regular turns was the all-stations goods to Basingstoke. We started from Woking at about eight in the morning and first called at Farnborough where we sorted the coal sidings and picked up wagons which came from the Royal Aircraft Establishment (RAE), these were hauled from the RAE by a little 0-4-0 tank engine called *Ironsides*. The track from the RAE to the yard at Farnborough ran down the centre of a road and it always amused me to see this little engine puffing along the road pulling its train of wagons. We also placed banana vans at the platform in the yard there, all the straw they contained was thrown out and burned. I don't know why this was done but rumour had it that the reason was to destroy any dangerous spiders which might have been imported.

Fleet was our next stop and here we serviced the coal yard, the goods shed and a breeze block factory. In those days, stations did not have large car parks and where a lot of motorists regularly used the station, as at Fleet, provision was made for them to park in the roadways of the goods yard. This provision consisted of a line of metal stakes with rope tied to them, which was supposed to keep the cars clear of the track, but often failed to work and we would have to bounce cars out of the way before we could start work.

One day our usual 'Monty' had been replaced with a 'King Arthur' No. 30777. As we propelled some wagons of ash towards the breeze block works, there were cars parked very close all along the line. I was keeping a sharp look out and one car, a very old Jaguar, was particularly close. Bert edged forward and the cylinders of our engine just cleared the outriders on the rear bumper of the car. I said, 'OK Bert, we are clear' and we moved forward again. We had not gone very far when we heard a load scraping sound from behind; we stopped and I looked back to see the old Jaguar and two other cars locked together. It turned out that the nuts securing the axlebox covers on our tender made the tender an inch or two wider than the cylinders which were the widest part of most engines. It demonstrates the weight and power of a large steam engine, we were hardly moving when the accident happened, yet the first car had moved about six feet from its original position.

My next promotion came in late 1962 when I moved to No. 2 link and was placed with another Bert, Bert Reed. He was much different to my previous mate, he was about 60 years old and was very short. I was rather dubious at first because he did not look a very happy person, but when I got to know him well we got along famously and I found he had a terrific sense of humour. This was just as well because that winter, 1962/1963, was one of the worst in living memory. It was good that we could laugh at the misfortunes which befell us or it would have been unbearable.

No. 2 link was better than No. 3, we were not rostered any ballast work and most of our duties were running turns. We only ever prepared or disposed our own engine and this was sometimes done for us. We worked freight trains between Reading and Redhill and between Woking and Salisbury, we had passenger turns to London and Salisbury, parcels to Southampton and at one time or another we went almost everywhere on the division except Bournemouth and beyond. To Nine Elms men we were 'Short road men' who didn't go very far at all and there was a joke at the time, that the golden angel on top of Guildford cathedral was put there so that Guildford men could go further afield. If they couldn't see the angel they wouldn't go.

One of our duties was the 'Angerstein' goods from Woking to Redhill. This train started at 4.48 am and was one of the earliest turns in No. 2. It was also the train on which I got my come-uppance as a newly appointed fireman, but all the times that I worked that train, I never stopped short of steam again. I came close to it but never actually stopped. As a matter of fact I can only remember stopping for a 'blow up' once while I was with Bert Reed.

During the time I was firing the worst problem we all faced was smog. This was thick fog which also contained smoke and all the chemicals contained in smoke. It was extremely dense and had a sort of yellow/green colour about it. When a thick smog came down, visibility was reduced to almost zero and was measured in feet rather than yards. When you were out in it the filthy muck settled on you and made you look as if you hadn't washed for a week. It also got in your mouth and nose and gave an awful taste in the mouth. Signals were difficult to see, especially the semaphore types and particularly the high semaphores between Brookwood and Basingstoke. They were on tall posts which were themselves on high gantries, many times I had to climb up gantries to see what position the signal was in.

When the winter really set in late in 1962, we were on a night turn. Our first trip was a freight from Woking to Basingstoke where we ran to the down yard and waited about an hour for relief, during which time we were required to move several times to enable our train to be sorted. We started the week in a thick smog which lasted until about Wednesday morning, all the time the temperature was below freezing and the yard at Basingstoke is in a very exposed position. That hour each night was real punishment, the '500' which we had offered little protection from the extreme conditions. On the third night the smog was gone but there was a blizzard and a fierce wind was blowing the snow right through the cab, it was bitterly cold and by the end of the week I was laid off sick. I was really ill for three days and during that time more snow fell so that when I returned to work it was nearly a foot thick. It was so deep that my motor scooter became completely stuck and I had to walk a mile to Effingham Junction to catch a train to work, when I returned in the afternoon my scooter was still in the middle of the road where I had left it.

The following weekend it snowed again and early on Monday morning we worked a goods across to Reading and onto the spur where we waited for relief. When the relief eventually arrived they had snow up to their knees and Bert remarked on it. 'Yes', said the relieving driver, 'You want to be careful down the footpath, the snow is deep down there'. When we got to the path from the spur down the embankment to the Southern lines, we could see what he meant. there were great holes in the snow where the other crew had walked and Bert decided that he would try a different route. As I climbed over the cables and started down the path, using the deep footprints as a guide, Bert went further along the embankment to find a more suitable way down. I heard a shout and looked up to see Bert up to his armpits in the snow with his macintosh spread out like a fan on top. I started laughing, lost my balance and fell over in the snow, still laughing. Bert shouted at me, 'Don't sit there like a silly sod, come and get me out', but he wasn't angry and it was the subject of much amusement afterwards.

He had a good laugh at my expense a few weeks later at Basingstoke when we were taking water. I was on the top of the tender of a 'Seventy Three' Standard and Bert threw the chain for me to pull the water crane round, I pulled on the chain but instead of the crane swinging round as expected, I slid across the tender top and over the side, still hanging on to the chain, I landed on the ground with a bump and finished up sitting on the drain grating. Luckily I was not hurt but Bert could see the funny side of it and said, 'That serves you right for laughing at me when I was in distress'.

That winter was so severe that lines of braziers were kept burning between the engines in the sheds to prevent water in the tenders from freezing. Engines were also stationed in convenient sidings at the foot of steep or long gradients to assist electric trains which had trouble picking up the current from the third rail. There was one at Witley, Havant, Bagshot and Effingham Junction, in addition every depot kept an engine at the ready just in case it was needed. All the snow plough attachments, which were normally kept on the ground at various depots, were fitted to engines which were allocated for the job. At Guildford our snow plough engine was a 'Q' class, but to my knowledge it was never used, we must have got off lightly in our area although we didn't think so at the time.

Old Bert had the appearance of being nervous and when he got excited his hands used to shake, but whenever we were in trouble I always found him to be cool and completely in charge of the situation. If we were getting short of steam and I kept looking at the steam gauge, he would hang his hat over it so that I couldn't see it. Then he would look out of the side and ignore what I was doing. He would say, 'When she blows off you will know you have enough steam, if she comes to a stand you will know that you haven't, so stop worrying'.

On one occasion Bert had been in an argument with a person at Woking Control and this person had said something which really upset him. The next day we were at Feltham preparing to work a freight to Basingstoke, I had found some hard coal at the back of the tender and was about to put it on the fire when Bert came up. 'Don't put that on the fire, save it', he said. I assumed that he wanted to use it for swapping for pea sticks, bean rods or some such thing which was a common practice in those days.

Anyway, I did as he asked and put the lumps of coal under the shovelling tray on the tender. As we passed through West Byfleet Bert said, 'Right, crack those lumps up and put them on the fire'. I was puzzled but did as he said. He then turned on the blower and as we approached the Control offices, which were beside the down line at Woking, he closed the regulator and shut off the blower. A great cloud of black smoke rolled off the top of the chimney and engulfed the offices. 'That will teach them to upset me', he said. He seemed a lot happier after that, until the following week that is, when he received a report asking him to explain why he had allowed his engine to make black smoke contrary to instruction. I never saw his reply so I don't know how he got out of that one.

The severe weather conditions lasted for weeks and weeks and eventually we ran out of coal at Guildford and had to get what we could from other depots and push the coal from the back of the tender when we were short. This situation lasted for a couple of weeks until one day when we signed on the running foreman told us that we had received a supply and we would be able to fill our tender.

We prepared our engine, a 'Monty', and I only made a light fire in anticipation of the good coal we were about to receive. When we were ready, we took the engine up to the coal stage and asked the crew there to fill it up while we went for a wash. Having washed and made a can of tea we returned to the engine which we had to take to the up yard to work a stopping goods to Reading. When I entered the cab I was horrified, instead of the nice lumpy coal which I was expecting, there was a tender full of rubbish. It was black but that was the only resemblance it had to coal, there were lumps of clay, tuffets of grass, tins, bottles and all manner of junk, it was a morass. Bert said, 'If that is all we have got we will have to make the fire up with it and hope for the best'. This I did but I had reservations about it and when I finished there was not a flame in sight in the firebox. We went up the yard with the blower on, hoping to liven the fire up before departure.

On arrival at the yard we were informed that part of our train had not arrived yet and would be about an hour. By the time we left the yard there were signs that the mess was trying to catch alight and as Bert gave her a good thumping up 'Pinks Hill' it burst into life. It also burst out of the chimney and as fast as I could shovel it in, it disappeared and reappeared like rain on the cab roof, the tender and the leading wagons. That old 'Monty' blew off all the way up the bank and my doubts were dispelled just like the coal.

Then Bert closed the regulator as we passed the summit and the fire went as flat as a pancake and we had to struggle up the slight gradient from Wanborough to Ash Junction. By the time we reached North Camp, our first stop, we were down and out. Before we could continue I had to throw out half the fire and make a fresh start, which made no difference at all as we stopped twice more before reaching Reading. I don't know where that coal came from but Bert reckoned that they must have dredged it up from Pompey harbour. The next day we didn't bother to take coal at Guildford, I pushed all the coal forward from the back of the tender instead.

One of the most interesting trips of my firing career was when the turntable at Reading was under repair. Tender engines had to go round the triangle at Reading West to turn, this job was done by Reading Southern men as there was not time for the train crew to do it. The duty we were on was allocated a 'Motor Tank' for the return trip to Redhill and having handed over our 'Monty' to the relief crew, we walked to the shed to collect the tank.

Our engine this day was No. 30032 and my driver, Joe Hawkins, remarked on the good condition she was in, beautifully clean and no sign of any leaks or steam blowing out. We went up to the station and attached our train, a three-car set. While we were waiting to leave, inspector Bolland appeared and told Joe that he was to ride on our engine as Redhill men had been losing time with these engines and he was trying to find out why. Joe said, 'You won't find anything wrong today, those Central men don't know how to handle a Drummond engine, they carry too much water in the boiler'. This was probably true as you could fill the boiler right up on most Brighton engines, if you did the same on a Drummond it usually caused water to get in the cylinders. It was normal to keep the level about halfway up the gauge glass. However, I thought he was being over optimistic but hoped he would be proved right.

I need not have worried, that trip must go down as the most perfect in my career, the engine behaved perfectly all the way and Mr Bolland was suitably impressed with the performance. When he got off he said, 'I think you were right Joe, I wasted my time coming with you today, still I am glad that I did, I wouldn't have believed it if I hadn't seen it'.

The only problem we had on this trip was that '32' was one of the original types and had a large 'pole' type reverser. As we were running bunker first the lever got in the way and the driver could not reach the regulator when he was notching up. We overcame this by me opening the regulator when I got the start signal from the guard and closing it when the driver wanted to notch up. Having notched up he could then reach the regulator. I don't think the inspector was very happy with this arrangement but he did not complain.

Another display of my expertise was when we relieved the 6.09 pm from Waterloo at Woking. The engine was down and out when I got on and inspector Smith told me that they had been in trouble all the way from London. I set to work and we soon recovered and had an excellent trip to Basingstoke; as the inspector got off he said, 'You made a lovely trip of that, well done'. My ego received a terrific boost which lasted a couple of weeks until I was working the 6.09 pm from Waterloo to Woking. I made a complete mess of it and unfortunately Mr Smith was again on the footplate; he must have changed his mind that evening.

With the arrival of spring in 1963, I moved to No. 1 link and so became a top link fireman. My new mate was a gentleman by the name of Ben Boyce. I use the word gentleman in all sincerity, I never heard him say a bad word about anyone and he rarely got upset, it was a real pleasure to work with him. The work in No. 1 was also pleasant, it was mostly passenger work with six of the 12 duties being on the Reading to Redhill service. The other six turns took us to London, Salisbury and Southampton, we were rarely spare and did not do any night work. For the year or so that I worked with Ben I can't remember any serious problems and any trouble was alleviated by Ben's cool approach to the situation. The only time I saw him flustered was as we were leaving Reading one day. We had a left-handed 'N' and as we were moving away a porter ran on to the platform and signalled us to stop. On the 'left-handers' the regulator lever was pushed down to open, which was opposite to the normal type. Not thinking, Ben pushed it down and the engine just stood there with the wheels spinning, half the fire disappeared up the chimney and cascaded down all over the station. Ben was very embarrassed by his mistake but soon had the situation under control.

He was a great help to me in preparing for my driving exam and any spare time we had was put to good use with Ben explaining some of the complexities of the engine or the finer points of the rules and regulations. I had started attending the Mutual Improvement classes, which were held weekly in the ambulance hut at Guildford, while I was with Bert Read. As I only had one year until I was 23 and old enough to apply for driving vacancies, it was a matter of some urgency for me to learn as much as possible in preparation. There was no formal training for the driving exam, it was up to the individual to gain the required knowledge, which was considerable, from wherever he could. Of

'Q1' class 0-6-0 No. 33025 enters Christ's Hospital with a Reading-Brighton excursion train on 7th August, 1961.   *John Faulkner*

'Q' class 0-6-0 No. 30543 at Gomshall & Shere with the 12.05 pm Reading-Redhill on 31st July, 1964.   *Author*

course I did have seven years of practical experience to draw on and during that period I had worked over most of the South Western system and performed nearly every type of duty, so I had a sound basic knowledge to build on.

The Mutual Improvement Class (MIC) was organised by drivers at the depot who acted as instructors voluntarily in their own time, senior firemen, or any fireman for that matter, also attended in their own time. BR supplied the premises for the meetings and such publications as were required, we studied the principles of steam traction in great depth and at Guildford we had two superb working models to assist us in this, one of Stephenson link motion and one of Walschaerts valve gear. I listened to what was said and watched the models working for ages before the penny dropped and all the things which had puzzled me for so long became clear.

After that I had a much deeper understanding of the engines I worked on and came to appreciate the engineers' problems and also the way that different drivers worked their engines. I was lucky with my new mate, he was an excellent driver who knew how to get the best out of an engine without thrashing it. With my newly acquired knowledge I was able to follow his driving technique and work out the effect it would have beforehand. Incidentally, it also made me more competent as a fireman.

We also studied rules at the MIC and this subject I found equally difficult. It is one thing to perform duties in compliance with complex regulations, it is quite another to be able to describe them in detail to the driving inspector in an office. Luckily the MIC instructors went to great pains to ensure that we understood the principles of the rules and usually illustrated them by using everyday situations which existed in our area.

The year 1964 was a big one for me. First of all in March I was married and in May I applied for a driving position at Nine Elms, the second event being prompted by the first. If I stayed in my present position I would probably pass for driving in a year or two and would then become a passed fireman. This attracted the same conditions as a passed cleaner, such as being booked a different turn every day of the week and never knowing what you were doing until the previous day. Being newly married I did not relish this prospect and decided to go for a proper appointment as soon as possible.

I applied for a vacancy at Nine Elms, I did not relish this much either, but it seemed the lesser of two evils at the time. My application was successful and I was to take up the appointment as soon as I passed the driving exam. My success was not due in any way to suitability or intelligence, it was purely on the grounds of seniority and the appointment would only apply if I passed the exam.

The next few weeks were my last chance to swot up on all the things I needed to know and I was really grateful for the assistance which Ben gave me in this respect. The main problem was that the things which I knew, I was fairly well versed in, but of course there was no telling what the inspector might ask me. Apart from several items which were a standard part of the exam, he had literally hundreds of pertinent questions to choose from. When the day came I was a bag of nerves and arrived at the inspector's office with some trepidation.

There were two of us to be passed out that day and we consoled each other with the thought that we were allowed three attempts before we would be classed as unsuitable as drivers and removed from the line of promotion. If you failed you had to take the whole exam again so we were keeping our fingers crossed that we would pass first time.

Mr Jupp, the inspector, greeted us warmly and told us not to be nervous as he was not out to catch us, but we should think carefully before answering the questions. The first part was a written paper which we both finished in the allotted time without too much trouble. The second part was oral and we found this more difficult. On one particular subject we both became dumbstruck for a while, but were reminded to think carefully before answering. I think it must have been a case of double nerves because as one of us remembered a relevant point it all came flooding back and we were on the move again. We went for our tea break feeling a little more confident and returned to continue the exam in better heart.

The other fireman was taking a position as an electric driver so he did not have to pass that part concerning the principles of the steam engine. He would go to the training school for three weeks before passing an exam on electric traction. I was on my own for the afternoon session which was to be all about the engine. I felt more comfortable with this subject, it had become my favourite at MIC. The afternoon passed quickly and at the end of it I was told that having proved myself competent on the first two parts I was to take the third part the following day.

This was the practical section and I was given the choice of working a train from Reading to Redhill or the 10.54 am from Waterloo to Basingstoke. I chose the latter as I thought I might have problems with the right-hand drive of the 'Monty' when stopping at stations on the Redhill road. The 10.54 was hauled by a 'West Country' and the crew were based at Basingstoke which meant that I would not be inhibited by having a fireman whom I knew and who knew me. If I made a mess of it I did not want my colleagues at Guildford to be eye witnesses to my failure.

I need not have worried, when it came to it I managed the train in a manner which old Ben would have been proud of and when it was over I was disappointed that it could not go on for longer. Mr Jupp was satisfied and told me that, subject to my passing the medical, I would be transferred to my new position as soon as possible. He congratulated me on passing the exam and after some words of advice about my future conduct as a driver said, 'I hope I don't see you too often, because if I do it will probably be because you are in trouble'. He then wished me good luck and I went back to Guildford, elated and wonderfully satisfied with myself.

I had my medical the following week and until then I received congratulations from my many friends and colleagues. Ben imparted some final words of wisdom, this final piece of advice held me in good stead throughout my driving career. He said, 'Always remember when working in the London area, there is only one signal for each line and you can only be on one line at a time, so concentrate on the signals which apply to the line you are on'. I always remembered that and never took a wrong signal in 15 years of driving.

I was sad to be leaving all my comrades, having been at Guildford for eight years and made many friends. I really felt as if I was leaving home and I was fearful of what was in store for me at Nine Elms, especially as I had hated the place so much as a visiting fireman. However, that was all to come, for the time being I was occupied with my farewells and I was reminded of the many noteworthy little incidents which I had shared with various drivers on day to day bookings.

These incidents are too numerous to mention here, but I can mention Les Willmot who nearly fell into the river at Reading whilst trying to walk to the Spur signal box in a thick smog. The man who spied on young couples who were out walking on the 'downs' using a brass telescope; until that is, one young lady he was watching turned out to be his daughter. The lad who went to the shedmaster's office and said that he didn't want to belong to the income tax any more. The fireman who went for a cup of tea and got talking, when he came back the fire had gone out on his engine.

All these things and many more are now but memories in the minds of those involved, or have passed into local railway folklore, but they were all part of the environment in which I spent the first eight years of my working life. Eight happy years despite the bad days, which are usually best forgotten. A visit to the motive power superintendent, Mr Downs, at Divisional Headquarters in Wimbledon, was the last part of the passing out process. He congratulated me, gave me some advice and wished me well in my future career. He said to me, 'Watch out for the one round the corner', referring to signals of course and it was good advice. He was a real gentleman and he knew the job backwards, so this meeting was quite pleasant. All that remained now was the actual move and this came on 1st June, 1964.

BR Standard class '4' 4-6-0 No. 75074 leaves Guildford with the 1.50 pm Reading-Redhill train on 24th October, 1964. *Gerald T. Robinson*

BRITISH RAILWAYS — EXAMINATION FOR PASSING AS DRIVER

(*) Examination (1st, 2nd or 3rd)

Staff No. .... Name .... ~~TYNSLEY~~ ~W

Seniority Date .... 52 Date of Birth .... Depot ....

Last Physical and Visual Examination

Date .... Physical Fitness .... ✓

Eyesight

	Right Eye	Left Eye	Both Eyes
Form Vision	6/6	6/6	6/6
Colour Vision		NORMAL	

I have examined the above-named as to his knowledge of the duties of a Driver of a
(*) STEAM/~~DIESEL/ELECTRIC~~ LOCOMOTIVE/~~MULTIPLE UNIT~~ with the following results:—

	Min. Mark	Actual Mark †
Part A (Oral)		
Applicable to all types of traction		
(i) Knowledge of Rules & Regulations & W.T.T.	Good	GOOD
(ii) Knowledge of types of Signals and their use	Good	GOOD
(iii) Knowledge of making out reports	Fair	FAIR
Part B (Oral)		
Applicable to all types of traction		
(i) Knowledge of the traction unit	Good	GOOD
(ii) Knowledge of the locomotive brakes, automatic brake, including A.W.S.	Fair	GOOD
(iii) Competency to diagnose failure and take appropriate action	Good	GOOD
Applicable to Steam traction only		
(vi) Knowledge of Fireman's Duties	Good	GOOD
Applicable to Diesel/Electric traction only		
(iv) Knowledge of principal auxiliaries (including train heating equipment—if applicable)	Fair	—
(v) Fire prevention	Good	—

Part C — see overleaf

CERTIFICATE TO ACT AS DRIVER

Depot .... Staff No. .... Date ....

The above-named has passed the technical examination in the duties of Driver of a
(*) STEAM/~~DIESEL/ELECTRIC~~ LOCOMOTIVE/~~MULTIPLE UNIT~~, and is approved to act in this capacity when required.

Signed .... District Officer   Date 25 - 6 - 64

Signed .... Regional/Line Officer   Date 26 - 6 - 64

*Delete items not applicable   †Insert Very Good, Good, Fair or Poor as appropriate.

	Min. Mark	Actual Mark
Part C (Practical)		
Applicable to all types of traction		
(i) Attention to signals and judging distances	Good	Good
(ii) Attention to Rules and Regulations	Good	Good
(iii) Care and manipulation of the traction unit including braking	Good	Good
(iv) Competency to diagnose failure and take appropriate action	Good	Good
(v) Preparation and Disposal duties of the traction unit	Fair	Good
Applicable to Steam traction only		
(vi) Attention to boiler and fire	Fair	Good
(vii) Knowledge of locomotive parts	Good	Good
(viii) Making and using trimmings	Fair	Fair
(ix) Care in and attention to oiling	Fair	Fair
(x) Ability to change a boiler water gauge glass	Fair	Fair
Applicable to Diesel/Electric traction only		
(vi) Operation of train heating equipment	Fair	—

The Candidate was employed as a driver on Steam Locomotives 34082 ; 34025
trains between Waterloo 1054 and Basingstoke and Return 13.13
under my immediate supervision on 17 / 6 / 64 and I consider that his capabilities as a driver are
SATISFACTORY/~~UNSATISFACTORY~~*

Date 20. 6. 64   Signed A. H. Jupp   Inspector

*Delete item not applicable

†Insert Very Good, Good, Fair or Poor as appropriate.

Chapter Four

Steam Driver: The Last Days of Steam

On the first of June 1964 I collected my belongings from my locker at Guildford loco and after a few last handshakes, caught the train to Waterloo and then to Vauxhall from where I walked to the depot at Nine Elms. I reported to the general office where I was introduced to my new shedmaster, Mr Gilchrist. After all the paper work was completed I was given a locker key and proceeded to the tatty concrete hut at the back of the shed which served as a locker room. Having deposited my bundle I then went to the 'list office' to arrange my route learning with the list clerk.

Train drivers, then as now, are governed by very strict rules and one of these rules is that a driver may not work over any route until he has learned all the main features on the route, such as gradients, signals, catch points, junctions, stations and sidings, etc. When he is satisfied that he knows the route thoroughly he has to sign a route knowledge card which lists all the routes normally worked over by drivers of the division. Each route has to be signed for individually and has to be re-signed every six months. It is important that the driver makes himself aquainted with all aspects of the route he is learning as he is responsible for carrying out complex safety rules and must know exactly what to do and where to go at any location.

It is particularly important to know signals, gradients, stations, junctions and speed restrictions as he may be called upon to work many different types of trains over the route and trains cannot be stopped quickly like a car, especially loose-coupled freight trains which were common at that time. The driver must be in full control all the time and run his train in accordance with local instructions as well as general rules and regulations.

I was told to learn the suburban routes to Chessington, Kingston, Hampton Court, Hounslow, Feltham and Staines, plus the complex section between Clapham Junction and Waterloo. I was placed in No. 6 link and although most of the work was preparation and disposal (P&D), there were also local running turns with empty stock, parcels and freight trains. There were seven links at Nine Elms at that time, Nos. 1, 2 and 3 with 24 sets of men, the others with 12 sets each. At least there should have been, but because of a shortage of firemen we either had a spare Nine Elms man or a daily on-loan man with us. The on-loan men came from far afield such as Salisbury, Brighton, Guildford, Feltham, in fact any depot that could spare them.

I spent the next three months learning the various routes although some times I was booked a duty, usually in the shed. When I felt that I was competent I signed the route card and prepared to take up my normal duties which for the next few weeks consisted of P&D work and light engines to and from Waterloo.

It was a bit of a shock to suddenly realise that I was responsible for the whole show myself. As a fireman I had driven various engines many times while the driver did the firing, but it is one thing to do it when another person is with you who takes responsibility for what happens; it is completely different when you are the responsible person, possibly with an inexperienced fireman who had to be watched all the time. As a matter of fact, my first mishap as a driver was due to my own inexperience. One day shortly after my arrival at Nine Elms, I was moving a 'West Country' from the disposal pit on to the turntable. There was a steep incline up towards the table and I had the regulator open when I reached the top of the slope; unlike the smaller engines which I was used to the 'West Country' kept on puffing when I closed the regulator (these types held a lot of steam in the steam chest). As I came on to the level table I realised that I was not going to stop, the engine crashed into the concrete block which marked the end of the line, luckily there was no damage to the engine or the concrete block, only my ego suffered.

My first proper driving turn came several weeks later. I was rostered spare and was booked a duty from another link by the list clerk. Because of my experience at Guildford I had quite a wide route knowledge which made me available for a variety of duties. This duty started by going to Feltham loco at about 23.00 where we prepared a '73' Standard. We then went to the 'down departure' section of the marshalling yard where we attached a train of coal hoppers we were to work that to Wimbledon via Chertsey.

It was a lovely night for my baptism, there was thick fog and the temperature was well below freezing. I was a little nervous but did not want to let my fireman see it, he was not very happy about the fog and it wouldn't have done much for his confidence to know that I was worried as well. We left the yard with 20 hoppers, loose-coupled, and six fitted box vans as a vacuum head. I had worked freight trains over this route many times as a fireman and knew the road intimately, which was just as well as visibility was down to a few yards and the signalling was all semaphore, very difficult to see in a fog if you don't know where to look.

The trip started fairly well and the tricky curves at Staines and Virginia Water were negotiated with no problems, but as we approached the junction at Addlestone I slowed the train to 20 mph, the speed limit when taking the left turn towards Weybridge. Then having tightened the couplings again in readiness for the difficult pull ahead, I applied more power and started the climb. It is not only the gradient which presented a difficulty on this section but the sharp curve all the way from Addlestone Junction to Weybridge, about ¾ mile. We were going well until the driving wheels started to slip, even a generous application of sand to the rails did not help, possibly because the freezing fog had caused the rails to ice up. Eventually we slipped to a stand and had to set back into the train and make a snatch start to get going again, I had to do this four times before we reached the main line at Weybridge and got moving properly.

It had taken 18 minutes to cover that ¾ mile and I was very embarrassed and disappointed to have had so much trouble on my first proper driving turn. I did not relish the thought of answering the report which was sure to come before long. We all learn by our mistakes and I am no exception, the rest of that week I used a different technique to negotiate that section and had no more trouble. The odd thing was that although my fireman had seen what a mess I had made of it, I overheard him later telling another fireman how clever I was to get the train moving again in that awkward position. Perhaps I was looking at the negative side of it, but it was a trip to remember whichever way you look at it.

Shortly after that I was sent to the training school for a week to learn the 350 hp English Electric diesel shunting engines. This was the first official training I had received since the firing course when I was 16 and I found it very interesting, it was also easier than finding out for yourself. I was supposed to go on another course for Drewry 204 hp shunters but they were withdrawn from duties in the London area so I did not learn them.

At first I hated Nine Elms, it was a dirty old place and parts of the depot were not far short of derelict. I did not know many people there and those that I worked with seemed a hard-hearted lot. After a while I settled in and came to accept my work mates as they were. I think the difference was that my mates at Guildford tended to be more serious and any bad feeling tended to last a long time. If somebody called you a bastard they meant it and it hurt, at Nine Elms the word was used almost casually and at times was nearly a term of endearment. If you had done something to upset somebody they would give you a good 'ear bashing' nicely laced with suitable obscenities and that was the end of it. Once I got used to it I found it to be a good system which avoided lasting ill feeling.

My impressions of my first six months at Nine Elms are mainly unpleasant. I see the depot spread out over a large area with heaps of coal and clinker all over the place and smoke rising in columns from the engines which had just been 'lit up', of engines lined up on the disposal pit or taking coal from the giant hopper, of being in the shed and seeing shafts of sunlight piercing the smoke and darkness through holes in the roof. As I said, it was not a very good first impression but as I became acclimatised to the place and got to know the people, I grew to like it and wished that I had gone there years before as a fireman. I made many good friends and really enjoyed going to work.

The top two links worked to Bournemouth and Salisbury and were trained on Western Region 'Warship' diesels which worked some of the Waterloo to Exeter services. Some of the men in No. 1 link were also trained on Brush type '4' diesels which sometimes hauled Southampton docks boat trains; apart from this everything was steam hauled. The link which I was in contained 12 duties, most of which were P&D work, although we also worked some empty stock trains between Clapham Yard and Waterloo. I had no regular fireman and because of this I soon came to know all the firemen at the depot. The good, the bad and the indifferent, there were some of each, a real mixed bunch.

It became even more mixed when a large group of redundant firemen came on long term loan from Glasgow in late 1964 to early 1965. They were a wild bunch but luckily most of the rougher ones went home after a short while and those that remained were pretty good. The only problem I had with them was that I couldn't understand what they said, they all spoke with broad Glasgow accents, but after a while their accent mellowed or my ear became attuned to it and that difficulty was eased.

About this time I was rostered my first regular fireman, a young lad on long term loan from Workington in Cumberland. He was not used to the multiple lines of the London area and was not happy when we were out on the road. He was also unused to disposing engines and made hard work of it, I found that I was doing some of his work as well as my own. He didn't last long and returned home after five or six weeks. There was talk of the end of steam but not many people seemed to worry about it, I was settled and was not looking ahead too much. I had registered a first preference move for Woking emu depot when I left Guildford and it was just a matter of waiting my turn, there were men senior to me to go there before I went.

Bulleid unrebuilt 'Battle of Britain' class 4-6-2 No. 34051 *Winston Churchill* approaches Vauxhall with the great man's funeral train on 30th January, 1965. *Brian Coates*

The big event of 1965 was the funeral of Sir Winston Churchill. 'Battle of Britain' class No. 34051 *Winston Churchill* was cleaned and polished to perfection for this event and she looked a picture as she left Waterloo with the funeral train, *en route* for Handborough in Oxfordshire. Even the '80000' tank which worked the empty train into Waterloo was sparkling in her black livery; that must have been the last big steam event in the country and a fitting tribute to the great man who had lived through the heyday of steam. It would not have been the same with any of the modern forms of traction and it was lucky that steam on the Southern lasted as long as it did.

It came as a surprise to me when I suddenly realised that all the older engines had gone, they had been withdrawn over a period and I had not noticed their passing. When I moved to Nine Elms there were still 'U' and 'N' classes about, there was a 'Q' class on the coal road shunter and 'Q1s' were still to be seen. I can recall working a 'W' tank as a driver and some of the '800' type 'S15s' were still in service. Now there were only Standard types and 'Merchant Navy'/'West Country' classes at Nine Elms; there were '73000' and '75000' tender engines, '80000' and '82000' tanks, occasionally a '76000' would appear but they were a rare visitor to the depot.

In 1966 the vacancy list was frozen and the link structure reorganised. There were now four links with 24 pairs of men in each, the dual link was disbanded and the drivers given the option of staying at Nine Elms or transferring to Waterloo emu depot. I was placed in No. 4 link and had a regular mate again, Paul Anderson by name, he was a very keen steam man and it was nice to have a fireman who was enthusiastic about the job.

I had an accident one night while I was oiling the middle big end bearing of a 'West Country'. I had wrapped a large newspaper round the brake gear spacer bar and tied it with a piece of string, this was for me to sit on as I found it easier than standing with one foot on either side of the pit and I did not get so dirty. To enable me to see what I was doing, I had placed a flare lamp* on

---

* A flare lamp was a metal vessel something like a miniature tea pot, there was a thick wick which passed up the spout from the body of the lamp, the vessel was filled with paraffin and the wick lighted where it poked out of the spout.

one of the angle brackets which fixed the cross braces to the main frames. As I sat on the spacer bar, busy with my oil feeder I heard an odd noise, it went 'Zoop, zoop, zoop', after a few seconds I located the source of the sound. Lighted drops of paraffin were dripping from the spout of the lamp, pretty blue drops that went zoop, zoop, zoop as they fell down, then I realised where they were going to, they were falling right onto the paper on which I was sitting and it was on fire.

I dropped from my perch and quickly removed the paper from the bar and stamped out the flames, then I reached up to retrieve the lamp. Unfortunately it was unbalanced and it fell into the pit where all the paraffin burst into flames all around me. I made my exit from under the engine at high speed, banging my head on the tender axle in the process. Paul found me sitting on the side of the pit rubbing my head. When I told him what had happened he said, 'Don't worry, I will fix something up for you so that it doesn't happen again'. A few days later he handed me a large brown paper bag. 'So that you don't set yourself on fire again', he said. The bag contained about 60 feet of electric wire with a bulb holder at one end and a connector at the other which fitted the lamp holders on 'West Country' and 'Merchant Navy' class engines.

The bulb holder had a miniature plastic shade on it and a boot lace attached so that I could tie it to my hat like a miners lamp, all I had to do was remove the bulb from one of the headcode lights, place it in my hat lamp and plug the other end into the headcode lamp. I could then go under the engine with both hands free to work with no fear of setting myself alight. It was a superb idea and I was delighted with it although some of the other men thought it was a big joke.

I sat on the spacer bar one night, oiling the big end, when the light went out. I was completely in the dark and I dropped the feeder, oil splashed all over me and I fell into the pit. I crept out from under the engine, covered in oil and smokebox ash and banged my head on the tender axle, smashing the lamp in the process. Unwittingly I had laid the wire over a pile of hot clinker in the pit and it had burnt though the insulation. That was the end of my patent electric hat lamp, I reverted to using a flare lamp after that and used it with extra care.

No. 4 link was a good one and we had a nice variety of work. We were not booked any Bournemouth or Salisbury turns but we worked to Basingstoke with the 02.30 paper train and back with a commuter train. We also had an evening train to Basingstoke at 17.09, working back with the 19.34 from Basingstoke, an up Exeter service. Another No. 4 turn was the 07.20 passenger to Woking where we were relieved by Guildford men, we then worked a freight to Feltham and a coal train from there to Nine Elms.

A duty which I spent a lot of time on was the Merton Abbey. This turn was originally based at Norwood Junction depot but for some reason it had been transferred to Nine Elms. A 350 hp diesel shunter was the engine used and there were two shifts on this duty. The early turn started by working the mixed goods from Wimbledon west yard to Merton Abbey where a long time was spent shunting the coal sidings.

Later we went up to the end of the line at Tooting where another coal merchant had his base. There was also a banana store there until it was burned down, it was not reopened after the fire. The line ended just short of the

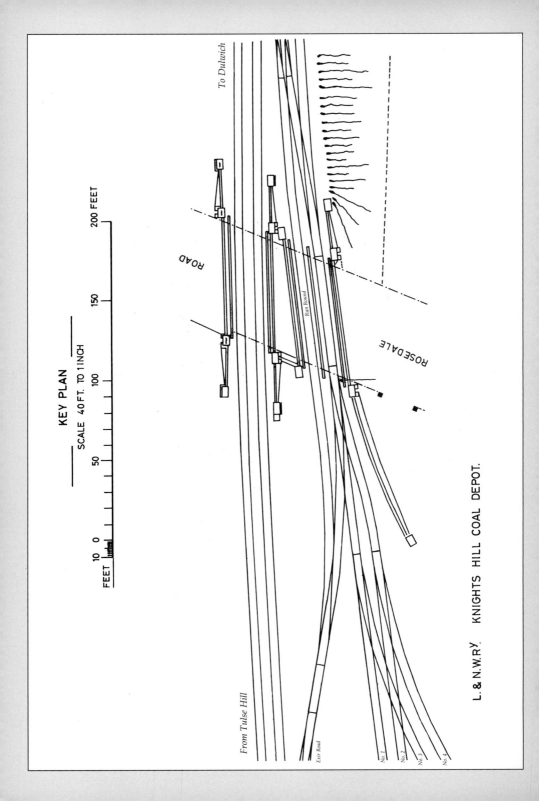

KEY PLAN

SCALE 40 FT. TO 1 INCH

200 FEET

50 · 100 · 150

10 · 0

FEET

To Dulwich

ROAD

Run Round

ROSEDALE

From Tulse Hill

Exit Road

No. 1
No. 2
No. 3
No. 4

L. & N.W.RY. KNIGHTS HILL COAL DEPOT.

Wimbledon to Streatham line and originally there had been a junction at Tooting and trains ran from London to Wimbledon via Merton Abbey. When I worked on the line it was operated as a siding all the way from the junction at Merton Park to the end at Tooting.

On returning from Merton Abbey the train was sorted in the west yard and we then set off on alternate days for either 'Brighton Yard' (Wimbledon) and Haydons Road or Streatham and Knights Hill. Brighton Yard was so named because it was originally built by the LBSCR; as a matter of fact there were still separate train crews at Wimbledon at that time, 'Central' men and 'South Western' men. The Central division trains operated from platforms 9 and 10 as they still do and the Central men never worked on the South Western lines.

On the days that we went to Streatham we had a long, slow climb up the steep bank from Tooting to Streatham Junction. The 350 shunters were a strong little engine but very low geared, their maximum speed at that time was 20 mph and on the steep gradient up to Streatham they would usually travel at about 8 mph. At Streatham we shunted the yard and placed the coal wagons in position for the coal merchant, we then reformed the train and set off for Knights Hill. This was a coal depot and was situated between Tulse Hill and North Dulwich, just beyond Tulse Hill tunnel.

It was an unusual yard for two reasons. Firstly, it was a former London & North Western Railway coal depot situated beside a LBSCR line just where the SECR line passed underneath, secondly, the layout was rather odd. The points leading from the main line and those at either end of the run-round road were marked with LBSCR plates, whilst the unusual set of points leading from the shunting neck to the sidings and the exit road were marked with LMS plates. The three-way points in the shunting neck had a very odd way of operating. If both left-hand blades were against the left hand rail (looking from the shunting neck), the route was set for the exit road. There were two handles to operate the points and pulling the first handle once moved one pair of points to the right, the road was then set in the central position giving access to No. 1 or 3 siding, No. 3 siding crossed No. 2 on a diamond crossing. Pulling the same lever a second time moved the second set of points and the road was set for No. 2 or 4 siding; of course No. 2 siding crossed No. 3 on the same diamond.

Pulling the first lever again caused no movement at all and it was necessary to pull the second lever which moved both sets of points together, back to the original position. The blades could only be moved to the right singly and only to the left together, so if they were both on the right (2 or 4 sidings) and you wanted to go to 1 or 3 they both had to be moved to the left with the second lever and then one set moved to the right with the first lever. It was a very complicated arrangement and often the cause of much laughter when the shunter got confused and placed the wagons in the wrong siding. He would sometimes set the points and then walk along the track to ensure that they led in the right direction. The accompanying plan of the layout will be useful when reading this description.

From Knights Hill we ran back to Wimbledon where the train was berthed, we then picked up another train and worked it across the single line to Mitcham where we were relieved. The late turn men spent some time shunting at

Mitcham before returning to Wimbledon to remarshal the train in readiness for the evening trip to Merton Abbey. This second trip did not go to Tooting but called additionally at the siding attached to the Triang factory. When the train arrived back at Wimbledon, it was sorted and all the wagons which had been collected on the various trips were formed into a train which went to Norwood Junction later in the evening.

The early turn Merton Abbey was a dangerous duty, especially in the summer when the school children were on holiday. There were several public foot crossings on the line and children obviously enjoyed playing on the line and making camps on the embankments. The problem was that they thought it was good fun to sabotage the railway by trying to derail the train. The driver had to be extremely careful, keeping a sharp look out for obstructions and examining all the facing points before passing over them. As usual, I learned the hard way. I was going towards Merton Abbey one morning when I spotted a large cardboard box on the track. I thought to myself, 'That won't do any harm, I will run over it'. I did and there was a loud scraping noise from under the engine. I stopped and discovered that the cardboard box contained an old refrigerator; I never took any chances after that. Actually it was very easy to forget that this was a busy London district, trees and bushes grew close to each side of the track and, looking along the line, it was just like a country branch.

I enjoyed the Merton Abbey turns, probably because they were not unlike the early work which I had done at Guildford. It had the same pleasant atmosphere about it and I met some unusual characters, which always added interest to the work. The only problems on these duties was the engine; the '350s' were really uncomfortable when worked on the running line.

Most of the other duties in No. 4 link were carried out in the hustle and bustle of the London area, although I was used to it now and accepted it as normal. One of our turns was the 'Kingston fish'; again, this train no longer carried fish, it was all parcel traffic. We left Waterloo with an '80000' tank at about 03.30, calling at Clapham yard to put off and pick up, our next call was Barnes where Callico boxes were off-loaded for the nearby hospital. They contained artificial limbs and when the boxes were returned empty, they were folded flat. Richmond was our next stop and a long time was spent unloading there before going on to Kingston. When we left Kingston the train was nearly empty and the call at Wimbledon saw the last of the parcels unloaded.

We then worked the empty vans to Clapham yard and after berthing the train we worked another van train to Kensington. There were two other turns over the 'West London' line to Kensington, these were the daily specials for post office workers, two in the morning and two in the evening. They were the only passenger trains to use platforms 1 and 2 at Clapham Junction and the only regular passenger trains on the West London. These trains ran until recent years when they were replaced with an all-day service to Willesden Junction. The specials were always known as the 'Kenny Belle', even in later years when they were formed of various types of rolling stock.

All the local turns were powered by either '80000' or '82000' tanks, but some 'Midland' 2-6-2 tanks of class '2MT' were allocated to Nine Elms for a time and were used in place of the standard types. Known as 'Teddy Bear' tanks, they were similar to the '82000' tanks and I always imagined that these small standard types were based on the '2MT' class.

It was with one of these 'Teddy Bears' that I nearly had a nasty accident at Waterloo which caused much laughter afterwards, although at the time it was decidedly unfunny. I was working an empty train to Waterloo for the 16.35 to Bournemouth, this train used to be the 'Royal Wessex' at one time and was still known as 'The Wessex' to Nine Elms men. As we rolled gently from Westminster Bridge into the station, I started to apply the brakes, but by the time we had passed the lift shafts halfway along the platforms I realised that we were not stopping. I made a full emergency application and braced myself for the crash as we hit the hydraulic buffers. The train suddenly stopped dead, only inches from the buffers. I just sat there, too shocked to move.

That may not seem very funny and in itself it was not. The funny part was that as we were running into platform 11 and above the buffers on that line was a concrete hut where the station supervisors worked. The station manager was in this hut and he was sitting at the desk looking out of the window, resting his chin on his hands, with a look of utter boredom on his face. As he realised that the train was not going to stop he made a series of movements, each one faster than the previous one. First he lifted his chin from his hands, then he stood up, he then ran out of the hut and jumped down the steps onto the platform all in one movement. He came up to my engine, red with rage, and said, 'What the hell do you think you are doing, you frightened the life out of me'. I replied, 'If it frightened you, what effect do you think it had on me, I was on the engine'. He apologised for shouting at me and asked if I was all right now.

I will always remember his face and his reaction that day, his eyes grew bigger and bigger as the realisation came upon him. Had I been using a Standard tank that day I don't suppose the problem would have arisen. I was not used to the action of the brake valve on the 'Midland' engine and had not reduced the vacuum level in the brake pipe sufficiently until I made the emergency application. Luckily the train stopped in time but it was a close shave.

Another of our duties took us to Guildford loco and it was nice to meet old friends on their own ground, I sometimes saw them in the London area but it was not often that I had a chance to talk to them for long. Occasionally I had a Guildford fireman booked with me when they were 'on loan' for the day, but this was not often now that I had a regular fireman. The character of the depot at Guildford had changed since I had left there, all the very old engines were gone, as were many of the more modern types such as 'Montys' and 'Charlies'. Now there were mostly the smaller Standard types there and it was not as I remembered it.

There were still several 'unconverted' 'West Country' class about and I enjoyed working on them, they ran much more smoothly than the 'converteds' and of course it was not necessary to go under the boiler to oil the axle. I had a frightening experience with an 'unconverted' one day. We had worked the 07.20 passenger train from Waterloo to Woking with one and were relieved by Guildford men. We went to the up yard to relieve Salisbury men on a freight, they also had an 'unconverted'; it was unusual to work the whole duty with this type and I was pleasantly surprised. After working a general freight up to

Feltham, we worked a coal train to Nine Elms; this was a heavy train and there was no vacuum head to assist the engine brakes.

As we approached Brentford the distant signal was at caution. Although we were not moving very fast the engine brakes would not slow the train down and it was obvious that we would not stop at Brentford. I sounded the whistle for the guard to use his hand brake but he either took no notice or his brake was ineffective. There is a deceptively steep incline down from Isleworth to Kew Bridge and on this occasion it proved too much for the engine brakes alone. Luckily the signals at Brentford and Kew were all clear when we passed them, because with the brake fully applied the train ran all the way to Grove Park crossing at Chiswick before coming to a stand. That was the only time during my driving career that I ever let a train get completely out of my control. Fortunately I was spared any of the dire consequences which could have resulted from my misjudgement; others have not been so lucky. It was a sobering experience and one which was not to be dismissed lightly. At such times one is reminded of the heavy responsibility one carries and the ease with which you can place yourself in a position you cannot control. I was always extra careful after that when I was working loose-fitted freight trains.

Paul had been promoted to the next link and was now a main line fireman. Strangely, he seemed to be unhappy with the job and after a while he left, the last I heard of him he was a driver on the Festiniog Railway in Wales. I was without a regular fireman again but I was not unused to it and it did make for variety. More variety came in the form of 'Warship' class diesels. The night turn to the Express Dairy depot at Morden had been taken away from Nine Elms and was now worked by a Western Region crew from Old Oak depot. They did not know the road to Morden and on the week that we would normally have worked the turn the driver was now booked to 'conduct' the Western Region driver over the route from Kensington to Morden, via Clapham yard and the main line. The 'Warships' were not allowed over the East Putney line because their AWS equipment was not compatible with the fourth rail system used by London Transport on that line. Sometimes this train was hauled by a 'Western' class which I found more comfortable than the 'Warship'.

Another of our night turns was the Waterloo shunter. This was a busy duty and many hours were spent sorting the vans which arrived during the night and making up the paper trains ready for the morning. An '82000' tank was ideal for this type of work and these were usually used on this duty. When an '80000' was on the job it was hard work, they had the same reverser as the tender engines and it was often very stiff when being wound into the reverse position, the '82s' were much lighter to reverse. The big Standards were sometimes used for shunting at Wimbledon, Surbiton and Tolworth. They were not really designed for such work and their use on these duties made the job harder than it need have been.

I used to enjoy taking engines up to Waterloo, although I rarely worked the train they were intended for. There was a lot of interest in steam engines at that time as most of the other Regions had changed over to diesel or electric traction. As the engine came back on to the train, the passengers would stand around to watch the coupling-up and they would ask the crew questions about their engines and their job. It was nice to speak to people who were interested in your work, some of whom were very knowledgeable. The 'West Country' and 'Merchant Navy' classes always generated most interest as they were an impressive engine to look at. A funny thing happened one day at Waterloo; we had just relieved Bournemouth men on their arrival and I was looking around the engine while my fireman was on the footplate. A man and a woman came up to the engine and the woman asked, 'Excuse me, is this a diesel?' The fireman replied, 'No madam, it is a steam engine'. At which point she turned to the man and said 'There you are, I told you so', and they walked away arguing. Not everybody was knowledgeable.

The year 1966 was one of unrest on the South Western division. Concrete plans were being made for the end of steam, the vacancy list at Nine Elms was frozen to prevent any more men coming to the depot before closure. The reason for this was that Motive Power staff were very restricted in what movements they could make between depots. Once they had had a promotion to become a driver they only had four moves which they could make.

Number one was the 'first preference' move which had to be registered when applying for promotion. The second was an 'accommodation' move which could be applied for at any time (but only once), this was a low priority move and was only allowed to take effect when there was an unfilled vacancy at the depot applied for. The third move was the 'mutual change over', this move could be made more than once but the person who wished to change had to be the same seniority as the person he wished to change with when there was link working at the depot. This was so that men already at the depot did not have their normal promotion chances impeded. The fourth move was the 'redundancy' move, this move took precedence over all other moves. A man who was at a depot not to his liking could use his accommodation move to get to a depot which was about to close, thereby becoming redundant and gaining an advantage by registering a 'redundancy' move and jumping the queue at the depot he wished to go to. Some men did come to Nine Elms for this reason, but the freezing of the vacancy list ended that; as men left or retired they were not replaced.

Guildford depot was also to close and the men were going to be transferred to Woking where a new mixed traction depot was to be established. Under the arrangements which applied at the time, when my turn came to move to Woking I would have to become a 'mixed traction' driver. This idea did not excite me at all, especially the thought of working ballast trains again. When I had originally applied for Woking there were only 12 drivers stationed there and they did no night work; all their turns were main line electric duties on the Portsmouth, Alton and Reading lines. I was very disappointed at not being able to take up the position I had expected.

At that time the arrangement was that the senior men at Nine Elms would transfer to a new 'mixed traction' depot at Waterloo when the steam depot closed. The junior men, which included me, were to go to the emu depot at Wimbledon Park. I thought that this was preferable to going 'mixed traction' at Woking and so cancelled my 'first preference' move and decided to let things take their course.

I attended the training school at Stewarts Lane depot for three weeks to learn electric traction. I found this course extremely difficult, firstly, because I didn't really understand the principles of electricity and knew nothing at all about such things as resistances, relays and the like. Secondly, there were so many different types of electric stock, which all had different equipment and different faults and failures procedures, that when I finished the course I was utterly confused. We learned 'Met Vic' suburban units ('Nutcrackers'), Brighton mainliners, 1936 ('BIL') stock, Portsmouth mainliners ('Nelsons'), 1941 suburban stock, 1951 and 1957 ('EPB') stock, Kent coast mainliners, Motor Luggage Vans ('MLVs') plus 'VEP' stock. The instructor really had his work cut out to teach us all this in three weeks.

The first week was spent in the classroom explaining the equipment and how it worked, the second week was practical, out on the track learning driving techniques and use of the Westinghouse and EP brakes. The third week was back in the class really getting down to the technical details and faults & failures procedures. The last day was the 'passing out' exam which was a terrible ordeal for me and I was extremely relieved when it was over and absolutely delighted when I was told that I had passed.

The senior men were being trained on 'Crompton' 1,550 hp diesel electric locomotives (later class '33') and electro-diesels (EDs) (later class '73'), but the junior drivers were only required to know emus in preparation for our transfer to Wimbledon Park.

The Bournemouth line was in the process of being electrified but although I was trained on emus I never worked on them. All my work except the Merton Abbey was still on steam engines. There seemed to be less steam engines about now and where once the depot at Nine Elms was full of engines, it was now half empty. The roads from about 15 to 25 were unused and those prolific yellow daisy type flowers, which always inhabit disused industrial sites, grew all over that section.

Generally the depot had deteriorated but being there every day I did not notice it, until one day I was asked to show a party around the shed and they commented on the run-down appearance of the place. The steep incline from under the coal hopper had become even more slippery than usual and it was often necessary to take a run at it. I did this one evening, I was trying to coax my 'Merchant Navy' up the slope without success and had rolled back down to the pit in order to try again. The track curved to the left just beyond the hopper and as the engine took the curve there was a load bang and the rail broke. Strangely, the engine was not derailed but there was a piece of rail about two feet long missing between the engine and tender so I was unable to move either way.

The running foremen were all old steam men and knew nothing about diesels. This was delightfully illustrated one night when the foreman came into the drivers' cabin and asked me, 'Do you know blue diesels?' 'No', I replied, 'I have only been trained on electrics'. 'Damn', he said, 'I have just had the foreman from Stewarts Lane on the phone complaining that our drivers only know red and green diesels, they do not know blue ones'. All week he was asking people if they knew blue diesels. Actually it was not the Stewarts Lane foreman who had phoned at all, but one of our drivers playing a trick. At that time the 'Warship' class was painted red, the Cromptons green and the new EDs blue.

The closure plans were altered late in 1966 and it was decided that none of the drivers would go to Wimbledon Park. Instead, 75 were to be transferred to the new mixed traction depot at Waterloo. Unfortunately I was No. 78 on the seniority list so I had no set job to go to, I would have to use my redundancy move to secure a position. I had to decide where I wanted to go before the closure when I would have to register the move.

In the meantime I continued in my steam-only role and I enjoyed some unusual duties. One of these was a special engine, an 'unconverted' 'West Country' which we had to take to Oxted on the Central division line to East Grinstead and Uckfield. There was a big tour organised by one of the enthusiast's societies and our engine was to replace the one which had worked the train thus far. We were to change engines and return to Nine Elms with the other locomotive. I had never been to Oxted before so it was an interesting trip, the conducting driver also found it interesting as he had not worked on a steam engine for several years. I found Oxted to be a pleasant place, the big steam engines seemed oddly out of place there but there was a tremendous excitement among the people who crowded the station and the special train.

Another special which I worked was a troop train from Aldershot up to Willesden Junction, where a diesel took over for the remainder of the journey to Glasgow. We had a 'converted' 'West Country' this day which made easy work of the eight-coach train, even up the steep climb up North Pole Bank to Mitre Bridge. On arrival at Willesden our engine was detached and the Midland driver who had conducted me from Kensington drove the engine through the maze of lines in the area. We eventually arrived back at Mitre Bridge facing the opposite direction (towards Clapham Junction). We then backed into the siding to await the arrival of our return working, which was an excursion from somewhere in the Midlands to Bournemouth. We were to work this train to Clapham Junction where we were to be relieved.

My fireman expressed his desire for a cup of tea but all three of us had used the ingredients which we always brought with us. The Midland driver said to my mate, 'If you take your tea can to the milk depot over there, they will sell you a can of tea for 6d. in the canteen'. My mate set off with tea can in hand, the Midland driver called after him, 'Bring some cakes while you are there'. Ten minutes later he returned with a can of steaming tea and a paper bag containing six delicious cakes. 'That will be tuppence each for the tea and 6d. each for the cakes', he said. 'What', said the Midland driver, 'Listen son, you are on the Midland now and on the Midland the fireman buys the tea and cakes'. My mate had a shocked look on his face as he realised that he had been conned into spending two shillings of his own money. The other driver never did pay his share so I paid half before we went home. I never knew that fireman to buy anything for anyone after that without first collecting the money.

Actually, that trip around the Willesden area was very unnerving, the conducting driver kept saying, 'Don't let her blow off' or 'Don't use the fire irons' and other such warnings. Of course, since the last time I had visited the area as a fireman on loan to Feltham, the overhead electrification had been installed and there were 25 kv wires just above the engine. The place looked a right mess with gantries and wires all over the place. Although the Southern third rail system had its limitations, it certainly had a better appearance and was less likely to kill you if you inadvertently touched it. I really felt uncomfortable that day and was glad when we left Mitre Bridge.

When I was firing my driver had been injured in a rather unusual manner by the third rail. We were preparing a 'Charlie' and I noticed that there was a split in the pet pipe. A fitter was called to replace the pipe, he was very reluctant to do the job and said, 'I have just washed and I am about to go home, can't you put up with it for today'. The driver replied, 'Never mind going home, we are not leaving the shed until you fix it'. The fitter completed the job in about five minutes flat, he didn't even bother to measure the pipe or cut it to the proper length. As we were going up Stouton Bank towards Woking I washed the footplate and when I had finished I threw the pipe out of the side of the cab as usual. There was a flash and a sharp crack and the pipe flew back into the cab at high speed, the metal nozzle hitting the driver on the head. He said, 'It seems as if that fitter wished that on me'.

Another incident with the live rail was when I was driving. I was working the 12.44 parcels from Guildford with a '73' Standard and was braking on the approach to Woking when I noticed the sound of steam escaping. The brakes on a Standard were steam operated on both engine and tender, the steam passing to the tender through a flexible pipe. Apparently the union which attached this pipe to the tender had worked loose and when I applied the brake it came off, the pipe was swishing around under the cab as the steam forced its way out. I did not know this at the time but when I examined the engine in the yard at Woking I found the defect and refitted the union. However, at the time that I first noticed the sound we were approaching a gang of men cutting the grass on the embankment, their lookout man was standing beside the track, leaning against the raised cable troughing. Just as the engine passed him, the flexible pipe touched the live rail, there was a 'Phooph' and a great orange flame. When the smoke cleared the man was right at the top of the embankment, I don't know how he got there but it looked like magic to me. Such were the hazards of working steam engines on an electrified railway. There were many more such incidents but I never knew anybody who was seriously injured, luckily.

During 1966 it was decided that all 96 drivers at Nine Elms would transfer to Waterloo when the depot closed and it would be necessary for them all to be trained on all forms of traction. Consequently I had to spend many weeks at Stewarts Lane training school. First came three weeks on the Crompton 1,550 hp diesel-electric types, then a week learning the braking techniques for freight train working with the new engines, another three weeks followed on the 1,600 hp 'EDs', plus several more weeks on various subjects related to the working of the new types including push and pull working with 'TC' units, 'REP' tractor units, etc. It took about 12 weeks in all. These courses I found to be easier than the first one, on electric traction, probably because I was totally ignorant on that first one whereas I now had the basic principles in my head.

After all the training, some of the duties were altered to include the new forms of traction. The line between Sturt Lane and Basingstoke was now electrified and some of the commuter services were now operated by electric trains. It was real luxury to be in a heated cab on a smooth riding vehicle and as they were new to me it was quite exciting. However, on the mixed duties I still looked forward to the steam part where this came at the end of the duty.

One such duty was the 17.09 from Waterloo to Basingstoke. The first part of this duty was worked with a 'KA' type Crompton hauling two four-car sets of the new 'TC' stock. At Basingstoke the train was berthed and the engine shut down, then after a short break we relieved a train up from Exeter. There were only three types of main line steam passenger engines running by this time, the 'Merchant Navy', 'West Country' and '73' Standard classes. There were still a few '75' Standards about but they were not usually seen on main line passenger duties. I always thought that it added interest to the job, waiting to see what would turn up.

There were more diesels and electro-diesels about at that time and many of the duties formerly worked by steam now had the new types as motive power for at least part of the day. Most of the Bournemouth trains were still hauled by steam and some of the Salisbury and Exeter trains also employed the traditional form of power.

The depot at Nine Elms had deteriorated further and in addition to the mass of weeds which covered the disused part, there were now dead engines standing about. They looked rather sad with their side rods removed and rust encroaching on their bare metal parts. The artist, David Shepherd, captured the atmosphere of decay in his wonderful painting entitled 'Nine Elms, the last hours'. I remember watching him while he was painting it and thought at the time that he must be a bit nutty, painting a picture of a near derelict engine in decaying surroundings. How wrong can you be, a print of this picture is now one of my prized possessions.

It is amazing how quickly the engines deteriorated once they were out of use. The name boards were removed from the 'Merchant Navy' and 'West Country' classes after several of them disappeared. This spoiled their appearance and they always looked incomplete without this decoration. The remaining engines had deteriorated in many ways, mainly little things like leaky steam valves, knocks and bangs and other items which at one time would not have been allowed to go unchecked. Probably the drivers did not bother to report minor defects as they knew that the end was near and some of the enthusiasm had gone from the job. In truth, there was not much glamour in clambering about under dirty engines with an oil can in the dark with a smelly paraffin lamp for a light. We all now had some experience of the modern forms of traction and I for one looked forward to being able to come to work in nice clean clothes and return home just as clean.

Actually, some of the steam drivers managed to keep exceptionally clean, but hard as I tried I always managed to get dirty and oily. I normally used two pairs of overalls in a week. I saw a Bournemouth driver oiling his engine on the pit at Nine Elms one day. He wore a spotless set of overalls and was standing at arms length from the engine. In one hand he held his oil feeder and in the other a white cloth, obviously he took great care in keeping clean and I wished that I could be as careful. As I approached him, he stepped down into the pit to go

The author's last steam trip was the 19.34 Basingstoke-Waterloo on 8th July, 1967, with 'Western' green BR Standard class '5' 4-6-0 No. 73029.

(Both) Author's Collection

under the engine; he immediately climbed out again and I noticed that his trousers had turned black for about six inches up from the bottom. Apparently the pit was flooded and somebody had thrown a load of smokebox ash into the pit, this ash was floating on the water and the driver had not realised that there was water in the pit. I did feel sorry for him but I could see the funny side of it. I was glad that he did not see me laughing as I walked away, that would have been rubbing it in.

The closure date, 9th July, 1967, came very quickly and in the last few months everybody seemed intent on having a last fling before steam engines disappeared forever. Some spectacular performances were recorded in this period and despite the minor defects previously mentioned, the engines were still capable of some really hard work. The last week of steam operation was upon us before we realised it. I was working the 17.09 down to Basingstoke that week and was delighted that at least part of my last week was on the main line with a steam engine.

The down trip, with a Crompton and '8TC' called at Woking, Farnborough and all stations to Basingstoke where we put the train away in the down carriage siding. The return trip was on an up Exeter service, departing at 19.34 and calling only at Woking and Waterloo. Being the last week I was determined to have a good run and was lucky to have a very good fireman by the name of Les Golding. For the first three days a converted 'West Country' was our steed and we had some very nice runs, the eight- or nine-car train was an easy task. On the Thursday Les was rest day and my fireman was Phil Bassett, one of the most experienced firemen at Nine Elms. This day a superb 'Merchant Navy' appeared and I looked forward to a spectacular trip, at least as far as Woking where the traffic started to get heavy. The trip lived up to my expectations and the 'Packet' performed beautifully with the light train. I was really pleased to have had such an excellent trip on the main line before steam traction ended.

The 8.30 am Waterloo-Weymouth passing Surbiton on 8th July, 1967, headed by 'Merchant Navy' class No. 35023 *Holland-Afrika Line*. This was the last rostered steam departure from Waterloo.   *John Faulkner*

I thought to myself that on the next day I would really have a go, being the last chance. As we stood on the platform at Basingstoke waiting for our train to arrive, there were crowds of people on the station waiting to see the steam engines before they finished. It was a very exciting atmosphere and we waited eagerly to see what type of engine we were to have on our last trip. As the train came into view I could see that it was headed by a Standard type and it arrived in the form of a Western Region green-painted Standard No. 73029. Chalked on the smokebox door was the slogan 'Farewell to Steam'. I was disappointed, I had worked on this engine before and knew it to be a poor tool. Anyway I decided to try my best with it, on the section between Basingstoke and Woking we never exceeded 75 mph and the engine proved to be just as weak as I had expected it to be.

To compensate for the disappointing performance of the engine there were hundreds of people alongside the line and on all the stations and bridges, all waving and shouting. It was very moving and I realised for the first time the historical importance of the occasion. This was the last steam-operated main line in the country and over a hundred years of development was coming to an end. I was subdued for the remainder of the turn and was not very interested in the excited people who crowded round the engine at Waterloo. For the past 11 years I had been taking part in the final stage of an era and hadn't realised it until the last day, it was a sobering thought.

After working an empty train to Clapham Yard we took our engine to Nine Elms and dropped the fire into the pit for the last time. Then we walked away from this filthy, dilapidated place where I had spent the past three years at work; three very happy years despite my early impressions.

Strangely, the end came suddenly; although I had known it was coming for the past two years that last week seemed to spring upon me. I left Nine Elms on the Friday night knowing that I would never return there. But there was no sad farewell and I looked forward to starting my new duties at Waterloo on Monday 10th July, 1967. I walked out of the Brooklands Road gate, past Ada's café, past the Brooklands Arms pub, the corner shop on the opposite corner and the row of 'Coronation Street'-type houses up to the Wandsworth Road and away to Vauxhall on a No. 77 bus. Many years later I visited the area by car, but all I could see was a large stack of concrete where the old buildings were, not a sign of the Nine Elms that I knew.

Some of the men were involved in towing dead engines away from the depot, but I myself never stepped on a steam engine again, apart from museum exhibits and locomotives on preserved railways. I did see some dead engines in the loco depot at Weymouth when I was on a training trip there after steam had ended.

When I started at Waterloo I was too busy learning new techniques and new routes to spend much time thinking about the past. It was a clean break and it just seemed natural to be working on the new forms of traction. Waterloo was divided into four links, three mixed traction links of 36 men and an emu link of 80. Most of the duties were single-manned now and I missed the company to start with, but after a while I got used to it. The long mileage duties were shared among all the links and Nos. 1, 2 and 3 all had turns to Bournemouth. I was in No. 3 link and I found the work in this group very interesting and varied.

It was all very exciting and a big improvement on the work which I had performed on the steam. I no longer had to go down the pit to oil the inside bearings of engines, I was always in a clean dry cab and the power was 'on tap' and did not have to be produced before you could use it. The thing I liked most about my new work was that when I started a turn, it only took 10 minutes to prepare the engine and when I finished it took only 10 minutes to dispose it. There was no fire or smokebox to clean and no waiting for coal or a pit to examine the engine on. Basically, all I had to do was switch off the engine and do a short check on various items and that was that, away home. It was a real luxury and I can honestly say that I never missed the steam engines. I should have enjoyed driving one again, but not the preparation and disposal which was part and parcel of the steam duty.

All that is long past now and will never be seen again. I think that I am fortunate to have experienced it at first hand. The fraternity still exists today, but the individuals have changed, the power of the locomotive or unit is determined by the design team and nothing the driver can do will alter the performance. It is a very efficient system but it does not leave much room for individuals.

Guildford Shed, on the last day of steam on the Southern Region, 9th July, 1967. The 'USA' 0-6-0T (on the turntable) had replaced the Adams 0-4-0T as shed pilot in the final years. To the right is rebuilt 'West Country' Pacific No. 34018 *Axminster*, its nameplate having already been removed.

Chapter Five

Transfer to Waterloo and Mixed Traction

In all, 96 drivers were transferred from Nine Elms to Waterloo, the arrangements for the placement of the men were carefully worked out by the joint Nine Elms/Waterloo Local Departmental Committee (LDC). Basically those emu drivers who were previously based at Waterloo would have the option of transferring to mixed traction or remaining purely emu, the ex-Nine Elms men were all to be mixed traction but could opt for the emu link if they so wished, all applications would be considered sympathetically.

In this way it was hoped to achieve a smooth transition from the old depot to the new, fulfilling the wishes of as many men as possible. It is a credit to the joint LDC and local Management that the transfer was a painless operation and was achieved just as smoothly as planned. It was also a vindication of the excellent 'machinery of negotiation' which existed in the railway industry in this country at that time. All the Nine Elms men were officially 'displaced' which gave them certain advantages when applying for vacancies at other depots and some of them used this to their advantage and moved to other parts of the Region.

To explain, an LDC is a committee consisting of members of the work force who are appointed through election by the staff, and local managers. They were able to discuss items of a local nature which did not infringe on national agreements. Rosters, link working, rest day rotations and leave rosters were some of the items which were discussed. In the case of the new depot they did an excellent job and produced a superb set of rosters which were fair to all staff. Everybody had a share of the 'good' work such as long mileage duties and also shared in the other work such as suburban, shunting, parcels and Waterloo & City work. I was in No. 3 link which contained many of the duties which were in No. 4 link at Nine Elms (my link), so I continued doing some of the same work with different forms of traction. This plus the Bournemouth, Portsmouth, Waterloo & City and suburban work made for a varied workload which I found very interesting.

The first few weeks were pretty hair raising and for my own part, if I had any problems with my engine or unit I would try to think of all the things I had learned at the training school. But after a while I settled down and became more comfortable; mind you, I still carried all my faults and failures books with me and found them invaluable at times. For the first few weeks of the new operation, inspectors from the training school would ride on various trains to assist drivers with any problems they might encounter.

One of the problems which I found was that all the new locomotives, the 'TC' stock, some of the older and all of the new emu stock were compatible for working in multiple. A book was issued from the training school listing all the various combinations which could be coupled in multiple and which connections to make in each case. This book I also found invaluable, it was not just a matter of coupling the units together and 'hey presto'; you first had to establish exactly what type of locomotives/units were to be coupled, consider what type of equipment they carried and what if anything needed to be cut out or altered on each unit. At times the whole train was formed of different types of units and this of course complicated the faults and failures procedures; a fault on one unit could affect one or more of the others and it was sometimes necessary to uncouple the units to isolate the fault and thus discover which unit was defective and what the fault was.

One such train was a Basingstoke service at about 17.00 in the evening peak, and if my memory serves me correctly it was formed something like this:

Front	'4VEP' (class '423')
	Crompton (class '33')
	'4TC' (class '403')
	'EDL' (class '73')

the train divided at Basingstoke, the emu going on to Eastleigh, the Crompton hauling the '4TC' to Salisbury and the 'EDL' going into the siding to work a van train away. It was also possible to have an emu train leading a Crompton or 'EDL' with a vacuum braked train on the rear but I personally never worked this combination. All these new practices took some time to get used to and I suppose in retrospect it was quite an interesting period. The Exeter line trains were hauled by 'Warship' class diesel-hydraulic locomotives and there were also some Brush type '4s' about (class '47') but I was not trained for either of these types.

An illustration of the sort of problems encountered with the new types of traction is provided by an incident which happened just a few weeks after the move to Waterloo. The running foreman, Bill Cruz, said to me: 'Behind the boat train on platform 10 there are a pair of Cromptons, when the train goes take the two Cromptons and put them on top of the boat train on platform 11'. That seemed a simple enough instruction so I went to platform 10 and having checked that everything was as it should be, I started the engines and waited for the train to leave. This was the first time that I had used two Cromptons in multiple although I had been well versed in the theory.

When the train moved away I released the brakes and opened the controller. To my dismay instead of the expected roar of the diesel engines all I got was silence and a bright blue fault light. The train disappeared from the platform whilst I sat there looking stupid. The fault light could mean one of many things and after some head scratching and reference to the appropriate book I set off to locate the defect. I found the problem in record time and returned to the cab well pleased with myself, even though the item which had caused the problem was one that I should have checked when preparing the engines. The original Cromptons were fitted with a 'lead and trail' cock in one cab and when working in multiple the cock in the leading locomotive had to be in the lead position, in the trailing locomotive it had to be in the trail position. Of course when the engines had arrived at Waterloo the cocks were in the correct position, but when I tried to drive from the other end they were wrong, a simple mistake soon rectified.

Back in the cab and ready to go again I confidently opened the controller; this time there was no fault light but the locomotives leaped forward, the amp gauge jumped to a very high reading and then gradually reduced as I moved up the platform at a steady pace. I intended to stop at the end of the platform to ask the signalman not to give me the signal until I had a chance to look at the locomotive

Above: Bank station, on the Waterloo & City line, with a two-car train on 18th January, 1967.　　　*P.H. Groom*

Right: The author looks out of the cab of Crompton No. 33025 at Waterloo in 1971. Jim 'The Spring' O'Halloran is seen alongside.　　*Author's Collection*

again. However, before I could get to the phone the signal was cleared so I decided to wait until I got back into platform 11 before doing an examination.

Unknown to me, an inspector had been watching my performance and when I set back into platform 11 he came to speak to me. He had seen the locomotives jump forward again when I opened the controller and asked me what the problem was. I explained what had happened, he said something about the load regulator and then disappeared into the engine room. The inspector was Bill Neal and he was acknowledged as something of an expert so I did not interfere.

Whilst he was in the engine room, another driver, Ted Dente, came up and asked me what the inspector was doing. I told him the story and described the symptoms of the present problem. He said 'Have you got a brake handle in the 'running' position on the rear loco?' I hadn't of course. On the original Cromptons it was necessary to have one handle in the running position on the trailing locomotive in order to release the brakes (the braking system was later modified to make this unnecessary). I was pulling the rear locomotive along with the brakes on, hence the snatching and the high amp reading. Ted went back to the other engine and placed the handle in the running position. When Bill Neal came out of the engine room his hands were covered in dirt and grease and he said, 'Try it now'. I did and of course there was no problem. 'That's fixed it', said Bill and walked away with a broad grin on his face and well pleased with himself. I dared not tell him what the real problem had been, he would not have been amused.

I was busy for some time learning the route to Bournemouth and having a refresher on the Portsmouth line. Most of the other routes I already knew but my new duties took me into places which I had only passed by before, so I had to have a look at them. Eastleigh marshalling yard was one, Bevois Park yard was another; there was also the new diesel depot at Eastleigh with which I was not familiar, the last time I went there it was a steam depot and some radical changes had taken place.

All in all the first few months were pretty hectic and I was always occupied with something new. Most of the duties were now single manned; the second men at Waterloo were not rostered with a driver, they were in a link of their own and the duties they performed covered the relevant parts of many drivers duties. We were thrown in at the deep end and it is surprising how quickly we learned to swim. For some time I was not trained for the Waterloo & City (W&C) line, I was waiting my turn to go on the course. I knew virtually nothing about this line and judging by the comments of those who did I wasn't missing very much. However, my turn eventually came and I spent another week at the training school learning all about it.

The W&C as it was usually known is a short underground tube railway, about 1½ miles long which runs from beneath Waterloo station to Bank station in the city of London. It was worked with specially-built rolling stock which consisted of separate motor cars and trailer cars. The motor cars had a cab at each end and could run singly, in pairs or in train formations, although they were prohibited from running singly in passenger service when I worked on the line. The normal formation was three trailer cars with a motor car at each end forming a five-car train. Outside the peak hours the trains were split and reformed so that two motor cars ran coupled together, as there were normally three trains running in the off-peak there was always one in the five-car formation.

There were two tube tunnels, one for the up line and one for the down. In 1967 the trains were booked to run at 2½ minutes intervals during the peak hours, each single trip taking 4 minutes. Outside the peaks the frequency was gradually reduced to 10 minute intervals. During non-peak times the crew would change ends at each end of the line and work the same train back and forth. During the peaks a turnover crew was provided, they travelled to Bank and on arrival worked the train back to Waterloo while the first crew got themselves in position to work the following train back. This arrangement was necessary due to the volume of passengers which made it very difficult to change ends in the short time available.

Having got over the first few months of interest in this new job, I soon adopted the widely felt attitude of utter boredom which over the years became an active dislike which never left me. The only consolation was that the early turns did not start until 06.00 (the first train was at 06.45) and the last train ran at 22.00, also, the four W&C duties in No. 3 link were mixed with main line duties on alternate days which made it a little more bearable. The emu link (No. 4) had 12 turns on the line and they worked them for a week at a time which I hated on the occasions when I was booked to cover one of these duties.

My own opinion was that it was a soul destroying job and I hated it intensely and watched the clock all day, feeling that I had done a week's work rather than a day when I went home. Some of the duties involved 18 round trips which meant changing ends 36 times, one duty contained a period of four hours of non-stop working with 12 round trips before the meal break. The passengers always referred to the W&C as the 'Drain', the crews always called it the 'Rat Hole' which is an indication of the general feeling about the line. Having said all that, the line was built as an extension to the London & South Western Railway, giving access to the City. This is still its function and as such it is a very important link, so however much it was disliked by the staff it was unlikely to go away and this was one of the reasons for my seeking promotion as described later in the book. (Although, as it turned out, the line was later transferred to London Underground.)

The W&C also gave me the opportunity to do something that I had never done before. When I arrived at work one day, the depot master, Arthur Jupp, asked me if I would mind taking part in a BBC radio programme. I agreed and went down to the 'Rat Hole' to meet the radio crew. The producer explained that he was making a programme about the 'City' and the people who lived and worked there (it was called *The not so square mile*). I was to talk about the W&C and its role in moving the city workers to and from work. The producer placed what looked like a tin can on a tripod in front of me and said 'Speak'. I was nonplussed for a moment but eventually plucked up courage and spoke to the tin can which made me feel extremely silly. I spoke for what seemed a long time, off the top of my head (or perhaps it was the back of my head). Eventually I ran out of things to say and the producer said that it was very good, I was quite pleased with myself. My disappointment came some time later when the programme was broadcast, my lengthy diatribe was reduced to several seconds and was partly drowned out by real life sound effects. This was my one and only effort at broadcasting.

Chapter Six

The Traction Units

The locomotives that I first used on my mixed traction duties were of three basic types, namely, classes '33', '73' and '08', although they were not known by these class numbers at that time. Some details of these engines may be of interest. Class '33', commonly known as Cromptons at the time, after the maker of the electrical equipment (Crompton Parkinson), was a diesel-electric locomotive of 1,550 hp, the diesel engine being made by Sulzer. They were introduced to the Southern Region in 1960, I first saw them at Feltham and Eastleigh where they were used on freight duties. They were a strong and reliable locomotive and basically very simple to operate, having fully automatic control equipment. Having taken the weight of the train with a small opening of the controller it was possible to open up fully and let the equipment increase the power as required, very rarely did an overload occur.

There were three variants of the class in 1967, i.e. '33/0', '33/1' and '33/2'. The '33/0' was the original type and apart from a few modifications to the braking systems they remained as built. The '33/1' was the push-pull version fitted with Westcode automatic remote control system, these had emu type brake and electrical connections above the buffer beam as well as the normal locomotive connections below the buffer beam. They were compatible for multiple working with all types of Southern Region emu stock built from 1952 to 1973, plus 'TC stock' and class '73' locomotives and of course other class '33s'. The '33/2' was similar to the '33/0' except that it had a narrow body to allow it to work on the Tunbridge Wells to Hastings route with its narrow tunnels, some of this type were also fitted with Hawker Siddeley fine control equipment for use at 'merry go round' terminals. The '33/2' type were commonly known as 'Thin Cromptons'.

Although only 1,550 hp (rather small for a mixed traffic locomotive) the Cromptons were a powerful performer and drivers were often surprised at the work that they could do. They were used on the Southern Region for every type of duty from shunting to express passenger services. From the point of view of the engine crew the Crompton was a diabolical machine. They were very noisy in the cab, they vibrated from end to end and everything in the cab rattled when working in the mid-power range. They were extremely rough riding at speed and at times the rolling and bumping could be quite frightening.

Having said all that it is now only fair to describe the credit side, first and foremost they were absolutely reliable and must have rated highly in the table of availability and mileage between failures. This must in part reflect on the servicing they received at the hands of the CM&EE staff but the main point is that the equipment was of sound solid design and not prone to failure. In fact the day to day servicing of these locomotives was minimal and on a typical visit into Stewarts Lane depot for fuel, the fitters there would check the sump oil, the circ oil (it drove the cooling fan), the brakes and associated equipment, the lights and any defects reported in the repair book. Then it was back into service,

Crompton (later class '33') No. D6504 arrives at Waterloo on 6th July, 1962, with the 07.03 Le Havre boat train from Southampton Docks. *A.G. Dixon*

Crompton No. D6541 approaches Wimbledon with the 11.30 Waterloo-Bournemouth West train. To the left is Durnsford Road sidings and the old SR power station. *Brian Stephenson*

A later view of D6516, now carrying the BR blue livery, passing West Byfleet with an up cement train on 4th July, 1969. *J.H. Scrace*

Class '73' electro-diesel No. 73132 is seen at Wimbledon Yard with the 11.37 Acton-Tolworth train on 13th June, 1974. *J.H. Scrace*

A new 'VEP' unit in 1967. It carries the original livery of all blue with yellow ends.

often in less than an hour. In service it was only necessary to keep an eye on the fuel level and a few other items, the general machinery was so reliable and self governing that it could safely be left to look after itself; a typical Southern motive power unit in fact. They could carry 800 gallons of fuel and, at something like one mile to a gallon on average, they had a fair range between servicing, although the fuel level was rarely allowed to fall below 100 gallons.

I used these locomotives for many years on a whole range of duties and never once had a complete failure. The auto-governing equipment worked so well that it was possible to open the controller fully with the train at a stand and the engine would give full power and regulate itself to start and accelerate the train with no fear of overload. When starting a train the diesel engine first revved up to maximum revolutions and the amp gauge would progressively rise to a maximum of 1,500 amps. Some time would elapse before the engine would move, unlike some other classes which would respond instantly to the controller. This mode of operation must have seemed strange to drivers who were not used to it; many times when I have been conducted on other Regions the conducting drivers have been reluctant to leave the controller open when the engine is revving but the locomotive is not moving. In fact the only time that the vibration was kept to a minimum was when the controller was either fully open or closed and regular drivers tended to use these two positions only, coasting when not on full power.

The other common type of locomotive was the 'ED', later known as class '73'. When first introduced they were numbered E60XX. In my opinion they were the best mixed traffic locomotive ever built, they could be used, and were, for anything and everything. They were basically an electric locomotive of 1,600 hp, not very powerful but adequate for most duties required of them. When they were used on heavy boat trains to Southampton docks two were coupled in multiple. The engine room also contained a 600 hp diesel engine which was used when shunting or running on non-electrified lines. This engine was very powerful at low speeds but as speed increased the power dropped off but it never ceased to surprise me what these little engines could do. They were compatible for multiple working with most types of traction units built after 1950. Provision was made on 'VEP', 'REP', 'TC', and 'CIG' stock to control the vacuum exhauster on the locomotive, the intention being that the driver could be in the cab of an electric unit with an 'ED' behind hauling a vacuum-braked train.

The class '08' shunters do not warrant much description except to say that as a shunting engine they were just about perfect mechanically, their only problem being that the designers forgot to allow for the fact that somebody had to drive the thing. They were at best uncomfortable and at worst positively dangerous to work on, with all sorts of pipework and associated joints, brackets, etc. all around the area where the driver was supposed to work; a rough shunt could cause injury to legs or head. Because of the 350 hp engine they were commonly known as '350s'. The later modification which appeared as class '09' was still called a '350' by the staff, but because they were fitted with air pipes at platform level for coupling with emu-type stock they were jokingly called 'push & pull 350'.

Crompton No. 33101 propels '4TC' unit No. 407 out of Woking station on 3rd June, 1977.
Les Bertram

'4CIG' unit No. 7425 with the 14.28 Guildford-Ascot train arriving at Warnborough on 4th September, 1977.   *Les Bertram*

350 hp diesel shunters at rest inside the new diesel depot at Feltham in 1966. *BR/SR*

350 hp diesel shunter No. D3462 alongside the old steam shed at Feltham on 6th December, 1967.
J.H. Scrace

'Warship' class diesel hydraulics at Waterloo on 18th March, 1967. The locomotives on view are, *from left to right*, an unidentified Crompton, No. D810 *Cockade* and, waiting to depart for Exeter, D869 *Zest*.
R.E. Ruffell

Because I was in No. 3 link and we did not go to Salisbury I was not required to be trained on the 'Warship' class (2,200 hp diesel-hydraulic) and only occasionally worked on them as pilotman to 'foreign' drivers over our routes. As an observer I was not very impressed with them but those who worked on them regularly seemed to like them and always extolled their virtues.

The Brush type '4' (class '47') often worked on the South Western Division and No. 2 link at Waterloo was trained on them. It was planned to train us all on this type but before this happened a strange machine (copied from Billy Bean I suspect) appeared on the scene. This was the type 'HB' electro-diesel, later class '74', an ultra-modern collection of electronic bits and pieces affixed to modified type E5000 electric locomotives from the South Eastern Division.

These became known as 'Big EDs' and of course the other 'EDs' then became 'Little EDs'. The big ones were much more powerful than the little ones at 2,500 hp on electric power but the 650 hp Paxman diesel engine never seemed to perform as well as the 600 hp English Electric unit on the earlier type. This was probably due to the different control systems. Whereas on the little 'ED' the engine would tick over in the normal manner and rev up when the controller was opened, on the big ones when the engine was started it would wind itself up to maximum revs and remain in that state until it was switched off. The power was regulated between the generator and the motors by the electronic equipment, the diesel engine had to keep the booster running at constant speed as it would when running on electric power. At least that was the general idea but sometimes the equipment would not perform according to theory and usually had to be switched off and left to cool down for a while. This often worked and when the engine was restarted everything returned to normal.

A lot of the problem with this type was that they encompassed brand new technology which nobody really understood from a practical point of view. When they went wrong there was nothing to examine when looking for defects, opening the equipment cupboards revealed a mass of wires and printed circuit boards. The basic theory of the equipment was simple. On the little 'ED' when the power controller was opened, the current from the third rail was fed through a bank of resistances to the motors, the resistances were progressively removed from the power circuit either by the driver using the manual notch-up lever or automatically when the lever was placed in the 'run up' position. With the big 'ED' there was none of this paraphernalia, the current through the power circuit to the motors was controlled electronically.

When the engine was 'cut in' the first thing to happen was that an enormous generator started up, the sound that this made was like the engine of a jumbo jet and the nickname 'Jumbo' was coined for these locomotives. When the power controller was opened, the power circuit was opened from the third rail to the motors direct, there was no bank of resistances and had the current been allowed to flow unhindered it would have been too much for the motors to take while stationary. Through the magic of modern electronic gadgetry the power produced by the generator (booster) opposed the power from the third rail and therefore limited the amount allowed to pass to the motors.

This control system was known as 'Buck and Boost' and when the equipment was operating as described above it was in the 'buck' mode. As the engine

Class '47' No. 47433 passes through Clapham with the Northfleet to Uddingston cement block train on 9th April, 1975. *R.I. Wallace*

Electro-diesel (later class '74') No. E6110 is seen at Surbiton with the 11.38 Waterloo-Weymouth parcels train on 3rd February, 1970, with Winthrop House overlooking the station. *J.H. Scrace*

speed increased the booster would oppose less and therefore allow more power from the third rail into the motors until it did not resist at all. The equipment would then change from 'buck' to 'boost' mode and instead of resisting the flow of power to the motors it would supplement it. All these operations were automatic and controlled by an on-board computer known as the 'logic box'. In theory at least it was possible to open the controller to full power when stationary and the logic box would work out what the locomotive was pulling and give enough power to accelerate without slipping. That was the theory but in practice it was found to be not a very good idea as the equipment did not always react as expected. I heard one driver telling a newly qualified man, 'Treat them like a woman, be nice to them, treat them gently but never trust them'. In my experience this was good advice as they proved to be very temperamental. When they worked as they were supposed to they were a very powerful machine but when they played up they could be frightening.

Some examples of the odd things that they could get up to may be of interest to the reader. As described above, the logic box would work out the load attached and give maximum power to pull it without slipping. As an experiment I once opened the controller fully whilst stationary with a light engine, I wanted to see how the logic box worked out that there was nothing attached and what power it would apply to accelerate a light engine. I got an awful shock because the power was first applied at about 400 amps while the logic box thought about it, then it did a totally unexpected thing. Having decided that the locomotive was pulling nothing it gave maximum power to accelerate without slipping, in the case of a light engine this was about 4,000 amps. The effect of this was terrifying, the locomotive accelerated from about 15 mph to 90 mph in under 30 seconds and I could do nothing about it as I was in my seat, pressed against the back wall and unable to reach the controller or brake until the acceleration eased off.

When the diesel engine was started it revved up until the load regulator set it at normal running speed. If the controller was opened before it had properly settled the amp gauge would jump back against the stop and the locomotive would leap forward. I called this negative amps although the engineers insisted there was no such thing, however, they could not deny that it happened when they saw it and huddled over their schematics trying to work it out.

If you gave the equipment an instruction you had to leave it alone until it had completed that instruction before giving another one or the system would go haywire. I once pressed the 'auxiliary power on' switch instead of the 'reset' switch which was next to it. The diesel engine started priming and the collector shoes lifted, realising what I had done I then pressed the 'auxiliary power off' switch to stop the sequence. The effect of this was that the diesel engine stopped priming and the shoes remained in the up position so I had no power at all, I coasted into Basingstoke like this and spent half an hour trying to make it work again, eventually shutting down completely and starting from scratch after a few minutes. This became an accepted procedure on these locomotives if not an official one.

Locomotives were originally numbered with a letter denoting the main type of power, 'D' for diesel and 'E' for electric with the type being shown by the first two numbers, thus the Cromptons were numbered D65XX, the original type being designated 'KA' and the push-pull type being 'KB'. The little 'EDs' were

Driver Whelton, of Waterloo, looks out of the cab of '2BIL' No. 2138 at Ash on 25th May, 1969.
R.E. Ruffell

'4COR' No. 3104 arrives at Guildford with the 13.50 Waterloo to Portsmouth Harbour on 10th October, 1968.   *J.H. Scrace*

E60XX, the six prototypes being designated 'JA' and the remainder 'JB'. (These two types could not work in multiple.)

Apart from the locomotives there were a whole range of multiple units, all of which I had been trained to drive. The oldest were the '4SUB'; built by Metropolitan-Vickers they were sometimes known as 'Met Vicks' but on the South Western they were known as 'Nutcrackers', because of a large circuit breaker located under the cupboard behind the driver which continually clicked and popped as the power circuit was activated. If the power was shut off when a high amperage was in the circuit this contactor would create a loud bang and flames would emit from the arc chute. I found this very frightening and was pleased that these units had virtually disappeared from the South Western and I can't ever remember driving one on my own account although I did ride on quite a few of them.

Most of the suburban services were operated by '4SUB' units dating from 1937 which were a big improvement on the Met Vicks. '2BIL' units worked the outer electric services to Alton and Reading and also the stopping services on the Portsmouth line. The fast Portsmouth services were operated by '4COR' units, these were known as 'Nelsons' because one of the cab windows was blanked off by the route indicator giving the front end a 'one-eyed' appearance. Some of the 'Windsor side' locals were worked by '4EPB' units and by this time so were the Guildford 'New Line' trains via Cobham. The service via Epsom to Effingham Junction was worked by 'SUBs'.

New trains had been introduced for the newly electrified Bournemouth line, these consisted of 'REP' tractor units in multiple with unpowered 'TC' units on the fast and semi-fast services and '4VEP' units on the stopping services. In the peak hours some of these trains were made up to 10 cars by the addition of a '2HAP' unit, a non-corridor main line type of '2EPB' which were introduced for the Kent Electrification scheme in 1959.

All the above types were in my repertoire and the Waterloo depot duties reflected this. For example, one duty entailed working the 06.46 semi-fast from Waterloo to Bournemouth with a 'REP'/'TCs', returning with a '4VEP' on the 10.12 stopping service as far as Woking, then taking on a train from Portsmouth which was formed of '10BIL'. This train was worked all stations to Surbiton then fast to Waterloo. Having spent the best part of the day in the comparative luxury of a modern cab with easy to use electro pneumatic (EP) brake, it was quite a shock to revert to 1930s technology with five two-car units in multiple using the Westinghouse brake. Making reasonable stops at stations required a lot of concentration.

'4SUB' unit No. 4678 at Clapham Junction with the 15.06 Waterloo-Chessington South on 18th September, 1974.   *Brian Morrison*

Chapter Seven

Time for a Change?

Having jumped in at the deep end and learned a few hard lessons I gradually grew in confidence and felt completely happy with any type of traction on any type of duty. In fact the great variety of work made the job most enjoyable, the only problem being the hours of duty which ranged over the whole 24 hours. As I lived some 30 miles from Waterloo it often meant travelling up on the last train at night and waiting to start duty early in the morning, or finishing late at night and waiting for the paper train to get home. However, I felt that the 'pros' outweighed the 'cons' and as I got to know all of the staff I had little trouble in changing turns for those which fitted my travelling arrangements.

A description of some of the duties will illustrate the variety. The 06.46 semi-fast to Bournemouth was one duty as just mentioned. Another was the 06.42 stopping train to Bournemouth, returning with the 10.56 semi-fast to Waterloo. At first this duty ended on arrival at Waterloo but in a productivity initiative many of the duties were altered and one of them was the 06.42. On arrival at Waterloo at 13.04 we had to work the 13.29 round the Hounslow loop. On the late turn No. 3 link worked the 14.46 to Bournemouth returning with the 19.12 'stopper' to Basingstoke; after relief at Basingstoke we worked the following semi-fast to Waterloo. We also worked the 18.30 fast train to Bournemouth and the 21.12 all stations back again; this was the slowest train of the day and did not arrive at Waterloo until about 00.30.

We worked two paper trains to Portsmouth, the 02.30 which called at Woking, Petersfield, Havant and Portsmouth, this train also carried the Isle of Wight papers. The other was the 03.40 to Guildford where we picked up the 'Bolton' vans before continuing to Portsmouth; we off-loaded papers at Weybridge, Woking (the vans for Woking and Farnborough were detached here), Guildford, Godalming and Haslemere. The Bolton vans contained mainly 'mail order' traffic which was dropped off at all stations except Farncombe and Rowlands Castle. Both these duties involved working back into London in the morning peak period, the 08.20 ex-Portsmouth on the 02.30 turn and the 08.56 vans on the 03.40. The 08.56 vans was a huge train with usually 22 to 24 vans on, albeit empty, they still took some humping up Buriton Bank. I always found the return working on these duties very arduous as I was obviously tired after being out all night and if the sun was shining it was in your face all the way.

Another interesting duty for me was the 07.06 parcels train to Woking. I liked this turn because it did not involve getting up at 03.00 and different trips were made on different days. After working the vans to Woking we went into the yard to pick up our train for the next part of the job. One day we went down the Portsmouth line to Liphook and Liss with military traffic, another day we would go to Aldershot government sidings, again with military traffic. Another trip was to 'Coxs Lock Mill' at Addlestone to deliver bulk grain in 'Presflo' wagons. I always enjoyed these trips as it was the same type of work that I started out doing at Guildford steam depot, I also met people whom I knew during that period. After the various trips we would go to Guildford and work the 12.44 vans to Clapham yard calling at Woking, Walton-on-Thames and Surbiton, putting off and picking up at each stop.

We also had two trips to Eastleigh which returned with freight trains, one to South Lambeth yard (Battersea), the other to Hither Green, with relief at Clapham Junction. We also retained much of the local work from Nine Elms such as the 'Kenny Belle' passenger trips to Kensington, the Vauxhall milk trains, the Morden milk and many empty stock working between Waterloo and Clapham yard. We continued to man the Waterloo shunting engines which were round the clock jobs (if you visit Waterloo at night nowadays it is difficult to imagine that there were two shunting engines fully employed for most of the night).

All this plus a whole multitude of electric inner and outer suburban services and the dreaded Waterloo & City line made for a very varied workload. I quickly became an expert.

At this time there were a lot of loco-hauled trains running, most of the Royal Mail went by train as did most newspaper and magazine traffic and a large amount of mail order and general parcels. The West of England service was also loco-hauled. The 350 hp shunters were kept busy all day at Waterloo but especially during the night when arriving parcels trains were unloaded and re-marshalled to form some of the paper trains (some came from Clapham yard already formed). Apart from the main line parcels trains there were many local services which dropped off vans at such places as Richmond, Twickenham, Hounslow, Staines, Wokingham, Surbiton, Walton, Woking and Guildford. These would be picked up on the return workings, many were taken to Clapham yard for marshalling into inter-Regional trains, others were taken to Waterloo for unloading.

Every night a huge train of loaded vans was assembled in the Kensington sidings at Clapham Junction. This then went up to Willesden where the vans were placed on various trains for the North. There were often too many vans to form the train within the sidings, it was then formed in two parts and put together by shunting towards the Kensington line with the front part and back into the siding to attach the rear part; the train then started away from outside the siding signal. The gantry supporting Clapham 'A' signal box collapsed in about 1965, this prohibited access to the Ludgate lines for some time. As a result a temporary parcels depot was set up on platforms 1 and 2 at Clapham Junction, (I believe that the parcels had previously been dealt with at Bricklayers Arms depot) but the work continued at Clapham Junction for many years afterwards.

The shunters in the Kensington sidings had no communications between themselves and Clapham 'C' signal box which was located at the country end of platform 3 and 4 and they would shout instructions to the signalman for the moves to be made at the top of their voices. One man in particular, a West Indian known as 'Bingo' Hilton, had a really loud voice and when he shouted from the bottom of the sidings his voice would echo all around the newly erected blocks of flats on the up side. Goodness only knows what the residents thought of it all at 2 o'clock in the morning, a voice booming, 'Up the middle out of three'; luckily for them this no longer happens.

Although I now considered myself an expert I was soon to be knocked off my perch. One Saturday afternoon in the summer of 1968 I was working the 12.30 fast train to Bournemouth stopping only at Southampton Central. It was very hot and it was not possible to have the side windows open in the cab of a 'REP' unit when travelling at speed, due to the drumming effect of the air as it passed around the front end of the unit which hurt the driver's ears. As I approached Brockenhurst I had a green light on the distant signal; the signals at Brockenhurst were a mixture at that time, on the down line there was a colour light distant, a colour light home signal, a semaphore starting signal on both down platforms and a semaphore advanced starting signal which also carried the distant for Lymington Junction on the same post. The green light on the distant indicated that the home, starting and advanced starting signals were all clear.

As I approached Brockenhurst I reduced speed for the 60 mph permanent restriction though the station, in fact I slowed to 50 mph and put my head out of the side window to get some fresh air. I did not look at the advanced starter as I knew it was clear. Having had my fresh air I closed the window and opened the controller fully for the climb up to Sway. As I rounded the bend towards Lymington Junction I saw the home signal at danger and despite an emergency brake application I ran past the signal at danger, stopping just short of the junction. The home signal at Lymington Junction consisted of a 'T' gantry with three signal posts on it; the left-hand one was for the Lymington branch, the centre one (higher) was for the main line to Bournemouth and the right-hand one used to be for the Ringwood branch. There was no signal on this post as the branch was long closed but the post was still there.

My first reaction when I saw the two signals at danger was 'where is my one?', my second reaction was to 'drop the handle' making an emergency brake application. When I stopped I did not have far to walk to the signal box; the signalman said that there was no damage done but there was a train at the intermediate signal between Sway and New Milton. When this train moved away I was allowed to continue. Three aspects of this incident caused me some distress. One was that I considered myself to be a good driver and was upset to think that I could make such a mistake. The second was the thought that if I had not seen the signal at Lymington Junction I might have charged through the section and possibly collided with the train standing at the intermediate signal, the consequence of which could have been disastrous. The third was that I was charged with the offence of passing a signal at danger and everybody knew that I had done it; although the punishment that I received was not excessive I felt really bad about it.

However, I soon recovered my confidence and got on with the job. I was now trained for all types of traction and signed for all routes required by my link position plus a few which were not required. This was useful for me as when I was rostered a spare day I would often get a job not normally in my link and I found this very interesting. The situation did not change much for the next few years until the closure of Feltham depot became imminent. The depot and the marshalling yard were to close completely and most of the drivers with the remainder of their work were to be transferred to Waterloo. At the time my wife was in hospital and I had two small children to look after. I appealed for help to the depot master (Arthur Jupp, he was the inspector who had passed me out as a driver); he arranged for me to be accommodated on duties which allowed me to carry out my domestic responsibilities while still going to work. It was a difficult period but without this arrangement it would have been impossible.

One of the jobs I was given was to learn the routes in North London where we would be required to go when the Feltham work was transferred, this work would take us to Willesden (Brent and Sudbury sidings), Temple Mills, Stratford, Purfleet, Hertford East and Cricklewood. I spent about six weeks riding about the area and preparing a coloured map. This was more difficult than it sounds as there was not a regular train service on all the routes and I spent a lot of time sitting in signal boxes at junctions waiting for a suitable freight train to carry me over the required route. When I was confident of my route knowledge Mr Jupp told me to take the 'Kenny Belle' Crompton when it had finished its trips and take other drivers with me to teach them the routes. I did this for about a month and found it a most interesting job. We would set out from Clapham Junction each morning and either go across the West London line via Kensington or via Kew and Acton to Willesden High Level on the North London line. Our progress thereafter was on request; I would stop at various signal boxes and advise the signalman where we wanted to go. Most of them were helpful but some were less so and a few arguments ensued.

One day I went into the signal box at South Tottenham Junction and spoke on the phone to Temple Mills box. I requested to go though Temple Mills yard then via the Channelsea curve, High Meads curve, through Manor Yard, back through the marshalling yard then down to Hertford East. On returning from Hertford I asked to go via the main line and High Meads curve to Victoria Park Junction then back to Clapham Junction via Camden and Willesden. I had prepared my request beforehand and reeled it off without thinking. The man at the other end of the phone must have got out of bed the wrong side that morning as he gave me short shrift and told me in unprintable terms that he was there to run a railway, not to play trains. Anyway, who did I think I was, wanting to go here there and everywhere at a minute's notice. After a long conversation in which I used great diplomacy I managed to persuade him that what I was doing was important and if he did not want to help he could explain why not to my boss. We eventually covered all the routes that I had planned but on later trips I made a point of only asking for one or two moves at a time.

When the Feltham men came to Waterloo the mixed traction links were increased to 40 men each and the emu link was also increased. Due to my lengthy period of route learning I was in demand for the North London work while other staff were still route learning and often came off my rostered turn to cover these jobs. I enjoyed this work as it was varied and often involved going to places not normal for Southern Region men. Often the conductor driver had not worked on a Southern engine so these trips had a double interest. The downside was that when you went onto the North London line you never knew when you would get back. They always seemed to be 'on the block' at somewhere or other and did not seem to be in the least concerned about pathways and the like. The timetable was a work of fiction and for a Southern man who was used to being chased for odd minutes lost it was difficult to understand; still, it was not all bad and I did find it interesting.

At that time most freight trains were double manned although drivers did not have a regular secondman. The running foreman asked me one day if I would help out by coming off my rostered duty to work a train up to Ripple Lane yard at Barking. He asked me if I knew the route and I confirmed this adding that I even had a map (the one I drew when first learning the routes). Unbeknown to me the secondman allocated to the job had been listening to the conversation and had seen me produce the map from my bag. He refused to come with me, telling the foreman that if I needed a map to find my way I should not sign for the route. He was adamant and eventually another man was found and we went on our way. When I got back a friend of mine spoke to me about this, he said, 'Is it true that you have to use a map to find your way about on the North London line?' When I explained what had happened he could see the funny side of it but I was ribbed for a long time afterwards about my map.

There were some days in each link rostered for route learning. I used these to best advantage and made a point of learning the road to Salisbury (I had not worked down there since I was a fireman). I also learned the road to Horsham via Dorking and various other bits and pieces which I had not learned before. Over a period I signed for all routes on the South Western division plus a few other useful lines on other divisions and Regions. I was quite pleased with myself that I was qualified to drive all types of traction, work all types of trains and work over any route possible at the depot. However, this knowledge was to work to my disadvantage; the conditions of service agreed between the unions and British Rail worked on the principle that drivers should be rostered a complete week's work in preference to daily booking. This was a good principle which allowed you to plan your social life at least a week in advance. Because I was trained for all traction and all routes I was always available for a week's work if I was spare and therefore never got a chance of getting the special duties which were booked on a daily basis, such as boat trains and special freights, etc. I did consider crossing off some of my routes to overcome this, but decided against it as it would have restricted my ability to change turns to suit my domestic arrangements. This is important when you have small children; working such odd shifts may not be everybody's cup of tea but I found it not too bad. I never took my family out on bank holidays, I would have a day off in the week instead and take the kids to the seaside when it was quiet and there were no traffic problems.

By the mid-1970s I had done virtually everything that a driver could do on the South Western and I decided to try something new. I applied to the LAMCO corporation for a job driving iron ore trains in Liberia, West Africa. This was not prompted only by my desire for something new but there had been a lot of industrial relations problems in recent years and I sometimes disagreed with others over the action to be taken. This sometimes turned

A LAMCO Corporation triple-headed empty iron ore train waiting in a passing loop in Liberia.   *Author's Collection*

unpleasant and I did not enjoy going to work, which was not like me at all. After making the application my wife and I were invited to attend an interview at an hotel in London. We considered that if we rented our house to the army for three years we could save enough from the salary offered to pay off our mortgage when we returned home. I would then have to find a new job as it was not possible to rejoin the motive power line of promotion at that time if you were over 26 years old. However, we did not consider this a big problem at the time.

The interview was very informal and the person who asked me various questions in a private interview did not seem to know much about driving trains. I was not impressed and on the way home we decided that I would not take the job if it was offered. A week later I received a letter from the company saying that I had been accepted for the job and would fly out in six weeks' time. Included with the letter was a packet of malaria tablets which I was to start taking immediately, an appointment to see a London doctor for a medical check and an introduction to a shipping company with a view to moving my furniture. This came as a bit of a shock and I had great difficulty in contacting the company to decline their offer. In the meantime my wife got more and more upset at the thought that I may have committed myself, especially as they said that I would have to go alone to start with pending allocation of suitable housing. However, this was eventually sorted out and I was to stay where I was; I was a little disappointed but decided to see what else I could do without going to Africa.

When the opportunity arose I applied to become a panel supervisor. I would remain on the roster as a driver in the normal manner but would be called upon to act as motive power supervisor (MPS) when required. In mid-1975 I was accepted and started training for my new duties. I was to have a week on each shift with various supervisors to learn the job, I would then be on my own. The jobs to be covered were the mixed traction supervisors at Waterloo and Clapham Junction (the former was a round the clock job, the latter just a day job), the main line emu supervisor and the Windsor line emu supervisor at Waterloo (the former was a round the clock job, the latter was two shifts, early and late turn). After a week on each shift of each job I 'took on'.

I had wanted something new to do and I was not to be disappointed. There was a lot more involved in the jobs than I thought. Typically the worker thinks that the supervisor doesn't do anything but of course he does as I was to discover. Not only did I have to ensure that there were staff on duty for all the jobs and that the rolling stock was available for them to work on (all this was pre-planned), but when anybody or any stock was missing for some reason I had to re-arrange the diagrams, etc. to make up for the missing part of the equation. To run a train you had to have three things, a driver, a guard and some suitable rolling stock. Keeping these three things together at times of disruption took some doing and as I gained experience I began to enjoy the job immensely and relished it when things went wrong and I had to put them right. This involved working closely with the station supervisor who had to control the passengers, the signal box regulator who had to guide the signalmen and arrange stock movements, and I also had to liaise with Control who had an overview of the situation on a divisional basis.

The MPS at Waterloo had quite a lot of power to arrange things on his own and in liaison with others but the main thing was to keep 'Control' advised as to what changes had been made to the planned working. I sometimes failed to do this and incurred the wrath of the line controller; however, I can honestly say that while I was doing the panel job I never fell out with anybody.

I did this work for five years during which time I applied for supervisory vacancies which came up, without success I must say. I found this disheartening as I felt that I was good at the job and deserved to have the chance to do it permanently. Towards the later part of my panel time I devised a system for monitoring inwards services in relation to the next working of each of the three requirements (driver, guard, rolling stock), I could not get anybody in the Motive Power department interested in taking this forward but the assistant area manager (operating), Gordon Hartnell, expressed some interest in the idea.

Chapter Eight

Station Supervisor, Waterloo

I decided that I would stand a better chance of getting the supervisory job permanently if I was in a supervisory grade, so when I saw a job advertised as station supervisor I applied for it. At the time there was no precedent for a Motive Power person to apply for such jobs and the only way that somebody could get into them was if they were taken off driving for some reason then worked their way through the 'traffic' grades. Although my application was submitted tongue in cheek it was accepted and I was called for an interview. Luckily for me the interview was conducted by Gordon Hartnell who had shown interest in my monitoring system and I felt that I had a head start. I was appointed as Station Supervisor, grade 'B' on 1st April, 1979, luckily I am not superstitious. Arthur Jupp, the depot master, called me into his office to congratulate me on my promotion and wished me well. Then he said, 'Before you go clear out your locker and hand back your Bardic lamp'. I thought that was a nice goodbye after 23 years' service in the department.

The new job involved working round the clock on three regular shifts which was a big change from the multiple shifts that I worked as a driver. I was able to plan my social and domestic life weeks or even months in advance. On the early turn I did not have to get up until 05.00 which I considered a luxury, on the late turn I was home by 23.00 which again was very nice as there was no chance of missing the last train home. The only disadvantage involved the change of shifts at weekends. The rotation of shifts went late, early, nights, and the week of nights was particularly difficult. It started with an early turn Sunday (I had to drive my car in for this turn unless I could come to an arrangement with the person I was relieving). I finished at 14.00 and got home just after 15.00, but had to catch the 21.00 train back up again to start my week of nights. There were no rest days on the night shift and the double Sunday turn followed by another six nights used to wear me out. However, it was not all bad as you will see later and I came to accept this as part of the job.

It was agreed that I would have one week working with another supervisor on each shift and would then take over on my own. I was quite happy with this as I felt that I knew quite a lot already and would have little difficulty in picking up anything new that I needed. Once again my illusions were to be shattered. There were three supervisors on duty for early and late turns and two at night. In overall charge was the duty station manager who also worked round the clock, the senior supervisor was normally in the station control room with the announcer and information board operators. My job was outside making sure that the staff were working properly and that the trains departed on time. There was another supervisor with a similar role on the Windsor side who looked after platforms 16 to 21. I looked after platforms 1 to 15 plus the concourse and various offices and facilities; at night I was responsible for the whole station.

I spent a week on each shift working with an existing supervisor, after which I was expected to take over control myself. I must admit that I was shocked at the amount of knowledge that was required to do this job properly. As a driver I had a typical motive power attitude that the railway would not run without the driver. I began to wonder if I had made a good move but I was in it now so I had to get on with it. I decided that one of my priorities must be to get to know all the staff by name and function so that I could supervise what they were doing. This proved to be more difficult than I imagined as there were something like 500 people on the station (not all at the same time of course) including platform staff, parcels staff, ticket collectors and all sorts of other people who did things which I had never even thought of. I set about the task which, as expected, took a long time.

I experienced resistance from some of the staff at first as they did not like the idea of a driver telling them what to do. I realised that I would have to prove myself before I would be accepted. I had no idea as to how I was going to do this and decided to appeal to my senior supervisor, one Jim Richardson. He was also an ex-driver who had been 'taken off' driving for some reason which he did not talk about so I hoped he would be sympathetic towards me. However, before I could do this fate took a hand one evening. I was on the night shift and after organising the staff for the night's work I started walking around the station on my 'get to know people' tour. I made a point on each shift of seeing all the staff on duty at their place of work. I found this useful in more ways than one but it was time consuming and it made my legs ache. I had been to see the staff on platforms 13 and 14 and spent some time talking to them. As I passed through the ticket barrier towards the concourse I heard a lot of very loud shouting and found a member of staff in a furious argument with a man.

Bravely (or stupidly as it turned out) I walked up to these people, told them to stop shouting and tell me what was going on. The staff member (Angelo Psaila) said, 'He is going to kill me'. I asked why and he replied: 'I don't know, he came up to me with a knife and said he was going to kill me'. I asked the other man if he had a knife; he totally ignored me and walked away. Using my 'walkie talkie' I asked the senior supervisor to call the police. I then followed the man; another member of staff came with me. As he went down the stairs towards the underground station he turned to us and said, 'Are you following me?' I confirmed we were and he responded, 'Well effing well don't' and continued to walk down the stairs.

We followed him into the long gallery which leads to the underground station and about halfway along he turned and came back to us. He asked, 'Why are you following me?' and I replied, 'You threatened one of my staff with a knife, you can't do that'. 'Oh yeah', he said, 'And what are you going to do about it?' I was about to make a run for it when a policeman arrived (phew!), so I said, 'Nothing, he will deal with it'. This constable was fairly short and the man was a giant, nevertheless he walked right up to him and asked if he had a knife. 'No' said the man. The constable said, 'Give me the knife' and the man said, 'No, I am not going to'. The constable repeated his demand and the man said nothing, but suddenly swung his arm, knocking the policeman off his feet and crashing him against the wall. The policeman picked himself up, brushed himself off, replaced his helmet, walked up to the man and again asked for the knife. The man said, 'No, I will give it to him'; turning round we saw two more policemen arriving, one of whom was as big as the man himself.

The man gave the knife to the constable whereupon two of the constables held his arms behind his back and marched him off to the police office on the station. All of a sudden he went berserk and set about all three policemen, a terrible fight ensued and I tried to call for help on my radio but it did not work underground. Eventually the police got the better of the man and took him away, a little worse for wear. Later, I went to the police office to make a statement and that was the end of the matter as far as I was concerned. I resolved never to put myself in that situation again.

Over the next few months I got to know all the staff, despite the total numbers. They worked in shifts and were spread over an area of about 12 acres. Eventually I was confident that I knew them all and set about building a relationship with them, this was less difficult and I found everybody very co-operative and even helpful. The senior supervisor on my shift was Jim Richardson and he was well respected by the staff so I assumed that this affected their attitude towards me and considered myself lucky to be working with a good team.

I gradually found that there was a lot more to running a railway than I had thought and that I still had a lot of learning to do. As a driver I thought I was the most important man on the railway and all the other people worked on the periphery in support roles. I was in for a rude awakening. In my new role I was responsible for a variety of staff doing a variety of jobs. It took a long time to get to grips with all this, especially as it had to be done while trying to keep up with the day to day running of the station. I was lucky to work with Jim Richardson as he was very supportive and helped me when I was out of my depth.

The three shifts were all different in the type of work to be done and this added interest to the job. The early shift 06.00-14.00 started with ensuring that all the staff were on duty and all the jobs were covered. Any shortfalls had to be sorted out before the morning rush started, this built up from about 07.00 and lasted until about 10.00. The morning rush was not much of a problem as the people arrived and disappeared immediately. After the rush was over, the off-peak travellers started to arrive and depart. These people were more of a problem than the regular travellers as they did not understand the working of the station or the train service and would need information. As I spent most of my time out on the station they would make a bee line for my gold rimmed hat; so if I had something important to do I would put my hat in a carrier bag which I always kept in my pocket for such emergencies.

Throughout the shift parcels traffic would arrive on the passenger trains and these had to be transferred to the parcels depot in the arches below the platforms. Red Star was a premium service and Red Star parcels were dealt with separately; they were immediately transferred to or from the Red Star office as they were booked to travel on specific trains. Station cleaning was a permanent job but because of the amount of people passing through in the peak hours it was concentrated after the morning rush.

The late turn from 14.00 to 22.00 was more arduous. After sorting out the staffing and ensuring that all the cleaning was completed it was time for the evening peak service. This built up from about 16.00 and lasted until about 19.00; the same people who had arrived in the morning peak were now going home, but they were not the same people by a long shot. Whereas in the morning they got off the train and disappeared, in the evening they arrived at various times and expected a train to their respective destinations. They were not concerned that there were problems in other areas which were affecting the service generally, they each wanted a train to Guildford or Basingstoke or one of hundreds of other places. Also, after a hard day at work they were in no mood to be messed about; I spent a lot of time on the late turn trying to keep people calm and help them get their train. This could be hard work especially if the service was disrupted, and I sometimes felt 'shell shocked' at the end of the evening peak.

The main line services were booked out at two minute intervals and the physical layout meant that it took about one minute and 45 seconds for each train to clear, this left only 15 seconds to spare on each departure. I used to see each main line train out of the station personally to ensure that we met this tight schedule. Luckily the departures were mainly booked from consecutively numbered platforms so there was not much walking from train to train. However, if any problems occurred on the suburban services I would have to leave the 'main liners' to the platform staff and sort it out; this was often more difficult than expected. On top of this there were the people to deal with, if people were taken ill or had an accident I had to deal with this as well and take them to the first aid centre or to an ambulance if one had been called. There were frequent incidents of this type.

Having got through the evening peak it was time to tidy the station again and this took up the remainder of the shift unless the service had disintegrated during the peak as it sometimes did, when I would be out on the platforms trying to sort it out. On some occasions I was required to work 12 hours to cover the early turn and half of the late turn. The evening peak was then a torture because I was tired before it started, on these occasions I would go home absolutely shattered.

The night turn started as usual by sorting out the staffing, but this was more difficult than the other two shifts because there was a specific gang of night staff and all the jobs were tightly scheduled to encompass the massive amount of work to be done. If anybody was missing I had to reschedule the work and get some of the late turn staff to stay on to cover parts of it. The night work consisted of several functions which were overlapping. The first job was to finish the normal daytime service which lasted until about 23.30, several parcels trains arrived at the start of the shift and these had to be unloaded as the vans were required for early morning paper trains. The newspapers started to arrive at about midnight, there were five trains to load, first the 01.45 to Yeovil, then the 02.15 to Weymouth, the 02.30 to Portsmouth, the 02.45 to Bournemouth and the 03.40 to Guildford. The papers arrived in a continual stream of road vans, which were unloaded and the papers sorted on to trolleys on the station concourse. Then these were coupled together in the correct order before being towed to the appropriate train by an electric tractor. The tractor would drop off trolleys at each of the rail vans and the loader or loaders would lift all the bundles of papers into the vans and stack them in the proper order for the wholesaler's staff to unload at their destination. They would then couple up the empty trolleys for the tractor to pick up on its return. This was a continuous operation and it was hard work but the staff rarely complained; if there was an interruption in the arrival of road vans it would cause us problems by upsetting the flow. The railway had to pay a penalty if the trains were late starting, except when the Newspaper Publishers Association (NPA) specifically asked for a delay to assist their production schedule, so we were always under pressure to get the job done in time and get it done properly.

The loaders were generally booked to load the first and third train or the second and fourth train, with everybody getting stuck in on the fifth one. The 03.40 was the hardest because it was obviously left until last and if the papers for the other trains had caused problems, staff would be late getting started on this train. When this happened there was always a pile of papers waiting to be loaded when the staff arrived so they had to clear the backlog before they could start the normal loading. I would have to move staff from other duties to assist in getting the 03.40 away on time. The up TPO (mail) train from Weymouth arrived at 03.36 and this had to be unloaded in double-quick time. When the paper trains were gone there was about an hour and a half to get the station cleaned up and sweep out all the berthed carriages before the morning services started between 05.00 and 05.30. Then the night staff would go onto the platforms to ensure that the first services left on time before being relieved by the early turn staff.

The supervisors' roster worked backwards in time so that all the turns could be covered in seven days. After a week of early turn I would work early turn Sunday from 06.00 to 14.00 then come back at 22.00 for the start of a week of seven nights straight off. After doing a double shift on Sunday I would be really tired when I went home on Monday morning and it would take me until Wednesday night to get into the pattern. Saturday night was always a bad night as the Sunday newspapers were always a lot heavier than the weekday issues. Extra staff were always required on Saturday nights and these were brought in from other departments just for the night. I had my work cut out trying to keep tabs on them, keeping them working at the required rate and doing the job properly which made a difficult job even more difficult. I was always shattered after a week of nights and it was a relief having the Monday morning off before starting the late shift.

The staff on the station were a real mixed bunch, they represented many nationalities and all ages from 16 to 65. I was concerned about this at first, never having worked closely with ethnic groups before, but I need not have worried as I had no trouble at all and in fact got on very well with all the staff whatever their age or ethnic background. There was a large contingent of West Indians, a similar amount of Asians and all sorts of other people such as Greek and Turkish Cypriots and West Africans. This mix gave the job an added interest although I did sometimes have difficulty in understanding some of them.

Another of my jobs was meeting VIPs and escorting them to or from their train or car. This did not include royalty who were dealt with by the area manager and the duty station manager. On one occasion I was told to meet Sir Geoffrey Howe who was Chancellor of the Exchequer at that time and his wife, Lady Howe, when they arrived from Southampton airport. I duly met the train and found the VIPs where I had expected them to be. I opened the door and Sir Geoffrey alighted first, I said 'good evening Sir' and he replied in the same vein, I turned to help his wife from the train and said 'Good evening Lady Howe'; she smiled and stepped down from the train. Unfortunately I did not notice that she had a very small dog on a lead and I trod on it. The dog squealed and Lady Howe said something like 'You great oaf' and walked off with her husband and the limping dog. I was left standing there feeling very embarrassed. Jim Richardson suggested that I should read a book called 'How to win friends and influence people'. I never did but I got the message.

One of our duty managers was Norman Fair. He was a nice person but he did like to wind me up. On one occasion there was a big blue limousine parked in the cab road in the middle of the station; this was prohibited for security reasons and Norman told me to get rid of it. I had several announcements made before I called the British Transport Police (BTP) and asked them to have it towed away. When they saw that it was a big limo. they were reluctant to have it removed, instead, they looked all around and under it and said that they could see nothing wrong with it. I was angry about this as if it had been my car it would have been gone in no time at all. I called the police again and they eventually placed a parking ticket on it. After some time a scruffy individual drove the car away. Norman ribbed me about it for the rest of the shift and I was beginning to get annoyed by the time I went home.

The next day after sorting out the staffing I walked across the concourse and spotted a Rolls Royce parked in the cab road. I said to the chauffeur, 'You can't park here, you will have to move'. He said, 'I am waiting for the Chairman, this is his car'. I asked, 'What Chairman?' and he replied, 'The Chairman of the Board'. 'What Board? said I. 'The British Railways Board, Sir Peter Parker', he replied. I then considered that I had gone far enough with this one so I told the chauffeur that he could stay there as long as he didn't leave the car. He agreed to this so I walked to platform 11 intending to go to our office on the raft. On the way I spotted Norman Fair with the area manager, Mr Adams, on platform 10. They were dressed in their 'bowlers' and were obviously waiting to meet Sir Peter Parker. I walked over to them and Mr Adams asked me how things were going. I replied that all the staff were on duty and the train service was running well but that I had experienced some trouble with a car in the cab road very similar to yesterday. Norman's ears pricked up until I said that it was a Rolls Royce and that I had ordered the chauffeur to take it away and park somewhere else. At this he went grey and then white, I thought he was going to pass out so I told him that it was only a joke and the car was still there. At this he went red and I thought he was going to explode. The arrival of the Chairman saved me and I made a quick exit. Norman Fair did not wind me up so much after that and he never mentioned the incident at all.

Although it was a hard job it was nearly always enjoyable and the people with whom I worked were first class. All had fairly difficult tasks to perform but they were always cheerful and could laugh at adversity. The senior supervisor was located in a office on the 'raft' which was a single-storey building above the barrier line between platforms 1 and 11. The office was known as the Solari because the person who operated the Solari departure/arrival indicator boards on the station had his control panel in this office. The Solari equipment was operated using floppy punched cards which were inserted into an electronic reader; various panels were displayed on the indicator boards depending on the pattern of holes punched in the cards. There was a full set of cards to cover all the planned service plus regular special trains. Special cards were cut when the train service was altered for weekend engineering work or other planned alterations.

There were three indicator boards on the concourse; one on the south side for main line suburban services; the main one above the entrance to platforms 13 to 15 which showed all the main line departures and arrivals plus the main side suburban services; another one on the Windsor side showed departures from platforms 16 to 21. In addition to these main boards there was a small individual indicator above each platform entrance and at each set of stairs from the platform subway. In the early 1990s a new control system was introduced which utilised a computer and eliminated the punch card system, although the actual indicators were not changed.

The senior supervisor worked in close liaison with the signal box regulator to ensure that the service was run as planned and they agreed any alterations necessary to resolve problems which arose. When there was severe disruption this became very difficult but Jim Richardson was always on top of it and we developed a system for dealing with such situations. Basically, when the service started to become severely disrupted I would go into the Solari office, make all the telephone calls and liaise with the drivers' and guards' supervisors which left Jim free to concentrate on making arrangements. This system worked extremely well and we often avoided the service falling apart completely. When this did happen it was a horrendous job trying to get it going again. One day it was so bad that Jim, the signal box regulator and the drivers'/guards' supervisors all agreed to put away the service plan books and make up the service as they went along. After about an hour we were on top of the situation and had a service to all destinations at fairly regular intervals. This was hard work but very satisfying as it went so well.

The author as station supervisor *(right)* with Duggie Goddard in the Solari office at Waterloo in 1980. *Author*

After several hours of this method of working Mr Adams came into the office with Mr Whitehall, the divisional manager. Mr Whitehall was angry and said to Jim in a fierce tone of voice, 'What have you cancelled?', just like that, no introduction or question about how we were doing. Jim was annoyed at his attitude and spun around on his chair with an equally rude reply, 'Nothing', he said, just like that and spun back to his work. Mr Whitehall went red in the face, very angry now he said: 'What do you mean, nothing, the service is a shambles and Control don't know what is running'. Jim turned round again and said, 'If you ask me what we have run I can tell you exactly because it is all recorded, but nothing is cancelled because the service books are in the drawer and we are making it up as we go along'. Nothing more was said and I continued to run back and forth to the various supervisors to ensure that we had crews for the trains we wanted to run. When this was confirmed, Jim would tell the signal box regulator, the Solari operator and the station announcer and get all the people loaded and the train away. Mr Adams asked me if there was anything he could do to help. I said that he could make a pot of tea which would help; I think he might have done it but Mr Whitehall grunted, turned and walked out without so much as a 'by your leave', Mr Adams followed.

Mr Adams decided that I would benefit from some formal training and I was duly booked to attend the National Examination Board for Supervisory Studies (NEBSS) course. This was run as an 'in house' course over a period of eight weeks, divided into four 2-week sections. The first three sections were held at the training centre at Beckenham and the fourth and all important section was held at the British Rail School of Transport at Darlington. An assessment was made at the end of each section to decide if you were to continue to the next section. I was quite proud when in 1980 I was presented with my NEBSS certificate by the divisional manager, Mr Whitehall. The circumstances were certainly different to the previous time that I met him.

Back to work and I tried to apply my new found knowledge to my job, with limited success. However, the theories that I had learned gave me a new outlook towards my role in life and my attitude changed considerably. Although my original intention in taking the job as station supervisor was to put me in a better position when a motive power supervisor's position became vacant, I now wondered if that was what I really wanted. There was a lot more to railways than I had thought and I wanted to know more so I took every opportunity to find out about things which were outside my normal remit. I therefore took a lot of interest in the parcels after they left the platforms and in the arrangements for managing the NPA contract for moving the newspapers, the arrangements for handling Royal Mail traffic. All the information I gathered proved to very useful in doing my job and I am sure that it helped me when I went for promotion.

I really started to enjoy the job and felt that I was on top of things. When the work patterns were amended to take account of the introduction of the newly agreed 39 hour week for conciliation staff I could see some flaws in the roster, one of which I rectified myself and wrote the alteration on the roster. I was called to the office of the personnel manager and told my fortune; he said that he was in charge of rosters and I should mind my own business. He was right of course but I was miffed at the way he had dealt with me.

Collecting the NEBSS certificate from Bernard Whitehall, he was the South Western divisional manager at that time.   *Author*

When Christmas came around, the personnel manager asked for volunteers from the night staff to work on Boxing night. As this was a Saturday night all the night staff were rostored rest day and entitled to be off and due to problems in getting home the previous year hardly any of the staff volunteered. Out of the 74 staff required to handle the Sunday papers on Saturday night only 12 put their name down. The personnel manager asked me what he could do about it and I was most unhelpful and told him that if he had only 12 people he would only get 12 people's work done. Later in the day Mr Adams called me to his office and asked me if I had told the personnel manager that I could handle the Sunday papers with only 12 staff. I laughed at this and repeated what I had said to the personnel manager and explained his earlier comment that he was in charge of rosters and I should mind my own business.

Mr Adams said that if we could not get staff on Boxing night he would have to cancel the contract for the night. This would cost a lot of money in penalties and must be avoided if at all possible. He asked me to persuade the staff to work and promised that the personnel manager would not interfere, he also agreed to provide transport home for those who needed it. I agreed to help but said that I could not promise anything at that stage. There were five paper trains on a Sunday: the 01.45 to Yeovil, the 02.30 to Weymouth, the 02.55 to Bournemouth, the 03.15 to Portsmouth and the 03.40 to Guildford. I revised all the work programmes so that we could do the job with only 64 staff and asked each of the night staff individually to work, with the promise of transport home if needed. I revised the programme again to do the job with only 56 staff but I could see that it was going to be difficult to achieve the full task with that amount of staff. I reported this to Mr Adams and he agreed that we should try to do it, and he would warn the NPA that there may be some problems.

At 22.00 on Boxing night all the staff who had promised turned up and I was delighted. I told them to go for a cup of tea and come back at 23.30 having decided that the cleaning duties would have to be sacrificed for one night. Where they went for their tea I don't know but there was nobody in the mess room. However, at 23.30 they were all back and ready for work. And work they did, with a vengeance, as the papers started to come in everybody was in position and the first trickle gradually turned into a flood. Because of the shortage of staff they had to load two vans each instead of one and if there were no papers at that time for their vans they helped out on other vans. The first two trains were away on time but the next two got progressively later despite all the best efforts of the staff; they were getting tired now and the full crew did not get on to the 03.40 until 03.30. there were papers everywhere and they were not loaded until 04.10 at which time there were still 15 road vans waiting to be unloaded. Jim decided not to unload these vans and sent them back, advising the NPA of the situation. With the last of the trains gone the staff went to the mess room, they were absolutely shattered. I thanked them for their efforts and set about arranging transport, they were all gone by 06.00.

On the Monday I went to see Mr Adams and explained the situation. He was pleased that we had done so well. I asked if he would write to the staff thanking them for their efforts and he agreed to this, in the event this letter was coupled with another letter of thanks from the NPA who were aware of our staffing problem and were well pleased with our performance. I have never seen people work so hard and I took great satisfaction from the fact that they had done so willingly at my request. This was one of the highlights of my railway career and is an event I shall always remember with affection, what a wonderful bunch of people.

This was only one of the many occasions that the staff supported me. Another which sticks in my mind was one night when the Lyceum ballroom disco was turning out very late at night, this was a regular event and always caused problems with youngsters who were mainly drunk, always noisy and some times aggressive. On this occasion a group of lads walked across the concourse and knocked over a line of advertising pedestals. I shouted at them and immediately wished that I hadn't because they turned on me and gave me a lot of abuse. I was trying to decide which was the best route of escape when I detected a change of mood in the lads, they were suddenly quieter and less aggressive. A voice from behind me said, 'Are you having trouble Guv?' I looked around and saw three of the largest members of my staff, all of whom were West Indians; they obviously had a good effect in this situation so I replied, 'No, these lads are just going to stand the pedestals up again'. After some hesitation while they were apparently waiting to see if one of them would lead a challenge to the three giants they stood the pedestals up again. Emboldened by the staff support I gave the boys a talking to and told them to get off the station despite their protests that they wanted to catch a train. As they left in a surly mood a BTP policeman came along on his patrol and asked if they had been causing problems. 'Not at all', I replied, 'They have gone for a walk'. Boy, oh boy, was I relieved, I thanked Messrs Austin, Chambers and Jackson for their help but they said that they were only too pleased to help and not a little disappointed that the lads had backed off. I was not disappointed as it would have been a massacre and I would have been responsible for it. I always looked for some back-up before confronting aggressive groups after that.

All this sort of activity was a world away from a cozy driving cab isolated from the public. I had not realised that this sort of thing went on and I was never very comfortable in dealing with it. The worst problem was people going to football matches, the so-called fans were mostly in various states of inebriation, very noisy and very aggressive, especially to rival 'fans'. One terrible day Portsmouth was playing at Chelsea and Tottenham was playing at Southampton; as the Portsmouth supporters returned through the station a large gang of Millwall supporters arrived and started fighting with their rivals.

Although the BTP had a lot of staff on duty for this event they were unable to contain the situation and Metropolitan Police officers were drafted in to assist. However, before they were able to take control a running battle took place which left a lot of people hurt, this took place among the ordinary passengers and many people were terrified. When the situation had quietened down the Portsmouth supporters were loaded on to a Portsmouth train with one section locked off from the other passengers and the Millwall gang were escorted away. The Portsmouth mob were forced to take off their 'Bovver' boots and they were piled in the guard's van, they must have taken some sorting out at their destination. All of a sudden a Metropolitan officer came rushing into the Solari office and asked if a train was due from Southampton. Jim said that it was and would be here in a few minutes. The officer asked for it to be stopped or there would be another riot on our hands. Luckily he was in time and the train was held outside the station for about eight minutes until the Portsmouth train had gone. This was annoying for our normal passengers but it did avoid further trouble; when the Southampton train was allowed in there was a lot of noise but the police were able to contain any trouble.

Because of this sort of thing I developed a strong dislike for the so-called football supporters and hated working on Saturday afternoons in the winter. Luckily I was not on every Saturday and other aspects of the job made up for this nasty bit, but I hated the supporters and stopped watching football altogether and avoided anything to do with it as far as possible.

Saturdays in the summer were also difficult but for a different reason. Thousands of people going on holiday passed through the station and had to be organised and guided. There were large inverted pyramid shaped boards hanging above the concourse with the letters A to J clearly marked on them. The station announcer would advise people for a particular service to form a queue under the appropriate letter and the same information was displayed on the Solari indicators. When the train was ready for loading I would lead the queue to the platform entrance before the indicator board was changed and the platform announced. The system worked well but some people could not understand it or did not want to queue and they caused me all sorts of problems. It used to amaze me, the number of people who set out for their holiday journey with a total lack of knowledge of the route to be taken or the train service. This sometimes led to passengers becoming aggressive when I tried to explain to them that they were at the wrong station or that they would have to change trains at some point.

One man was furious when I told him that he would have to travel by ferry from Portsmouth to Ryde on the Isle of Wight. He said that his wife could not travel by sea and we should advise people that they had to catch a ferry. He would not have booked the holiday if he had known. I had the devil's own job in convincing him that it was not my fault and that most islands have water all around them.

One day a well spoken lady called out to me. 'Young man', she said (that made my day as I was 41 at the time), 'I want to catch the 11.10 train to Bournemouth'. I replied, 'I am sorry but there is not an 11.10 train to Bournemouth, it leaves at 10.35 and it has just gone, there is a semi-fast train at 10.46 or another fast one at 11.35'. 'They told me it was 11.10 and I want to catch that train', she said. I explained the situation again to no avail, then I asked her if she was actually going to Bournemouth. She replied, 'No, I am going to a little place near Bournemouth'. I established that the 'little place' was actually Gillingham, so I directed her to the 11.10 Exeter train and she went away happy. You had to be very careful when people asked you questions because for some reason they don't ask the question that they want answered. For example: 'Is this the Portsmouth train?' 'Yes sir.' 'Does it stop at Liphook?' I sometimes found this exasperating but gradually developed a technique for dealing with questions so as to establish exactly what people wanted.

During my time as station supervisor I received unending support from the senior management team and I was very grateful for this. Jim and I were allowed almost total freedom to run the station our own way when on duty, as long as we achieved the end result we were allowed to get on with it. I found this invaluable in my later career as, without realising it, I was becoming accustomed to making and backing my own decisions.

Class '33' No. 33012 passes through Vauxhall with the 13.00 Waterloo-Exeter (St David's) on 5th September, 1979.   *J.H. Scrace*

The assistant area manager (commercial) was an unusual character by the name of Reginald Streeter. Although I liked him and got on well with him I did have difficulty in following his train of thought at times, he often made decisions without discussing things with the people concerned and this also caused problems at times. One particular incident went into the long list of stories often repeated by railwaymen when they get together. Mr Streeter came into the Solari office one day and said to Jim that the paper cutters on the 02.30 Portsmouth train had complained that the brakes on some of the 'Brute' trolleys were not effective and when the train was braking heavily they sometimes rolled down the van which was a danger to these staff. This was a serious problem and Mr Streeter suggested that the trolleys be tied to the side of the vans so that they could not move. Jim agreed to this and said that if Mr Streeter would provide the rope he would ensure that all the trolleys were tied up. That was the end of the subject until a few weeks later when Mr Streeter phoned to say that the rope he had asked for was arriving on a certain train from Portsmouth.

I sent a man to collect the rope and when he had done so he called me to have a look at it; I was amazed and immediately burst into very loud laughter. I called Jim down and he joined in, we could hardly stand up for laughing. Mr Streeter had apparently asked a friend in Portsmouth to supply some rope and he had sent a huge coil of the sort of rope with which ships are tied up. We could hardly pick it up never mind tie knots in it and Jim said that perhaps we could use it to tie the vans together instead of the trolleys.

There is a sequel to this story. The rope was put in a store cupboard and forgotten about. One night there were some people examining the station roof using a rail mounted 'Cherry picker'. The person in charge asked me if it was all right to push in the hydraulic buffers with his machine so that he could reach part of the roof. I told him it was all right but if the buffers did not come out again he should tell me. After he had done his inspection he told me that the buffers were stuck in so I had 'The rope' loaded on to a trolley and taken to the relevant platform. I told this person, 'If you tie this rope to the buffer of your machine and on to the hydraulic buffer and gently tug it the buffer will come out'. He said 'Do you know who I am?' I said, 'No'. He said, 'I am the Regional Civil Engineer'. 'Nice to meet you', said I. He said, 'Do you realise that if you attach that rope to my machine and to the buffer it becomes a lifting implement and is therefore subject to relevant Health & Safety legislation'. I was ignorant of this so I decided not to use the rope and called the machinery fitter from under the station to free the gland on the buffer. I was suitably chastened and vowed never to be caught like that again and made a point of reading up on Health & Safety legislation; this also came in useful later in my career.

Looking back on this period of my career the thing that comes to mind every time is the humour. I have an active sense of humour and often see the funny side of things which others miss. It sometimes got me into trouble but most of the time the people I was working with joined in and it made the job a lot of fun. It would take up too much space to recount all the stories but here are a few of the more memorable ones.

One of the relief station managers was Bill Atkins, he was a West Country man and had an accent to go with it. One night Jim and I were joking with him about a song we had heard on the television. The song was sung in a West

Country accent and went something like this: 'Where be that blackbird to, I know where he be, he be up yon wurzle tree and I be after he'. We all had a laugh about this, but during the night Bill decided to do an inspection of carriage cleaning. He was obviously not aware that this work was done after the paper trains had gone and kept calling Jim on the radio to report that carriages were not cleaned. Jim decided to follow him with the CCTV cameras as he went up and down the platforms. When he saw that he was beyond the phone on platform 1 Jim dialled the number and Bill had to walk back to the phone.

Jim said, 'Can you tell me if the two units on platform 1 are coupled together?', Bill looked and said that they were. 'Good', said Jim, 'they are supposed to be'. When Bill went up platform 3 Jim did the same thing, this time asking if the units were uncoupled. We thought this was funny and Jim placed the camera on platform 5 for a repeat performance. He moved it from left to right and zoomed in and out but could not find Bill. As he was doing this he kept saying, 'Where be that blackbird to' and suddenly a voice from behind him said, 'You won't find he out there'. It was Bill who had crept into the office unseen. I think that was the only time I saw Jim lost for words.

Another of the relief managers was Bert Hughes, he was a smashing chap but did not know much about the train service at the terminal. He would go out onto the concourse and when people asked him questions he would call on his walkie talkie, 'Watrail 1 to base, where is this or where is that'. Towards the end of the week Jim was getting a bit fed up with this so when the late turn Manager handed his radio in, Jim turned the battery round so that it would not work. On this night before coming to work I had seen that Oscar Peterson was on the television at 11.30 pm. After I had sorted out the staffing I went back to the office and Jim said that Vera, one of the announcers, had a portable television in her locker and we could watch Oscar Peterson until the papers started coming in. I was pleased with this and we started to set up the television. While we were doing this Bert came in, he knew that we should not be doing this and promptly took his radio and left the office. Jim had forgotten all about the battery being turned around.

To our disappointment we found that Oscar Peterson was only on Southern TV and we could not get it in London so we put the TV away and got out the service books and started checking and entering amendments for the forthcoming timetable changes. Bert was out on the station and we forgot all about him, but just after midnight we heard very loud footsteps in the corridor outside the office and Bert burst through the door, all flustered and red in the face. When he saw what we were doing he visibly relaxed and said, 'I have some visitors for you', introducing Mr and Mrs Cawley. Mr Cawley was a senior officer in the operating department.

Apparently Bert had met the Cawleys on the concourse and Mr Cawley had asked if he could show his wife the Solari office. Bert had readily agreed to this then suddenly realised that when last seen by him we were setting up the television to watch Oscar Peterson. In a panic he called on his radio but got no reply, not surprising as the battery was turned round. Bert said later that he had never been so relieved in his life as when he saw us both gainfully employed on company business. Jim had no intention of letting him out on the station without his radio working, he was going to call him on the PA and tell him what he had done but in messing about with the TV and then starting work on the amendments he had completely forgotten.

In September 1981 my son who was 15 at the time, had a terrible accident which put him in hospital for nearly seven months and left him disabled. This put me under a lot of pressure with my family life and work became more difficult to cope with; however, with the support of the management, my colleagues and the staff I came through it. Looking back on that period it was the unending support that helped me. It was a difficult period anyway, with numerous bomb threats and other security scares to deal with in addition to the normal problems of running a service.

Having been through that trauma I started to look at my future. My original intention had been to take the station job in order to improve my chances of getting the motive power supervisor's job. Having spread my wings and found out a lot more about the industry I was not so sure if that was what I now wanted. I arranged an interview with Mr Adams and explained my quandary. He agreed that reverting to the Motive Power Department would be a backward step as it is a very narrow field. He suggested that I try for a job as assistant station manager (ASM) when these new jobs were advertised as part of the forthcoming re-organisation.

This was known as Line Traffic Management, stage 1 (LTM 1) and the management structure was to undergo considerable alteration with the area managers' areas being merged and taking on some of the functions currently at divisional level. A lot of station managers' positions were being done away with and replaced by managers based at the main stations who would have a number of assistants depending on the size of their areas. For example, the station manager at Surbiton would take on the areas of the station managers at Claygate and Walton-on-Thames and have three assistants. This did not mean much to me as I had never been involved with the Traffic Department and did not know what had gone before. However, Mr Adams felt that this would be a good move for me and I believed him.

When the time came I applied for the positions as ASM at Wimbledon, Surbiton, Woking and Basingstoke. I was interviewed for all of them at once and about a week later Mr Adams called me to his office, saying, 'I have some good news and some bad news for you'. I said, 'Well give me the good news first' and he told me that I had been appointed as ASM at Surbiton. The bad news was that LTM 1 came into effect in two weeks and I was to 'take on' from that date. I had some rapid learning to do and the next two weeks were filled with all sorts of extras on top of my normal duties. This was hard work and in retrospect I wonder how I coped with it.

Having got to know the staff very well in the past three years I wanted to say goodbye to all of them so I also spent a lot of time on that. I mentioned to one man that I had thoroughly enjoyed my time in the job and that I had never had any trouble at all from the staff. He said that this was because they all held me in high esteem for my action in saving Angelo Psaila's life. I was puzzled by this until he explained. Apparently, after the incident with the man with a knife in the subway the story went round that this man had threatened to kill Angelo and I had tackled him and had him arrested. This was not exactly my view of what had happened but nevertheless that was what the staff thought and it did me no harm.

Chapter Nine

Assistant Station Manager, Surbiton

I took my station manager's 'rules' with chief inspector Ron Russell in his office at Clapham Junction, I found this particularly hard as rules were not my favourite subject but nevertheless I passed, to my great relief. My period as station supervisor was a turning point in my career; I had learned an awful lot about the industry and had also undergone formal training which was to prove invaluable. I was also aware of my previously blinkered motive power attitude and could see the stupidity of it. I used to cringe when some of my former colleagues started being awkward as some of the things they said were stupid beyond belief. If they could have stood in my position and seen what they looked like I am sure that they would have adopted a different attitude, because normally they were very sensible people who did a professional job and were rightly proud of it.

I moved my belongings to Surbiton in November 1982 and started another new direction in my career. The station manager was David Gould. I had never met him before but he came through the traffic grades in the Ascot-Guildford area so I probably came across him at some time or another. However, we had a lot in common and got on very well together. There was one other ASM at first, this was Jeff Hawkins and again we got on well. There should have been three ASMs but we were one short at the start of the new organisation. David and Jeff did a good job of teaching me the things I needed to know, most of which related to the booking office as this was the bulk of the work at the 10 stations under our control. It took me some time to become confident in checking and signing accounts. I made one mistake when I signed a monthly account before it was complete. I had checked all the figures leading to the monthly balance and told the clerk to transfer the figures and send off the account. He sent it off without entering the remaining figures and the account did not balance by £800. The auditor came to follow up the discrepancy and admonished me for signing the account before it was completed; another lesson learned which was to have serious ramifications later in my career.

Another of our main functions was managing/supervising the signalling centre at Surbiton. This was a 1960s panel box which controlled an area from just east of Surbiton to Cobham on the Guildford 'new line', the main line nearly to Woking including branches from Weybridge and Byfleet to Addlestone and also the branch line to Hampton Court. This again was completely new to me and took some time to get into. I understood the principles of signalling and knew the applicable rules but I had never been a signalman or worked in a signal box, never mind an area panel box.

How would the signalmen take to an ex-driver giving them orders? Lots of similar questions were raised in my mind but the staff were very good to me, often advising me when things went wrong. I quickly became proficient in this aspect of the job and found it interesting as I understood both the signalman's and the driver's point of view when disputes arose. Getting to understand the Signal & Telegraph (S&T) department proved to be more difficult. Technical staff were based in the panel building at Surbiton but they tended to keep to themselves and only get involved with signalmen when dealing with problems. Part of my problem was that I knew little of the technical aspects of the equipment. I had to take what I was told on trust and make my decisions on this information. Having said that, the S&T staff always helped as much as possible to keep the service running and I had few problems with them. I also had close contact with the Permanent Way (PW) department for the first time and this proved interesting as well.

I learned a lot about operating a railway and I had to learn fast as several incidents happened in the first few months and I had to deal with them as I was the only Manager on duty at the time. The one which caused me the biggest problem involved an allegation by the Regional Control office or 'Control' as it was known. I was 'on call' and Control called me at about midnight to say that they suspected that there had been a signalling irregularity but could not get a proper answer from the signalman involved; they requested that I interview the signalman to find out exactly what had happened. I arrived at the panel at about 01.00 and found that everything was quiet, the signalman was very calm and could not understand why I had been called out. I asked him to describe the events of the evening leading up to the time that the incident was alleged to have happened. He did this and it was a very complicated story and I had to check my notes with him several times before I was satisfied that I had all the relevant information.

The background of the incident was that detection was lost in the normal position on the points leading from the down slow line to the down Cobham line at Hampton Court Junction. This had happened earlier in the evening before the night signalman came on duty and a safe working arrangement had been set up between the signalman and the S&T staff. Under this arrangement, while the S&T staff were working on the points, down slow line services were diverted to the down fast line and returned to the down slow through a pair of points beyond where they were working. If a Cobham line train was coming the signalman would contact the S&T staff on site and wait until they advised him that they were clear of the line before setting the route and clearing the signal. This arrangement was still in operation when the night man came on duty although I was not aware of this at the time. I was cross that I did not know as I was on duty at the time of the original problem, but had not been advised as I should have been.

The following is the sequence of events leading to the incident.

1. The station supervisor phoned the signalman to say that there was a man on the station threatening people with a knife, the police had been called and were on their way but he wanted trains stopped so that the man could not escape until they arrived. The signalman turned his emergency stop signals to danger and stood looking out of the window towards the station to see what was going on.
2. A driver phoned to say that a signal had gone to red in front of him and he had passed it at danger. The signalman told him why the signal had gone to red and to set back behind the signal and wait for a change of aspect.
3. All lines were blocked and a queue of trains soon formed on lines in the area. The drivers of all these trains phoned in at different times to find out what the problem was.
4. To ease congestion, the signalman at New Malden switched some of his trains from the down fast to the down slow line, the first of these was a Guildford via Woking service, when this train arrived at Surbiton the signalman there directed it onto the down loop platform line.

5. When the police had removed the man from the station the supervisor advised the signalman to allow trains to run again, which he did and cleared all his signals. Unfortunately, from the down loop it was only possible to go on to the down slow line so the Guildford via Woking train went down this line towards where the S&T staff were working on the points at Hampton Court Junction.

The driver of the Guildford via Woking train stopped at the junction signal at Hampton Court Junction and phoned the signalman to advise him that he was there. The signalman told him to pass the signal at danger and obey all other signals without first checking with the S&T staff, the result was that the train went onto the Cobham line and nearly ran over the S&T staff in the process. The driver stopped at the next signal and reported that he had been diverted to the wrong route. During the time that this was happening a de-icing train had terminated on the up slow line and was reversed to the down slow line; unfortunately when this movement was complete the signalman could not get the points back to the normal position.

With the driver calling in, the new points failure and the S&T staff phoning to find out why they had nearly been killed the signalman became very confused, especially as the service was now disrupted and trains were not running as booked. Control were advised that there had been an incident and had been trying to get to the bottom of it without much success, which is why they called me in. When I was satisfied that I had enough information I went to my office and wrote it all out in report form. It was a good report but there was something missing and it worried me. After a long time trying to figure out what was missing I gave up and drove to Woking where I put my report on the area manager's (AM) desk with a note to say that I thought that something was missing and would speak to him in the morning.

When I spoke to the AM (John Norman) in the morning he said that he wanted the signalman in for interview the next day and that he was not to work that night. He also asked me to think about what I thought was wrong with my report. I discussed this with David Gould but still could not find the answer. I arranged for the signalman to be off duty that night and attend for interview with the AM and myself the next day. One of the first things he said when asked if he knew of the special arrangements was that he was on nights and did not know what the late turn staff had done. When signalmen change over they are supposed to advise each other what the current situation is and should have told this man about the special working arrangements. After a long interview we were no nearer to getting an answer as to exactly what had happened.

We had a recess where we discussed the attitude of the signalman and what had happened. I still felt that something was missing so the signalman was recalled and we went through the report again. Suddenly it came to me and I asked for another recess. The signalman claimed that he was not aware of the arrangements made by the late turn staff but in fact he had been on duty for two hours before the incident happened and had carried out the procedure correctly at least three times before the incident. So his claim that he was not made aware of the arrangements was a lie to try to cover up his mistake. When confronted with this he tried to bluff his way out of it instead of admitting his error. Mr Norman immediately suspended him from duty pending further enquiries, in the end he was taken out of the panel until he had received further intensive training.

The Surbiton management team, *left to right*, David Gould, Steve Price, the author and Ted Beausire.   *Author*

I learned a lot from this incident but the main thing was that when investigating incidents you should take careful notes of everything that may possibly be relevant as well as what is said, and study it in relation to the facts that you know about the incident. I had missed a vital point because I should have noted the signing-on time of the signalman when I first went into the panel. I never made the same mistake again and made a note of everything even if it seemed irrelevant at the time.

A totally different incident gave me a further insight into the way that people think. I was working at Walton-on-Thames checking accounts and preparing cash for a security pick up. I decided to go to Surbiton for my lunch so that I could speak to my colleagues while they were all together. As my train entered the next station, Hersham, I saw a member of the staff standing on the platform, there was nothing wrong with this of course and I took no notice. On arrival at Surbiton I went outside to a 'take away' for some food; I took it back to the office and had just arrived there when my colleague Steve Price said that there had been a break in at Hersham and rushed off to investigate. I ate my food and Steve phoned from Hersham with an update on the situation; the member of staff claimed that he had just arrived at the station and found the booking office door broken open. I thought this was strange as I had seen him on the platform some time before he claimed to have arrived so I caught the next train to Hersham and spoke to the investigating BTP detective. I told him that I had seen the man on the platform as my train passed and when he confronted the man with this evidence he broke down and admitted that he had broken the door himself and stolen the money. He apparently did this after my train left the station; he was suspended from duty and later dismissed after being convicted of theft.

One of the more difficult cases I had to deal with concerned a member of the platform staff at Walton-on-Thames. When the booking office was closed the platform staff would sell tickets from an excess fare book. They wrote out the details of the ticket and gave the top copy to the customer and kept the carbon copy in the book. They were supposed to pay the money in daily and the chief clerk would check the details in the book against the fare manual and ensure that the money collected matched what was entered in the book. Each member of the staff was issued with two books one of which was in use while the other was being checked, they were usually changed over daily.

The chief clerk told me that there had been some discrepancies in the payments made by a certain member of staff and this had been going on for some time but no action had been taken. I withdrew the current book from use and gathered the books used over the past three months together; it took me hours of painful checking before I could detect a pattern and understand what was going on.

Basically, the man had spent some of the fares money and when asked to pay it in had withdrawn some money from his bank account and paid that in; this had happened several times and his payments were in a complete mess. He was using the fares money for his own use until he got paid. When I eventually got to the bottom of it and submitted my report it did not make good reading and reflected on all the staff. The man was charged with theft but the Magistrate refused to convict him due to his ill health. It was a sad case and I got no satisfaction from it, especially as the man concerned used to be a driver whom I knew quite well until his health failed and he was given a station job as light duty. He was transferred to Wimbledon Park as a carriage cleaner as punishment.

The station manager was fully responsible for everything that happened within his area, operating, staff discipline, checking rosters and payrolls, dealing with customers and generally managing the area. It was a big job and David Gould was on top of it, he knew everything that needed to be done and ensured that it was done. I am a bit of an organiser and was allowed a certain amount of freedom in arranging the way that we dealt with various aspects of the job. One of the things which I introduced was a weekly list of weekend train alterations affecting us. All the information was produced by headquarters staff and we had a 'proof' copy of the information about a week before publication. My list enabled staff to see at a glance any alterations which affected their station without ploughing through the whole book and they were able to advise customers and put up suitable notices in good time.

When the Audit department was disbanded David decided that we would carry out local audits to ensure that standards were maintained in the booking offices. This was a new experience for me and I had to write down the procedure in order to ensure that I carried it out in the proper order. This proved useful and we operated the procedure at several of our stations with varying degrees of success. One chief clerk thought that we did not know what we were doing and was upset when we found a discrepancy in his ticket stock, we were pleased as we felt that this justified the work we put into it.

There was a fierce storm one day and during the evening the signalman told me that a Salisbury-bound train had broken down near Hampton Court Junction. It was standing on the down fast line and the driver was having problems rectifying the fault. I got another train to drop me off at the location and went to investigate. The area was on a high embankment and the wind was howling across the exposed lines, it was difficult to keep my footing. When I arrived, the driver was in his cab and told me that he had located the problem but was not sure what to do about it. I telephoned the signalman and requested the up fast line be blocked and trains be cautioned on the down slow line so that we could work around the failed train in safety. Because of the wind noise it was difficult to hear trains approaching and there was not much space for us to avoid them. The only safe way was to lie on the ground beside the train.

The train was formed of a '4VEP' multiple unit and a '4TC' trailer unit with a Crompton (class '33') pushing. The train would divide at Basingstoke with the 'VEP' going on to Southampton and the Crompton/'TC' going to Salisbury. One of the collector shoes had been knocked off the 'VEP' and the power cable had wound around the axle causing a short circuit. This was a common problem if a collector shoe was damaged. On examination I discovered that the driver had 'paddled up' the remaining shoes and had tied the paddles in place with rope, but had not removed any of the shoe fuses. I had the current isolated and placed a short circuiting bar on the live rail. I then unwound the cable, cut it off and removed the fuse, untied all the knots in the ropes and removed the paddles. The current was restored and the train was able to proceed normally.

The driver came from Salisbury and I suspect that he spent most of his time on diesel locomotives and not very much on electric units. The things that I did were standard procedures and he should have known what to do; luckily with my background I was able to assist otherwise he would have been there for a long time. Even though I knew what to do it was not easy to deal with in that location, especially with the weather conditions as they were. In the situation he had reached he would never have moved until a fitter or some other expert had arrived to help. I was late going home that evening and was glad when the train reached my station at Hook in Hampshire. As the train departed from the station there was a huge flash and a bang. I thought, 'Oh no not again', however, the train kept moving so I went to see what had caused the flash. I found a large grease can, of the type used by the PW staff for filling flange oilers, stuck between the running rail and the platform. I removed it and phoned the signalman at Basingstoke; he said that he would get the driver to examine his train when he arrived at Basingstoke.

Imagine my surprise the next morning when I heard that there had been a train crash at Fleet the previous evening. Apparently, shortly after the train on which I was travelling passed by Elvetham bridge between Fleet and Winchfield a large pine tree was blown down and fell across the line; the semi-fast Bournemouth train ran into it and was derailed. This was a serious incident and I considered myself lucky to have missed it by such a short time. In the report on this incident my reporting of the flash at Hook was part of the sequence of events but I don't think it was relevant.

I was able to use my driver's skills on another occasion, again on my way home, this time it was nearly my undoing. A PW man was examining the line near the aqueduct at Frimley and had left a rubber mat on the live rail. These mats were placed over the live rail so that the inspector could lie across the rail to examine the running rail. The front left-hand collector shoe was broken off when it hit the mat. I heard a loud bang and the driver making an emergency brake application, when the train stopped I asked the driver if I could assist. I knew him well from my time at Guildford and he agreed. He walked forward about a hundred yards to the signal post telephone to arrange for the current to be isolated, when the isolation was confirmed he called out to me that it was 'off'. As a safety precaution I placed a short circuiting bar on the live rail, there was a flash and a bang as the current was not off at all; had I not placed the bar on the rail I would have worked on the train assuming that it was 'dead' and I could possibly have been dead myself. The PW inspector came to see what had happened and went to another phone beside the Guildford to Reading line to ensure that the current was definitely off. This time it was all right and I disentangled the shoe lead from the axle and cut it off so the driver could continue on his way.

I reported the facts of this incident and the area inspector at Woking, Barry Cornick, investigated and obtained an explanation. The location where the train had stopped was on an overlap section between Eastleigh and Woking electrical control rooms and was fed from both ends. When the driver requested the current isolation he spoke to the signalman at Basingstoke, who in turn arranged the isolation with the electrical controller at Eastleigh and advised the driver when this was confirmed. The Eastleigh controller should not have confirmed the isolation to the signalman before ensuring that the Woking feed was also isolated.

Again my caution had saved me from possible injury or even death and vindicated my attitude of never assuming that something is fact just because somebody says so. I had adopted this attitude many years previously as a driver, when a signalman had allowed my train to enter a section of line which was under an engineer's possession. Having got into this position I refused to move again until I was assured by a third party that it was safe to do so. My thinking was that if he could make a basic mistake like allowing me into an occupied section he was capable of anything. I spoke to the divisional controller at Wimbledon and it transpired that there were two tamping machines in the section ahead of me, they were about to start tamping the track but the signalman had asked for the current to be restored to enable me to reverse my train out of the section.

If the current had been switched on when the machines were tamping the result could have been serious. There was an inquiry into this incident and the signalman was disciplined. I remembered some good advice that I received from Mr Stan Downes, the motive power superintendent many years before. I was not happy about the single manning on '350' shunters when running on the main line because of the restricted view when running engine first. He told me to stick to my guns if I felt strongly about it, if it turned out that I was wrong I would have to bear the consequences of my action. This was good advice and held me in good stead throughout my various jobs.

Back to Surbiton. I learned a lot from my experiences and formed lasting friendships with my colleagues there, I thoroughly enjoyed the job and was upset when rumours started in 1984 that a re-organisation was in the offing. The rumours gradually became fact, this scheme was to be called Line Traffic Management, stage 2 (LTM2). In this reorganisation the 'Divisions' were being disbanded, the area managers' organisations taking on most of the functions, one of which was responsibility for the former Motive Power Department (a radical departure as Motive Power had always been a separate department). This now became an integral part of the area structure with a train crew manager reporting to the area manager. The area managers had a lot more authority, being totally responsible for running their own area and reporting directly to Regional Headquarters.

I was nominated by my colleagues to represent them at the consultation meetings. I found this process very interesting but was disappointed when the points I raised were brushed aside and I was told that the process had already been applied 18 times to other areas on the Region; decisions had been made and there was nothing more to be said. I could see that the checking system which we had established in the booking offices could not work with the proposed staffing levels and I said so. I was told that there would be a new system but I felt that it would not be as thorough as the existing one and said that if I was involved I would make my views known.

The response was that it was a good job that I would not be involved. This was a surprise to me as at that time I did not know what I would be doing in the new organisation. I was soon to find out, however. The following week Mr Norman, the area manager, telephoned me to ask if I would be interested in being a train crew supervisor (TCS) or traction inspector at Woking. I said that I would be interested in the TCS job but not the traction inspector as this would mean flat money and I could not afford that. He said that he was going to a meeting on the next day to place the displaced people under the re-organisation and would take my views into account.

The day after this meeting he phoned again to advise me that from the next Monday I would be the traction inspector at Wimbledon Park. I was upset about this and Wimbledon Park was awkward to get to from where I lived. I talked at some length with David Gould about this and eventually came to accept it; at least I still had a job and I could use this as a base to find a position more to my liking. In fact David was worse off than me, he had been allocated the job as train crew manager at Salisbury. He had little experience of train crews and even less of the Salisbury area which spread from Basingstoke to Templecombe in Somerset, so he was not looking forward to his job either.

I phoned Arthur Mathews, the area manager at Wimbledon who would be my new boss and I was not impressed with what I heard. I said something like 'I suppose that you think that I shall walk in next Monday and just do the job'. He replied, 'Yes, you have the background and I am relying on you'. I had previously had some dealings with Arthur in his position as divisional operations manager and he had apparently been impressed by my handling of various operating incidents which was why I was now on my way to Wimbledon. I had not had any direct dealings with the Motive Power Department since 1979 and I had to dig out all my old technical and conditions of service books to refresh my memory. Also, some things had changed, new trains had been introduced and modifications made to others, I was not looking forward to it at all.

It was a sad day when we all said goodbye to Surbiton. Starting from scratch we had worked together and built something really good, we were on top of the job and had good systems in place to control all aspects of managing the area. However, the re-organisation was a fact so we all went to our new jobs resolving to try to build something as good as Surbiton. I have fond memories of some of the more light hearted things that happened at Surbiton and when I meet my ex-colleagues we often laugh about them. Jeff came to work one day with the address of a company which was marketing a new product for removing graffiti. We were all interested in this as graffiti was a big problem in our area. I phoned the company and the conversation went something like this.

Company rep.: 'Hello.'

Me: 'Hello, this is Surbiton station.'

CR: 'Which station?'

Me: 'Surbiton station.'

CR: 'Yes which station?'

Me: (A little louder) 'Surbiton station.'

CR: (A lot louder) 'Bus station?, Police station?'

Me: (A little quieter) 'No, railway station.'

CR: 'Well that's settled that, what can I do for you?'

Me: 'I understand that you are marketing this product.'

CR: 'Yes we are.'

Me: 'Do you think that we could have a sample to try?'

CR: 'No you can't.'

Me: 'Well I only asked.'

CR: 'And I only told you.'

With that he put the phone down so that was the end of that. My colleagues thought it was hilarious and 'Well I only asked' became a catch phrase in the area.

On another occasion David had mentioned that our accommodation arrangements were far from perfect. He had an office on the footbridge and we 'assistants' had one next door so it was necessary to go out and in again if we wanted to speak to each other. Jeff suggested that we had a hole cut in the dividing wall which was made of plasterboard and that a sliding door be fitted, which we all thought was a good idea. The next day David was sitting in his office when he heard a strange noise, he looked up and was surprised to see a power saw appear through the wall. Within 10 minutes there was a door-sized hole in the wall with a smiling Jeff standing on the other side. The next day Jeff fitted a sliding door and the job was done much to everyone's surprise and pleasure. Entrance to both offices was now though our door and communication was much better after that.

One day Jeff and I were in our office and David was sitting in his, telling us about an incident which involved Arthur Mathews, the divisional operations manager. As he was telling his story our door opened and in walked Arthur Mathews. I said fairly loudly, 'Hello Mr Mathews'; David said, 'Don't mess about' and was visibly shocked when Mr Mathews appeared in the connecting door. Luckily nothing derogatory was being said and Mr Mathews was not aware of what the conversation was about but I can still picture David's face.

One thing worth a mention at this point is that while I was at Surbiton we were involved in converting the former goods yards at stations into car parks. They had not been used for goods traffic since the BR Board decided to pull out of the general wagon load goods business. Car parking had been arranged in the former yards but they had not been surfaced or marked out for the purpose. This was now being done at many stations and it seemed strange to me because I could clearly remember going into the various sidings with the local goods trains. Things had certainly changed.

Chapter Ten

Return to the Motive Power Department

I discovered that the train crew manager at Wimbledon who would be my immediate boss was Derek Hayter. Derek had been a passed fireman at Guildford when I first started; I had worked with him many times as a fireman and got on very well with him. Our accommodation was located in the depot at Wimbledon Park. I went up to the office one afternoon and he showed me around and explained the job to me. I was to have a desk in his admin. office along with the chief clerk and the list clerks. I did not know any of them but I was introduced to them and they seemed a pleasant bunch. In fact I would not be spending much time in the office as most of my new duties involved monitoring drivers' performance and investigating incidents. After this visit I was a little happier about the job.

When I left Surbiton on the Friday I loaded all my personal belongings and equipment into my car and took them home. On the Sunday I drove up to Wimbledon Park and sorted out my office space so that I was ready to start work on the Monday. Leaving was not as traumatic as when I left Waterloo. I had not been there long enough to make any close relationships with any of the staff, but I was sad to be leaving the management team which had worked so well. This included managers and staff at the area manager's office at Woking who had been very supportive.

On the Monday morning I reported for work at 08.00. I found that there was a train from Hook which called at Wimbledon at 07.45 which was very convenient. There was a similar service at 16.45 for my homeward trip and this was to be the pattern of work while doing this job. Although I would have to get used to flat money, I did not have to work shifts or weekends and I had no 'on call' commitment so my social life was going to improve. My first morning started with a visit to the area manager, Arthur Mathews. He introduced me to his other managers and staff and explained what they all did. He also explained what he expected from me and I realised that although I would work with Derek Hayter it was Arthur Mathews who carried the ultimate responsibility and I would have to achieve the objectives he set for me. Arthur kept a big book in which he recorded all the relevant facts and figures about his area and used it to judge the area performance. All his managers were required to provide him with monthly statistics about their activities and explain any failure to achieve the set objectives.

One of my set objectives was to ride with every driver at the depot at least once every six months and report on their performance. There was no existing system in place for doing this in my area so my first priority was to work out a system. I went to the depot and had a further meeting with Derek, I explained the objectives that I had been given by the AM (or it could have stood for Arthur Mathews); he already knew this and he gave me some more objectives of his own. By the end of this meeting I could see that I was going to enjoy myself. Most of my tasks had no existing procedures for achieving them and I would have a free hand in setting them up. This is just the sort of thing that I like doing and I went home that afternoon feeling really good.

I spent most of the first two weeks in the office studying the rosters and diagrams and working out how I could ride with all the drivers at the required frequencies. I established that by riding on certain trains I could see two or three drivers on the same day and if the right drivers were on the duties I would easily reach my target. I also established that by combining some of my other duties with monitoring drivers I would be able to cover a lot of my objectives. It was a matter of planning what could be done on a daily basis, checking the drivers rosters with my riding programmes and selecting the best plan for the next day. Having worked it out in theory I set about the practice. After some initial problems and minor alterations to my schedules I started to make good progress so that at the end of the first month I had something to show. Derek was pleased and so was the AM but having got started I found other problems which had nothing to do with objectives or statistics. The most important was that since leaving the department in 1979 the class '455' units had been introduced and I knew nothing about them. It would be difficult for me to judge a driver's performance if I did not know how to operate the unit myself.

To overcome this I arranged to attend a drivers' course on '455s'; this was important as much of the work at Wimbledon Park involved these units. However, I could not just ride with drivers on one type of unit so I had to revise my planned schedule so that the rides were split between main line and suburban duties. I found the course very interesting especially the practical part of it, not having driven a train for several years I was surprised how easily I picked up the technique again. However, the new trains were very different from the types that I had worked on, they were very fast in acceleration and had a device which ensured that acceleration was the same whatever the loading. They also had disc brakes and this took some getting used to as braking caused very little noise. With the old units you could feel the braking performance by the sound and vibration; the disc brakes seemed to lose efficiency as the train slowed but I was not sure whether this was a fact or just an illusion.

I learned a lot from the course but one thing stuck in my mind, almost anything that went wrong on a '455' caused either the train brakes or the parking brakes to apply; basically any problem and the train stopped. Imagine my surprise when I read in the control log that two '455' units had divided on starting from Waterloo and the driver was not aware of it until he stopped at Vauxhall and there was no guard on the train to signal him away. This just could not happen. I found it hard to believe and as it was one of my drivers I set out to investigate. I knew the driver well, he was one of the most reliable men at the depot so I was able to rely on his evidence as to what had happened. Having listened to his story I was still unsure of the cause but one fact had emerged. He took the train from the depot formed of two '455' units as booked; on arrival at Waterloo the guard had problems with the sliding doors and asked for a fitter to examine them. To avoid delay the station supervisor told the crew to take another eight-car train in the next platform, the passengers were transferred and the train departed, or part of it did.

The engineer's report said that the locking pin in the coupling had been slightly damaged which had caused the units to come apart, despite this fact I was still puzzled, when the train parted it should have stopped automatically. The explanation came when I examined the stock working for the previous night. The train which parted had arrived at Waterloo as two separate trains, the driver of the second arrival should have coupled them together, the shunter was not in attendance when he arrived so he bumped the units together in the normal manner and left it there. The shunter arrived later, coupled the control jumper and brake pipes and also left the train.

The driver had not pressed the couple button in the cab or done a 'pull away test' and the shunter had not checked the coupling properly; due to a burr on the locking pin the coupling had not engaged properly. Because the couple button had not been pressed the two units were separated electrically through the coupling, so when the driver opened the controller the leading unit operated on its own. Had the coupling held, the rear unit would have prevented the front unit from moving as the brakes were still applied on that unit. The coupling came apart and the front unit went away on its own, pulling the control jumper and the brake pipe off the other unit.

The fault lay with the driver and the shunter on the previous evening for not carrying out the coupling procedure properly. The crew in the morning were also at fault as they failed to carry out a brake continuity test when they changed trains. Had the guard asked for a test he would have realised that something was wrong and would not have pressed the starting bell. This was something else I learned, the starting bell circuit passed through the control jumper and not the coupling as most of the other control wires did. All the staff involved were disciplined but for me the lesson was not to look at what actually happened in isolation, there is usually a root cause which is not always obvious.

Most of the drivers at the depot were old hands and some had been at Nine Elms when I was there so it did not take me long to establish myself with the staff. However, there was a group of new staff who came from all over the country, mostly from the North. They had come to Wimbledon Park to get their driver's job as promotion was slow at their own depots. By taking a job at another depot and registering a move back to their own depot or another depot of their choice they could ensure that they would move back at the first opportunity. This was a common practice in those days and had been for a long time. The problem was that these people came from far away and had no local knowledge of either routes or traction units. Sometimes the person would spend the first six to nine months in training and do little actual work. This obviously had an excessive cost on the depot budget as these people were being paid while in training and other people were being paid to cover their work, often at overtime rates.

Derek was working on ways to overcome this problem as it was causing chaos with his budget figures. His chief clerk had to produce weekly statistics which showed staffing utilisation and they did not look good. Between us we worked out a training programme which reduced the unproductive time of new drivers and I had to ensure that they achieved the targets set. The basic plan was that new drivers awaiting traction training would do route learning on specific routes, mostly in the suburban area. I had arbitrarily set time limits for each route based on my own route knowledge. As soon as they were traction trained they were available to work over these routes which made them instantly productive and also gave them practical knowledge. After this stage they were allowed time to learn the other routes required for their link position. I deliberately left the main line work and best paying jobs for this second stage, which was a good inducement for the new staff to qualify as soon as possible.

The training programme was fairly successful in reducing unproductive time and Derek was pleased. I was less pleased as some of these new staff showed a definite lack of motivation and commitment and I had problems getting some of them to follow the schedule. If a driver said he was not competent on a route there was not much I could do about it except give him more time. However, we eventually got on top of the problem, sometimes using the disciplinary procedure to enforce compliance. Luckily, the drivers' LDC was very positive about this, they could see that these people were causing problems for the existing staff and they endorsed the principle of the training programme and did not complain about discipline being imposed.

Although I was enjoying the job and had achieved a lot since I first started, the flat money was causing me problems with my finances and I decided to try for another position which would pay better. The problem was that most of the jobs which paid better involved round-the-clock shift work and I had got used to working near normal hours. I applied for two positions as train crew supervisor, one at Eastleigh and one at Woking, both fairly easy to reach from where I lived. I was appointed to the job at Eastleigh as from the 23rd July, 1984 but Arthur Mathews said that he would not release me until he had found somebody to replace me. This proved more difficult than expected, as he was being very selective about whom he appointed, so for the time being I carried on as traction inspector.

In the meantime I was offered the job at Woking which was a grade higher and I decided that out of the two jobs, this would be my preference. After about three months of waiting a replacement was found and after some time training him I was released on the 3rd October. When I went to see Arthur Mathews to say goodbye, we had a long talk about my future and he suggested that I should apply for the job as his area depot manager. In fact he asked me why I had not applied for the job when it was first advertised. I said that I did not know much about carriage cleaning which was a large part of the job and I had seen the present manager at work and he seemed to be under enormous pressure. He asked me what I had known about commercial work before going to Surbiton and I had to admit that it was not much. He almost convinced me that I should apply but I agreed to think about it and let him know. After this discussion I set off for home carrying my belongings with me.

John Norman was still the area manager at Woking, whom I knew well from my time at Surbiton. He welcomed me back to his area and suggested that as the train crew manager, Roy Vigors (another of the drivers from my days at Guildford), was going on leave for three weeks, I should cover his position. After some consideration I agreed to this, I was honoured that he had such faith in me but I was a little concerned because there were people senior to me who might question why they had been passed over. However, there were no such problems and I set about finding out what needed doing in the coming three weeks. Arthur Herbert was the chief clerk and I had a long meeting with him on the first day. Roy was a good manager but his filing system left something to be desired. On the floor in one corner of his office was a neat stack of papers about two feet high and I searched all through it to pick out odd pieces which I thought might be relevant to the items which Arthur had highlighted for me.

The first day was a long one but at the end I was happy that I had prepared for the three weeks to come. Only one thing worried me and that was the LDC meeting which had been arranged for the Wednesday. I had been given the agenda but had no idea what other business might be raised. I had attended such meetings at Wimbledon Park but had never been 'in the chair'. Drivers' LDCs had a reputation for being difficult and I was not looking forward to it at all. Wednesday came all too quickly and I went to work with some trepidation. I knew all the members of the LDC as they were all either drivers or firemen at Guildford when I was there; however, I was not sure if this was an advantage or a disadvantage. I opened the meeting by saying that as I was only covering the position for three weeks I was not prepared to get involved in any long term items, these would be deferred until the next meeting. The meeting went well and I was able to deal with most of the items raised without any problems.

One item did give me a problem and this was the question of payment for rest days *not* worked. I had never heard of such a thing but this was apparently a local agreement whereby if a person was booked 'Rest day off', they were on a rotation system which dictated who was next to work. If they were next to work but somebody lower down the list actually worked they could claim payment as if they had worked. If the list clerk was unable to contact the first to work he would try the next on the list until he covered the job which was outstanding. The people he was unable to contact would claim that the list clerk did not try to contact them. I had never heard of such a thing and said so at the meeting. Despite my saying that I would not get involved I agreed to look into staff complaints that some of the claims for payment had not been dealt with for over six months. The meeting ended peacefully and I was quite pleased with myself. Afterwards I asked Arthur to find all the payment claims that he could and let me have them the following morning with his comments on each one if possible.

The next day he presented me with a pile of claim forms which went back for up to six months as the staff had claimed; on most of them he had written 'unable to contact'. I spent some time considering what to do next and eventually decided that to be fair and consistent I would decline all the claims. If they had not worked they should not get paid, whatever the excuse. I spoke to Arthur about this and he thought it would cause problems at the next meeting. I spoke to John Norman about it and he agreed with me but could see that there would a problem which Roy would have to deal with; it was agreed that nothing would be said until the next meeting. Roy was not pleased when he came back but he said that at least it had brought it out into the open and the problem could be resolved.

During the first week in this job I received a letter from the motive power 'head office' advising me that there was a vacancy for a shunting driver at Strawberry Hill depot. There were six drivers in Roy's area who were on light duties working as station staff, messengers, etc. The tone of the letter suggested that if these six drivers did not apply for the position they would lose their benefits. To explain, if a driver became unfit for normal driving duties he would be accommodated in a job which did not involve main line work such as yard or depot shunting. If such a position were not available they could be accommodated in another vacant position such as station porter or anything else which their limitation allowed. Their allocation to such duties was approved by the BR doctor and they were regularly re-assessed. They retained their driver's rate of pay less one pound per week and were hourly paid at this rate; some of these people earned more as porters than they did as drivers.

I telephoned the BR doctor at Southampton to discuss the implications with him and he suggested that he come up to Woking the next day to discuss each case individually. This he did and he was angry, not because the people were to be asked to take up the vacant position but because of the threat to take away their benefits if they did not apply. He said that he and only he would decide whether people were fit for a job or not and some of the people had suffered heart trouble and would not be allowed to drive, even in a depot, and they certainly did not need or deserve to be threatened. The result of this meeting was that the doctor wrote to head office stating that none of the six were fit enough to apply for the vacant position. I think he did this because he was angry that he had not been consulted; however, after this the six people were not forced to apply for the job. My own view was that whoever was behind the letter had shot himself in the foot and achieved the opposite of what was intended; as far as I know nothing more was heard of this.

I found quite a few letters from youngsters who wanted to be drivers which had not been answered. They were being held as there were no vacancies at the time. I decided that they deserved a reply even if there were no vacancies and after some discussion with the personnel manager I drafted replies which suggested that they should apply for another type of job in the first place, such as porter or signal lad and make internal applications for Motive Power jobs when they came up. I understand that several people followed this advice and eventually joined the line of promotion to driver so I did achieve something in my three weeks as train crew manager at Woking.

I agonised over what to do next. The job I was appointed to at Woking as train crew supervisor was three shifts around the clock and seven days a week. It was grade 'E' which was the highest supervisory grade and, with extra payments for night and weekend work, it would pay well. I calculated that it would be about £15,000 gross per year which was good money in 1984. The job as area depot manager at Wimbledon was graded MS1 which was the first grade of management and would pay just over £9,000 per year. On the other hand it was a day job and it was a step up the ladder. Having already worked as a TCS at Waterloo and worked around the clock as station supervisor I was not keen on going back to shift work again. After long discussions with my wife and friends and colleagues, I decided to take a pay cut and move forward and phoned Arthur Mathews to let him know. He was pleased and agreed that I could move back to Wimbledon the week after Roy Vigors returned so that I had time to hand over to him.

Chapter Eleven

Area Depot Manager, Wimbledon

I said goodbye to John Norman again and went back to Wimbledon on 29th October, 1984. Arthur Mathews said that he would give me a period to learn the job and that Ron Harper, the relief manager, would work with me during this period. I knew Ron from when he was assistant manager at Clapham Junction and got on well with him; he showed me around my new area which consisted of Wimbledon Park depot, East Wimbledon depot and Clapham yard. I was to be responsible for depot operating (receiving, sorting and dispatching stock), carriage servicing (mainly cleaning) plus many other aspects associated with these functions. After a week of this introduction the AM called me to his office and told me that Ron was required elsewhere and that I was now on my own. This was a bit of a shock as I had hardly got my feet under the table and did not know many of the staff as yet. But that was that, I was on my own.

I had a staff of 216 and a wages bill of £1.8 million. I had to supply about 70 per cent of the electric train stock for the morning and evening peak services. The whole of the Southern Region loco-hauled stock was based at Clapham yard and a large proportion of the newspaper and parcels van fleet. I was responsible for all of this on my own. (Looking back I wonder how I managed it.)

The two locations were very different. Wimbledon Park and East Wimbledon were in fact one large complex with the repair depot at East Wimbledon. This was a new depot and stood on the site of the old Durnsford Road power station which used to supply power for the electric trains in the suburban area. I was responsible for operating in the whole area except inside the repair sheds. Clapham yard consisted of 52 sidings, some of which were electrified but most were not; between the peak hours a lot of electric stock was berthed in the yard. Each day the newspaper and parcel trains were received and reformed ready for the night services. They went out in set formations but came back on all different trains and had to be sorted again. There was a repair depot for loco-hauled stock and my supervisors worked closely with the engineering staff to ensure that vehicles were released for servicing or repair. Apart from the regular stock, anything moving from other regions or divisions on to the South Western invariably came into Clapham yard first before moving on to its final destination. This traffic was very diverse and included some freight trains, movements of new rolling stock, special trains, the Royal train and the Pullman stock from the Venice Simplon Orient Express (VSOE) which was privately owned. It was a hub in the railways of South and West London and was a very busy place.

It took me some time to get used to all the paper work which had to be done regularly but after a while this came easily. More difficult was getting to know the staff. There were a lot of them and as they were not all in the same place or at the same time, I could see that this would take some time to achieve. At Wimbledon Park I had yard supervisors who worked around the clock and a carriage cleaning supervisor, Fred Kimber, who worked days. When Fred was not there the yard supervisors were responsible for the cleaners. A similar situation existed at

Class '455' units lined up for cleaning at Wimbledon Park *c*.1986. *Author*

Jim, the cab-end cleaner at Wimbledon Park at work on '4VEP' unit No. 7755 *c*.1986. *Author*

Clapham yard although the carriage cleaning work was very different; Jim Brown looked after the carriage cleaning.

The staff were a mixed bunch, about a third of them were of West Indian origin but there were representatives from many nationalities which added to the difficulty of getting to know them. There was a lady chargehand at Wimbledon Park called Silvia Baines. She was a union representative and I did not like her at first. Arthur Mathews told me that she was a good person to have on your side so I took his advice and went out of my way to get to know her. This was a good move as the staff respected her and once we got used to each other I found her very helpful, but if she did not like what I was doing she did not hesitate to tell me so.

As I got to know the routines, responsibilities and especially the people I began to enjoy myself. I always left my office door open when I was free and the staff came to me without hesitation. I listened to what they had to say and learned a lot about what went on at the depot. The depot engineer was Dennis Barrett and I worked closely with him, he was good at his job and we struck up a working relationship to our mutual benefit. He kept me informed of what was going on in his part of the business and I tried to ensure that he had the units he needed at the time he needed them in his workshops. This relationship grew and spread to our respective staffs so that we had a good team spirit and no problem was insurmountable. There were problems but they were dealt with and were never allowed to interfere with the smooth running of the depot.

This job involved a lot of liaison with many people in other railway departments and I made a lot of new contacts. I worked closely with the Divisional Control over allocation of rolling stock for the peak services and with the chief mechanical & electrical engineer's (CM&EE) over movements of new rolling stock through Clapham yard to Strawberry Hill depot for commissioning (the class '455' stock was still arriving). I also worked closely with the operating department on the day to day arrangements for stock working and with the special trains department for preparation of special services. It was a busy job but an enjoyable one. Silvia Baines asked if the staff could have a Christmas party in the accommodation block and I agreed after ensuring that this would not affect the work. It turned out to be a big party with the area manager and my predecessor also present; unfortunately some of the people drank too much and spoiled it. I resolved not to allow this again and told Silvia to arrange a party 'off site' next year.

Carriage cleaning was a large responsibility and I concentrated a lot of my energy to getting this aspect right. The supervisors and staff were very good and once I was clear in my mind what was needed they co-operated in making it work. I was quite proud of the standard of work that we were turning out and I showed my interest by doing daily inspections of the finished work. This was appreciated by the staff (at least some of them) and when senior people visited the depot the staff did not like it if they did not inspect the work. In fact our reputation spread beyond the Southern Region and the area manager from Liverpool came to visit with his cleaning manager on the suggestion of his Regional Director. He was suitably impressed and it gave my staff a morale boost to think that the work they had been doing was so well known.

The job was not always so happy and I had my share of problems to deal with but I got enormous satisfaction when the problems were resolved amicably. One big problem arose because carriage cleaning was considered by some managers as unimportant. If they needed to cut back on spending when their budget started to go pear shaped they looked at carriage cleaning first as an easy way to cut costs without affecting the service immediately. Arthur Mathews called me to his office one day and dropped a bombshell; he said that to reduce his budget all overtime at the two depots was to cease immediately. I was to tell the staff that day and implement it by the next week.

I could see that this was going to be difficult to implement without causing friction with staff and disruption of the work. After considering how to approach the matter for some time I decided to go in head first and deal with any problems as they arose. I called the LDC together and told them straight that all overtime was to cease from next week. Their reaction was predictable and quite volatile. After a short and heated meeting they asked for an adjournment to consider their position, to which I agreed as it gave me a breathing space to consider my next move.

When the meeting re-convened the LDC presented a sensible case for retaining some of the overtime which was very similar to my own thoughts on the matter. However, there was one stumbling block which concerned how any overtime was to be shared and this aspect instigated a long and fruitless discussion. Then I had an idea which resolved the matter in minutes. Basically, there were two types of people working at the depot, those who were the family bread winner and those who worked just for the extra money. I proposed that only those who were bread winners should have overtime and this was accepted. As it happened most of those involved worked in the two shift gangs so it would be easy to allocate any overtime.

Less easy would be selling it to the AM. His instruction had been to cut out ALL overtime but somehow I had to persuade him that some was needed, which in my opinion it was. I took my proposal to the AM and explained that I had agreed a cut of 75 per cent with the staff but that I considered that the other 25 per cent was necessary and important in getting the job done properly. After some discussion, and with some reservations, he agreed to my proposals so I went back to the LDC and the changes were implemented the following week. I was pleased that the cut had been fairly painless for me and the LDC felt that they had saved some of the earning power of the staff.

Not long after this Arthur Mathews went to a meeting of area managers from the Region and had a disagreement with somebody from the South Eastern section about carriage cleaning. There was a fleet of stock used on that section known as 'Jaffa Cakes' due to the orange and brown livery in which they were painted. The paint was in very poor condition and this person claimed that they needed repainting. Arthur said that all they needed was cleaning and offered the services of my staff at Wimbledon Park to prove the point. He told me what was expected and asked me to arrange for extra staffing over the weekend to do the work. The extra cost would be borne by the Region and not come from his budget so there was not a problem of overtime working. I called the LDC and they agreed to the work being done so I asked for volunteers and put together a special group for this extra special work. The result was outstanding and the person from the 'South Eastern' was suitably impressed; it was agreed that this extra weekend work should continue until the whole fleet had been cleaned.

In fact the staff had got back more overtime than they lost in the first place so they were happy. They were also proud of being selected for this project as it showed everybody what a good job they were doing. They worked extremely hard scrubbing the outside of the coaches with an acid cleaner and thoroughly washing the insides with detergent, any graffiti was removed and the upholstery vacuumed. Word spread about what we were doing and we had visits from all sorts of people to watch the work in progress, some managers sent staff to work at the depot for a week at a time to learn the job properly.

Another job which we carried out was on a two-car 'EPB' unit which had been parked in a siding at Waterloo for staff training for about six months. This unit was required at Oxted for use as a temporary waiting room while the station was being renovated. Unfortunately, while it had been at Waterloo it had been used as a bedroom by vagrants and the interior was filthy. It was full of old paper, cardboard and discarded clothing and smelled horrible. I had difficulty finding anybody willing to tackle the job, eventually two of the staff agreed to do it on condition that they had special clothing, etc. and access to a shower afterwards. They made a lovely job of it but I doubt if the people who used it at Oxted were aware of the work that had gone into getting it clean.

The carriage washing machine at Wimbledon Park had been installed in the 1930s as had the one at Clapham yard. The machine at Wimbledon Park was very heavily used and it was decided to replace it with an up to date type using the latest technology. The CM&EE departmental head explained what was planned to be installed and we discussed timescales for the work to be completed. It was not just a case of demolishing the old machine and building a new one as the concrete aprons on which the machine stood were also to be replaced and this involved replacing the track as well. I arranged meetings with various interested parties such as the timetable and rolling stock planners and the depot engineer. After much discussion we had agreed how to tackle the project and it was given the go-ahead. The drivers' and guards' LDCs had agreed to special working arrangements so if the engineering work went to plan we should have no problems.

When work started the shunting staff had to deal with a near-normal service with a few cancellations whilst having only one washer road to shunt the incoming and outgoing trains on to gain access to and from the depot. They did an excellent job and the whole project went well with no major problems. That was until the engineering work was finished and we started to use the new machine. There were teething problems galore and the technicians spent many hours adjusting and modifying various parts. The machine had so many safety features built into it that the slightest problem would cause it to fail (unlike the old one which was very simple), but when all these problems were sorted out we had an excellent washing machine which made the cleaning job much easier.

Another project which caused less of a problem but took a lot of careful planning was the building of a wheel turning lathe. There was not a suitable machine available to us on the Southern Region and stock had to go to the Midland Region for wheel turning which meant that they were out of commission for long periods, especially after the autumn leaf fall season when wheels were more likely to develop a lot of flat spots due to slipping and sliding on the wet leaves. The new lathe shop speeded up this process no end and enabled a four-car unit to be re-profiled in one shift which meant only one day out of service. This was an enormous benefit to the division and stock availability improved considerably.

There always seemed to something going on at the depot in the way of improvements which all added to my workload. As well as the new rolling stock arriving and special trains to be cleaned the main train shed was repaired, the tarmac walkways between the yard sidings were renewed, the staff accommodation was renovated with new flooring, asbestos lagging was removed from the pipe work in the train shed and new communication equipment was installed in the shunters' control cabin. Another project which proved to be a big benefit was the installation of a computer controlled system to manage the lighting in the main train shed. Basically this system measured the amount of natural light in the shed and adjusted the power to the lights accordingly, they could be on at a quarter, half, three-quarters or full on and switched off automatically when it was light enough. This system was expensive to install but the energy conservation manager told me later that it had paid for itself in the first year after installation.

Similar works were carried out at Clapham yard but to a lesser extent; my main problem there was controlling the loco-hauled rolling stock which was getting a bit old to say the least. Some of the coaches were vacuum braked and they were limited to certain services, some of the newspaper and parcel vans were 'dual' braked and could be used on any train. One three-car coaching set was used on the 01.45 Yeovil paper train and returned on the 06.15 from Yeovil which was the first commuter train of the day from that area, the stock was awful and I was ashamed of it. One weekend this three-car set went out on a special into Wales and due to a derailment near Severn Tunnel Junction it did not come back as programmed. Luckily we had another set in the yard at the time so we used that, it was air braked and was in excellent condition so we kept on using it; apparently it belonged to 'Regional Railways' and I soon had calls asking for it to be returned. I held on to it for about four weeks with various excuses but eventually I received an order from British Rail Headquarters to return it as soon as possible.

I spoke to the person who issued the order and explained my position saying that I did not want to put the poor quality stock on the 01.45 service again. He was very helpful and eventually arranged for some newer stock to be transferred to me to replace the old three set. Unfortunately, when the coaches arrived they were all first class so I arranged for the labels to be removed and the yellow stripe at the roof line to be painted out. The new coaches went out on the 01.45 on the Monday morning and I was pleased; I was less pleased when I was told that the AM had received many complaints from passengers on the 06.15 that there was no standard class seats and they had to stand all the way. They were not used to having luxury stock on their humble train and thought it was all first class. However, they soon got used to it, it was probably the best stock running on the West of England line at that time.

As an attempt at image improvement, I had arranged for one of the cleaners to be fully employed in cleaning off graffiti and chewing gum. These had been a big problem but once they were tackled on a regular basis the situation improved immensely. One bank holiday weekend a group of graffiti 'artists' attacked several units which were berthed in a siding at Basingstoke, they made a real mess of the

Car No. 76484 from set No. 7777 after it had been attacked by vandals. These units were taken out of service for re-painting. *Author*

units and Dennis Barrett said that they would have to be taken out of service for repainting. Dennis and I agreed that we would not allow any trains with graffiti into service until it had been removed or the units painted. This policy was also very successful and there were no trains on the South Western seen in service with graffiti. Imagine my surprise some time later when I read that a group of senior people had been to New York to study the graffiti problem on the subway there and had come back with exactly the same policy. They could have saved a lot of money by coming to Wimbledon Park instead of going to New York.

I was called to a meeting with the AM one day. This was at the request of the rolling stock section at BRHQ. A lively young chap came to explain a new computer based system for keeping track of passenger rolling stock; this was called POIS and was already in place on the Midland Region, it was now planned to extend it to the Southern. I listened intently to what was said but at times I found it hard to follow. The basic idea was similar to TOPS, the freight tracking system, except that POIS relied on set working with set formations of coaches and vans running on a regular basis and maintenance being programmed for the complete formation at the same time.

When he had finished his explanation I said that although this was a good system it could not be applied in its present form on the Southern as the rolling stock did not run in set formations. The trains left Clapham yard and were divided *en route*, returning on different and separate services; when these trains arrived in the yard they were broken up and re-marshalled for following services. The only formation which was not broken up was the eight first class coaches of my boat train set which tended to stay together unless something special occurred.

He thought about this for some time and then said that this could be overcome by marshalling the trains so that the coaches and vans with specified numbers were placed in certain formations. At this I saw red and told him that if he thought that we would shunt most of the stock in the yard each day so that it matched the numbers in his computer system, he could think again. The system should support the work not dictate how we do it and create more work than necessary. The meeting ended with the AM telling the young man to think carefully about how this system should work before trying to implement it on the Southern.

The CM&EE chief, Max Millard, sent a letter to his manager at Clapham yard that as a particular repair on certain coaches was proving to be difficult and expensive, they were not to be repaired but taken out of service until further notice. This put me in an awkward position as we had little spare stock and would not be able to cover special work or stock failures. I spoke to the manager concerned but he was adamant that this policy be carried out. These coaches were gradually taken out of service and we became very short of stock. The crunch came when a special train was arranged to take guests to the opening of new accommodation at Woking Homes. (Woking Homes was originally a home for orphaned railway staff children and was known as the 'orphanage', the old building had been demolished and new smaller buildings put up in its place; these were to be for elderly people as the function of the charity was changing with the times.) The boat train set was 'out' and eight standard class coaches were booked for the special. We did not have eight to spare so I spoke to Trevor Adams who was then regional operating officer. He said that this special was very important for the Region and must take precedence over normal services.

My yard supervisor made up the special as instructed and had the task of finding enough stock for the remaining services. He did well in this but finished up by using all the odd stock in the formation for the Brighton to Plymouth service. Five of the eight coaches were BCKs, coaches with second and first class compartments and a guard's brake compartment, the guard had plenty of accommodation to choose from. The following day I received an irate call from the AM at Brighton to ask what I was playing at, putting all those odd coaches on his train. I explained that I had no choice but he was not impressed. The irony of this was that Max Millard, who had issued the instruction for the coaches to be withdrawn, was involved in the Woking homes charity and was an instigator of the special train. Anyway, the upshot was that words were spoken above my level and some more coaching stock was supplied, so it worked out well in the end.

The AM called me to his office one day to tell me that it had been decided to alter my area of responsibility. Instead of having Clapham yard I was to take on the three stations of Wimbledon Park, Southfields and East Putney. This would make my position geographical rather than functional. I was not very happy about this as it would mean taking on a lot of new functions such a booking offices and station maintenance as well as operating the line where the service was provided by London Underground. However, the locations would be easier to reach but I would have to concentrate my mind on things other than yard operating and carriage cleaning.

Once this change was implemented the first thing that happened was that a programme of station renovation was commenced, I was closely involved in this and found it very interesting. The programme started at East Putney and led to the first disagreement of many. On the island platform there were some old wooden buildings which were in very poor condition. They were a nuisance to the staff because tramps and dead beats often broke the doors open and used them to sleep in. I wanted to demolish these buildings and just leave the platform canopy; I was overruled and it was decided to renovate the buildings. I thought that this was a mistake and a waste of money but I had to accept it.

I was in a meeting with the depot engineer one day when I was advised that East Putney station was on fire. I called a taxi and went there immediately, there was an enormous fire and it was the disputed buildings which were burning. Unfortunately the platform canopy was also badly damaged and had to be demolished so we finished up with nothing at all on the island platform. Despite suggestions to the contrary I can assure you that I was in no way responsible for destroying those buildings; I was not amused when certain people started calling me 'smokey'.

When it came to renovating Southfields station we had a big problem. The platform level buildings were continually being attacked by vandals and were in a terrible state. After some discussion as to what to do it was decided to demolish these buildings, with a train every few minutes there was not really a need for a waiting room. I advised the local authority of our intentions and they agreed to the work being done, although they were not happy about it they could see the reason why. Unfortunately it was election year and the local MP got to hear about it. He persuaded the AM that we should have one more try at renovating the buildings, much to my dismay. The toilets were demolished but the other buildings were restored. On my suggestion, all the doors were changed to 'outward' opening so that vandals could not kick them in. This was successful and together with acrylic windows and steel mesh over the windows much of the vandalism was prevented.

When the tennis championships were held in June each year there was a huge number of extra people to deal with and this was another aspect of the job which was new to me, although these people were generally no trouble, unlike the football supporters who behaved like animals. The football problem became worse when Wimbledon football club was promoted to the first division; they had caused little problem previously but now they would get so-called supporters visiting from Liverpool and Manchester and other such places. I was called to the club to discuss transport arrangements with the police and club officials, etc. The club chairman was enthusiastic about how wonderful the promotion was. I told him that it was the worst thing that could have happened from my point of view and I was not looking forward to it at all. He tried to reassure me and took me out onto the terraces where contractors were busy building cages to keep the opposing fans apart, to me it just about summed it up. All I could hope for was that they would be relegated next season and things would return to normal.

The first time they played Manchester United at Wimbledon the fans were collected at Euston station, herded on to an underground train which ran non-stop to Wimbledon Park, from there they were escorted to the ground by mounted police. The same procedure applied for the return trip after the game. I thought it was a disgrace and felt sorry for the local people who for most of the time suffered no conflict in the area except for finding a parking space.

Another dramatic change came about shortly in that the position of AM Wimbledon was removed and the area came under the control of the area manager, Waterloo. Mr Alan Futter held this position and soon everybody was busy reorganising. I could see that I was going to become isolated in my patch as the AM Waterloo would have more important things to do and would not have the local commitment of Arthur Mathews who was actively interested in carriage cleaning and depot operating. I was right about this but although I was isolated it seemed to bring me closer to my staff which made for an amiable atmosphere. Another good thing was that Peter Hobkinson who was the operations manager in the Wimbledon area was to hold the same position in the new enlarged Waterloo area. He had been very supportive when he was at Wimbledon and I was sure that he would continue to be so.

There was a terrible snow storm one night in January 1987 and I went to work the next day ready for a long stay. This was just as well as the snow continued all day and we had problems keeping the depot running. That night I slept on the 'sick bed' in the ladies rest room so that I could be on hand for the early morning start of service. This was a good move on my part as we had terrible problems getting trains out of the depot. The snow was of the dry powdery type which was to become famous in later years as 'the wrong type of snow'. It certainly was the wrong type for us because as fast as we cleared a track to move a train the wind covered it with snow again if we did not make the move quickly. What made it worse was that Control kept changing their minds as to what stock they wanted out which led to many heated arguments. Having just spent half an hour getting a train out to the exit signal, to be told that it was not wanted does tend to try your patience. As the day went on another problem arose, some of the trains had been berthed since the previous evening and had become frozen to the track, they would not move under their own power and before we could get another unit to assist, the snow blocked the siding again. It was a horrendous day.

As a matter of interest the comment about the wrong kind of snow was not as stupid as the press made it out to be. Normal snow in this country is fairly wet and tends to stay where it falls, the electric motors on British trains are air cooled, the air being drawn through vents in the motor casing. This works perfectly well in normal circumstances but because the snow was dry and powdery it was blown into the air vents on the motors and caused problems, not only on traction motors but other electrical equipment which hangs beneath the train body.

There was a special train booked out about noon, this consisted of two 'chopper' controlled '455' units and a party of railway engineers from Scandinavia was going to ride on it from Waterloo. We had a big problem getting it out of the shed at East Wimbledon depot and were going to have an even bigger problem getting it out onto the main line. I phoned the operating officer, Mr Adams, to ask how important this train was and the answer was 'Extremely important' so we persevered and eventually got it out of the depot. Apparently the engineers were impressed with our ability to run such a train in those conditions, another feather in our cap.

We lost a 'brownie point' on a later occasion, the launch of Network SouthEast branding. We had a train painted in the new corporate livery (toytown colours, some called it), and the train was moved from Selhurst depot to East Wimbledon in the dead of night and hidden in the train shed until moving to Waterloo for a press call when everybody would see the new livery for the first time. When I went home the previous evening I left strict instructions with the supervisors that they must not tell anybody where the train was, to prevent anybody from taking photos and pre-empting the official press release. Unfortunately the supervisors took my word literally and refused to tell the crew who came to take the train to Waterloo where it was berthed, with the result was that the train was late for the press release and I had to make excuses which were not completely true.

Because I was now responsible for booking offices I was involved locally in the introduction of APTIS, a computerised ticket issuing system which also kept accounting details and would make the chief clerk's job a lot easier in keeping the monthly accounts. I was in dispute with the accounting centre at Derby because I refused to sign the monthly accounts on the grounds that I had not checked them and therefore could not say if they were correct. I remembered the telling off from the auditor when I was at Surbiton, and what had been said at the consultation meeting for LTM 2, and there was no way I was going to certify anything without knowing that it was correct. This argument went on for some time but I did not give in and eventually my chief clerks signed their own accounts. There was just not enough time in a day for me to check the accounts properly. The checks were carried out by roving clerical staff when APTIS was introduced.

I was not happy with this situation because I like to be in control of all aspects of my job, but that was the system which had been introduced so I made spot checks on certain key points and signed to indicate that I had found them correct. This problem was to have implications some years later and in a way it vindicated my stand against signing the accounts. But more of that later.

A rumour went around the depot, I don't know where it started, but the result was very funny. It was rumoured that the Government had agreed that some Vietnamese boat people could come to Britain and the British Rail Board had agreed to employ some of them on humanitarian grounds; we were to have 10 of them at Wimbledon Park. One person in particular, John, was extremely angry about this. Another of the staff, Steve, was very good at drawing cartoons and there were soon a lot of drawings posted about the depot showing John fighting with the Vietnamese. I was impressed with the cartoons and when Steve realised this I was inundated with his works which mainly showed the depot staff in various situations. He was clever at getting expressions and gestures into his drawings and it was amazing how accurately he depicted members of the staff although they did not always agree with his interpretation. I kept all his drawings and I can still laugh at them after all these years.

Another man, Lionel, was an excellent artist and produced a lovely oil painting of a 'Lord Nelson' for me. It really surprised me that people with this sort of talent should be cleaning trains but I never asked the reason. Lionel was also something of a musician and had in the past had music published and recorded. What other talents he possessed I did not find out because he moved to Plymouth; I would like to think that he used his talents to obtain a job more in keeping with his obvious skills.

A sad thing happened one morning. One of the staff, Genny Romanelli, an Italian lady, arrived for work just before 08.00. She told Fred Kimber that she did not feel well, so he gave her a drink of water and told her to sit in his office for a while. A few minutes later she collapsed on the floor, Fred called an ambulance and I arrived while they were waiting for it. Sadly Genny was dead on arrival at hospital. The staff were shocked and very upset as Genny was a very popular person. When the funeral arrangements were made everybody wanted to go, obviously I could not allow this or we would get no work done for the whole day. After a long discussion I agreed to allow 20 of her closest friends to attend. I arranged to borrow the depot engineer's minibus which could carry six people, the staff arranged another bus for the remaining 14 people.

On the day all those who were attending arrived suitably dressed for the occasion, the flowers were beautiful. I chose five people to share the depot bus with me and the others waited for the hired bus. When it arrived it was not a minibus at all but a 20 seater midi-bus and it was painted bright red. We arrived at the cemetery and waited in our buses inside the cemetery gates. It was a horrible day with drizzle drifting on the wind, a typical day for a funeral in fact. The cortège arrived led by a shining hearse and a large black limousine, followed by a motley collection of cars in various states of repair. We joined the end of the procession in our bright yellow 'railway' bus and our bright red midi-bus, I felt very self conscious as we drove slowly around the cemetery to the graveside.

We all stood in a semi-circle as the minister conducted the service, it was a sombre scene. As the coffin was lowered into the grave a West Indian lady who was standing on a raised flat gravestone, collapsed and rolled off. Somebody called out, 'Quick, call an ambulance'. I ran to the limousine (the hearse was gone by then), and asked the driver to take me to the cemetery office. We sped through the cemetery at an undignified pace and I rushed into the office to call an ambulance. The ambulance arrived after a short while and I stood on the running board to direct the crew to the grave. The ambulance raced through the cemetery with its siren blaring and me in my mourning clothes hanging on the side. The lady was taken to hospital and all the mourners went on their way. We went back to the depot.

Somebody made a big pot of tea and we all sat down and talked about the day's events, especially about me in my suit hanging on to the side of the ambulance with the siren blaring; apparently it looked very funny from a distance. It was obviously a sad occasion and Genny was genuinely mourned by all the staff, however, I am sure that Genny would have laughed if she could have seen it.

I was advised that there was a scheme afoot called Unified Depot Management (UDM); I was not sure of the detail but basically the CM&EE Department was going to take over the running of all depots on the Region including operating and carriage cleaning. I did not know what this would mean for me, if I would continue in my present position under a new boss or if I would have to find another job. Before long it became clear, I was out of a job again but this time there was no general reorganisation to scoop up displaced people such as myself so I was worried. I had a meeting with the AM and the operations manager and it was suggested that I take up the position of relief manager for the area. I was not too keen on this but there was not much choice.

I was to cover the station managers at Waterloo, Clapham Junction, Wimbledon and Epsom and would do special duties as required. I was to have an office at Wimbledon but would not spend much time there as I would be out and about in the area most of the time. The fateful day came all too quickly and the staff arranged a 'Leaving do' for me; they bought me a stereo radio for my car and when it was presented by Dennis Barrett I had to fight back the tears as I made a short speech of thanks. I felt really bad that I had to go as I had a strong bond with the staff and was proud of the work that we had done together. I was really sorry to be leaving and I was very sad when I carried my belongings down to Wimbledon.

Chapter Twelve

The Clapham Junction Accident

In January 1988 I took up my new position. The first job I was given was to prepare a contingency plan for the new area, this was to be based on a similar document which existed in the Southampton area. I had assisted David Gould in preparing a smaller project at Surbiton so I had some idea but this was to be a lot bigger and cover any eventuality. I gathered a huge amount of information about the area, not just from a railway point of view but also about alternative bus services, bus and coach companies who could provide vehicles at short notice, etc.

Having gathered all the information I set about putting it down in an easy reference form, this took me a long time but I was pleased with the result and it was accepted by the senior management. I did this project in between covering the various managers and although I enjoyed it, I did not enjoy the interruptions that the cover work caused. In fact I did not like the cover work at all as it was difficult to start things when you would not be there long enough to finish them, it was also difficult to pick up things that other people had started. I did have six weeks in the Epsom area when the station manager was in hospital and this was enjoyable, this job covered 12 stations from Motspur Park to Dorking and the Chessington branch. Much of the area was fairly rural, it was totally different from the hustle and bustle of the area between Raynes Park and Waterloo which I was used to. I also covered the SMs at Wimbledon, Clapham Junction and Waterloo and these positions put me in contact with people that I had known from my previous jobs, especially at Waterloo and Clapham Junction.

The on-call commitment was based on the position I was covering which was a bit unsocial and I found it difficult to plan my social life. Most of the call outs were related to booking office security when alarms were set off or just went off; in my previous job most of the call outs were related to operating incidents. When I was called out I first had to go to the base station for the area to collect the relevant keys and I had to take them back again when I was finished. This added to the time spent out on calls and made the job more difficult.

Some of my time was spent in the administration office at Waterloo and this was useful because I was able to learn the basics of using a computer. I had taught myself to type when I was station supervisor at Waterloo and once I had found out how to get into the computer system I found it really useful as it was easy to change things if you did not like them. I asked if I could have formal training in using the computer but was told that there was none available.

There was a live exercise on the Waterloo & City line one Sunday. For the purpose of the exercise a train carrying people made up as casualties was stopped in the middle of the down tunnel, a 999 emergency call was made from Control stating that there had been an explosion on a train in the tunnel and the emergency services and railway staff had to deal with it. The exercise was called 'Operation Drain'. I was nominated to be the duty manager on the day and had to pretend that I did not know what was going on. My instructions were to do

The 10.39 vans train from Southampton to Clapham is double-headed by class '47' No. 47053 and class '73' No. 73101 *Brighton Evening Argus,* seen at Woking on 28th February, 1987.
D.R. Franklin

Intercity-liveried class '09' diesel shunter No. 09012 *Dick Hardy* on display at the Network Day exhibition at Waterloo on 1st October, 1988.   *Brian Morrison*

nothing until I received a call from Control, and then to deal with the situation in my own way as it developed. There was no procedure as far as I was concerned so I would have to use my experience and local knowledge to deal with the incident. There would be a debriefing afterwards when the problems encountered in dealing with the incident would be highlighted.

I was concerned that I would be found to be lacking in dealing with such an incident. I was tempted to do some preparatory work to avoid this but Peter Hobkinson said that this would lessen the value of the exercise. The point was to learn from the experience as an organisation and if I was too prepared we would not learn very much, we would just congratulate ourselves on how good we were. On the day I purposely got involved in something else to try to make it realistic. This was a good idea and when the call came I had to rush down to the 'Drain'. As I arrived the police and fire brigade were also arriving, they obviously did not know where to go so I had to direct them and although I had not prepared I soon found myself in the thick of it; it is surprising how easy it is to forget that it is only an exercise. While I was busy at the Waterloo end I received a message that the fire chief had asked for my presence at Bank station urgently.

I had not expected this and had no idea how to get to Bank. I asked the police inspector with whom I was dealing if he could help. He called somebody on his radio and told me that there was a car waiting for me in the cab road. I delegated responsibility for the Waterloo end to a permanent way supervisor who had recently arrived and went and found the police car. I told to the driver to take me to the Bank. He replied, 'Where is the Bank?' That stumped me because I had never been there by road so we had to look in his A-Z of London to find the way. I don't know if this was part of the act but if it was it was very convincing. We set off with the siren blaring and soon arrived at Bank station.

I went to the Fire Brigade 'control' van and introduced myself. The fire chief was a bit aggressive towards me and demanded to know if there was any asbestos present in the coaches involved in the incident. I telephoned the BR Control who replied that some of them did while others did not, it depended on the coach numbers which were in the tunnel. I asked Control to try to find out the numbers of the coaches. The fire chief said that if there was any asbestos present he was going to withdraw his staff. He was pretty convincing and again it was easy to forget that this was only an exercise.

I was told that there would be regular liaison meetings between the fire brigade, police and ambulance service and I was required to attend every one of these. I was surprised to find that the British Rail Director of Safety was there as an observer, I had not been told that the exercise would be so high profile. The police superintendent asked me to find some information for him and this involved my going down to the platforms; while there the ambulance staff were having a problem and asked me to help. Because of this I missed the next liaison meeting and the fire chief was furious. I made a point of attending all the others. I learned a lot from this experience, especially about the organisation of the various emergency services when dealing with a major incident. I also learned that it was not my job to do things but to be near the control point and be involved in controlling things.

The view from Clapham 'A' box towards the yard. This had been the subject of Terence Cuneo's famous picture.   *Author*

The view from Clapham 'A' box looking towards Waterloo. The building in the centre distance is the carriage washing machine.   *Author*

The emergency services also learned a lot. The ambulance staff found out how difficult it was to carry a person on a stretcher half a mile uphill from the tunnel centre to the surface. The police had laid a telephone cable from the surface at Bank down into the tunnel to set up a forward control point. This was fine until they tried to bring it back up again, the further up the hill they went the heavier the roll got and they were really struggling when they were near the surface. It was a really useful exercise for all concerned.

The debriefing took place during the following week and we did not come out of it too badly, at least I did not disgrace myself. After this I returned to my normal duties and the exercise became just a memory. I was in the administration office one day in December 1988 when I was told that there had been a collision and derailment at Clapham Junction. I phoned Control for information but all they could tell me at that time was that there had been a collision and derailment and that it was considered a major incident.

I phoned Clapham 'A' box and confirmed with the signalman that all lines were blocked and the traction current isolated. He also was not sure what had happened but he was aware that it was serious and he was shaken. I went to see the AM to advise him about the incident and he told me to take some of the clerical staff from the operating section, go to Clapham Junction and do what ever needed to be done. On arrival at Clapham I sent two of the staff to assist the station supervisor and located one more at the platform end to take details of anybody coming from the site of the incident and also stop anybody going on to the track who was not authorised.

I walked along the track, meeting several people who were in a state of shock. I saw driver Alex McClymont, who had started work at Guildford on the same day as me; he was badly shaken but refused to leave the scene when I advised him to seek medical help. As I passed through Freemasons' bridge the sight I saw was unbelievable. There was a terrible wreck piled up by the embankment and firemen were swarming all over it trying to rescue the people inside. I had never seen anything like it and at first I was stunned.

As I stood there, Mr Pettitt, the General Manager, came up and offered me his mobile phone but I had just decided to check that the site was totally safe so I declined and set off to do my checks. John Noorani, the station manager at Clapham Junction had carried out all the necessary safety precautions so I headed for the fire brigade control van to see what the situation was. The area around the site was crowded with people from the emergency services, firemen were getting people out of the wreck, ambulance staff were treating them and taking them away and the police were keeping the area clear. It was a text book operation but I doubt if those people who had taken part in Operation Drain and similar exercises ever expected to find themselves dealing with a real situation such as this.

I asked the senior fire officer who was his on-site contact with BR, he said that he did not have one so I put my name down and waited for instructions. I phoned Control and gave what information I could and then set about assisting in any way I could. Control had told me that the breakdown cranes were ready at East Wimbledon depot and Clapham Yard, the fire officer said that a 100 ton road crane was on the way but had not yet arrived. After some time when the road crane had still not arrived he agreed to use the rail crane although he was not keen as he felt it might endanger his men on the track. I asked Ernie King, an area inspector, to go to Clapham yard and get the crane on to the site. I then went up to the wrecked train to find the fire officer in charge to tell him what was going to happen.

Having done this I was making my way back to the control van when the cover slipped off of a body which was being lifted up the embankment. It was a young woman with light coloured hair, and I went completely numb. My daughter Geraldine, who worked in the British Transport Police office at Waterloo usually caught the same train as me but this morning she was late getting up and would catch a later train; the train which had crashed was two trains after my train from Hook. I went to the police control van in a state of shock. Inspector Bob Davidson allowed me to use his very busy phone to contact the Waterloo office, to my immense relief my daughter answered the phone. I spoke to her for a short while, told her to phone home to tell my wife that we were both all right then I went behind the van and was physically sick.

When I felt better I went back to the fire brigade control van, they told me that the rail crane was coming on to the site and asked me to ensure that it was done safely. When this was done and on my way back to the control van I met a senior member of London Underground staff who told me that he had a powerful radio telephone which we could borrow if we needed it. I accepted gladly as until then I had been forced to use the fire control van phones which were nearly always busy with more important things than my business. We set up a railway control point in a PW personnel carrier and installed the phone in there where the GM and his assistants could keep in contact with other railway personnel. Later in the morning Alan Futter stopped me and asked what I was doing; I told him that I was still liaising with the fire brigade. He told me that this was no longer required as the control point was now established, and I was to go back to Waterloo and try to keep the service running on the Windsor lines as well as possible so that we were ready for the evening peak.

The interior of Wimbledon Park signal box in 1988.   *Author*

At Waterloo I went to the station control room and tried to assess the situation which as expected was pretty chaotic. The TCS came to me and said that he was worried because earlier he had phoned a driver, Arthur Creech, who lived in Basingstoke, to come to work on his rest day to cover a vacant job. Arthur had not arrived and although he could well have been delayed by the Clapham incident it had been several hours now without word from him. I managed to contact Ernie King on the site and told him of my fears; he called back later to say that it was thought that Arthur was one of the fatalities in the crash. I was upset as I had known him well from my time as a driver at Waterloo.

It was a terrible day and one that I would not like to experience again. Strangely enough, apart from the period when I thought that my daughter was a victim, I coped with it well and suffered no ill effects, possibly because I had practised in Operation Drain and was not overawed by the emergency operation. When I have thought about it since then I picture the scene as a series of photo frames. One picture which always appears is of people walking along the track in their socks although I don't remember noticing this at the time.

Some time later the GM came to the AM's office and thanked all those who were involved in the incident. It is the sort of thing that can't happen but it did. It had a profound effect on everybody but luckily the cause was found very quickly so that everybody was aware of the reason for the accident. The inquiry held by Sir Anthony Hidden QC was very thorough and the recommendations very firm. This was to have an effect on my future career although I did not know it at the time.

In 1989 another reorganisation was in the offing and again there was uncertainty but, as the details emerged, I could see that I was out of a job again. Basically, part of the Waterloo area was to be taken over by the area manager at Feltham, leaving only Waterloo and Clapham Junction in the Waterloo area, although the AM at Waterloo would remain responsible for signalling in his previous area, to allow continuity in the progression of WARS (Waterloo Area Resignalling Scheme). Under this scheme the individual signal boxes in the area would be decommissioned and the signalling controlled from a new signalling centre at Wimbledon.

The interior of Wimbledon 'A' signal box in 1988.   *Author*

Chapter Thirteen

Station Manager, Wimbledon

When details were published I applied for the position of station manager at Surbiton, which was a job that I knew well and was vacant at the time. As the scheme was restricted to the areas concerned and the job was the same grade as my present position I felt that it was a formality and was quite happy to wait for the move. Unfortunately, it was not a formality, the AM at Feltham had different ideas. He offered me the position as station manager at Wimbledon which I did not want. Having covered all the station managers' positions in the area I knew that the Wimbledon job was the most difficult of all and I felt that it was under graded. Anybody would have to be mad to take on this job at the same grade as the much quieter jobs at Surbiton and Epsom. I made my views known but to no avail; I was told that I could take it or leave it so I had to take it, but I was not happy about it. In my new position I was responsible for 11 stations, Earlsfield, Wimbledon and Raynes Park on the main line, the three stations on the East Putney branch and five from Motspur Park to Chessington. To make it more difficult, I was responsible for operations in my area but had no responsibility for, or authority over, the signalmen

I was awaiting the outcome of my application for re-grading on the grounds that I had covered MS2 positions for more than 25 per cent of the past year so it was possible that I would get a higher grade anyway. I started the new job on 1st January, 1989 and had decided to make the most of a bad job. This was to prove more difficult than expected because of the 'Norbiton Wall'. This imaginary barrier had the same effect as the Berlin wall in that it kept me out. I don't know if this exclusion was on purpose, and I expect that the functional managers in the Feltham area would deny that it existed, but both myself and the SM at Epsom, Peter Dixon, certainly suffered from it. I went to area meetings at Feltham and although the other participants were friendly it was noticeable that there was little or no interest in what happened on my side of Norbiton. I worked hard to bring my patch up to standard but was discouraged by the AM who made his own decisions without consulting or advising me.

During my time at Wimbledon I was permanently involved in station renovation work which started with all the stations having their lighting renewed and special equipment installed in readiness for 'driver-only' operation. Although the plans were never implemented the equipment was installed ready for the new form of working. The station at Wimbledon was repainted as were several of my other stations, the final project involved paving the whole of the high level area and the District (London Underground) side concourse with terrazzo. I dealt with all the problems associated with this work largely on my own with little assistance from Feltham. David Gould who was now the commercial manager for the area was more helpful but he had many other problems in addition to mine. On top of these problems, a senior figure at the Health and Safety Executive passed through Wimbledon station every day and often picked me up on various items to do with the renovation work. He did not hesitate to threaten to close the station if Health and Safety requirements were not strictly adhered to.

I was also closely involved with the local authority, London Underground and London Buses in planning a major reorganisation of the station forecourt and street layout. It was planned to construct a bus depot just off the street, build a road down the side of the station and around the back of adjacent shops, rearrange the taxi rank and generally improve the facilities at the station. The British Rail Property Board were also involved in this process and at the preliminary meetings each party made their views known; gradually the plan was developed to include as many items as possible raised by the various parties. A lot of money was spent on surveys and various other exercises and the plan was progressing well, or so we thought. At a meeting in my office London Underground quite unexpectedly announced that they would not support the scheme unless there was an entrance to the District side of the station at concourse level direct from the new road which was to be built at the side of the station. The BR Property Board would not agree to this as it would take passengers away from the retail outlets at street level which were an important source of revenue at the station.

The outcome of this was that the scheme was eventually put 'on ice' and I had no more dealings with it. I had spent a lot of time and energy on this scheme and with little or no help from Feltham I had to deal with all the various parties, including the local taxi drivers' association who were particularly adamant in their views, especially as they were also in conflict with 'mini cab' companies who were trying to muscle in on their territory. It was difficult enough doing my normal job without all these added problems and it really began to get me down.

I sometimes felt that other people were actively working against me; one such occasion was when I planned to move the station supervisors to an office on the District side of the station and make them responsible for some aspects of running my other stations. The office move depended on the telephone systems being moved which should not have taken long. As time went by I got more and more frustrated. I spoke to the technical services manager to try to get the telephone work carried out as soon as possible, he told me that the AM had put a stop on the work. I phoned the AM to ask why and he said that he did not think the move was a good idea. I had kept him informed of what I was planning and he had raised no objections at the time. He had decided to block the planned work but failed to tell me, no wonder I was getting disillusioned.

In another instance I had complained about the difficulty I was having in getting the stores that I ordered and that my store room was almost bare. One day a van turned up and delivered all the stores that I had asked for. The following day the personnel manager and her assistant came to Wimbledon and asked to see my store which of course was well stocked. After three months of waiting I suspected that it was a set up and did not take kindly to the suggestion that I was complaining about nothing.

The personnel manager was not much help either. One of my female staff had a breast removed and I asked the personnel manager to visit her when she came home from hospital. She declined and suggested that I should visit her. I did not think that this was the right thing to do but eventually persuaded my wife to come with me, I still found it embarrassing and was annoyed with the personnel manager. I was even more annoyed when one of the staff was diagnosed as having motor neurone disease. I advised the personnel manager and asked her to visit this person to advise him of his entitlements. She did not visit him at all and one day when she was holding a 'surgery' at Wimbledon I saw this man walking across the station. He could not talk by this time but I ushered him into the room where the personnel manager was and she then had to deal with him.

When the booking hall and bridge were being resurfaced I had the old ticket collectors' boxes removed and when the floor was complete I had some newer boxes installed which had been redundant from the Chessington branch when the stations were de-staffed. I ordered new direction signing for the booking hall and overbridge as the old 'light boxes' were really tatty and the control wiring had been removed with the old boxes. The signing did not arrive and as the old equipment had been removed there were no signs at all so we had to use hand written notices. I phoned the signing company and was told that the AM had told them not to do the work. I was furious and I could see that I was not going to get anywhere, so I wrote to the AM setting out my objections and asking for a personal interview to try to sort out what the problem was and why I was being treated in this way.

Shortly before this Alan Futter had moved over to work on the new Eurostar project and the AM Feltham had taken responsibility for both Feltham and Waterloo areas. I did not send the letter as I thought it might be construed as 'whingeing' on my part, also as he was responsible for both areas I felt that he had enough on his plate without my complaints. It was mentioned at an area meeting that somebody was required to do a special project related to the implementation of the recommendations of the 'Hidden' report into the Clapham crash. After the meeting the AM asked if I would be prepared to do this work. I jumped at it as I saw a chance to get out of the situation I was in, the pressure was becoming unbearable and I was totally demoralised. The station manager at Kingston, Brian Humphreys, was to take over my job while I was away and I was happy to leave it in capable hands.

The project involved investigating the current situation regarding staff leave entitlements with a view to setting up a system to ensure that all current and outstanding leave was taken in the current year. The next objective was to ensure that staff were rostered within the guidelines laid down in the Hidden report. After some time gathering information I devised a chart to set it out in ready to use format. This proved to be very interesting and I could see that there were going to be some problems in changing staffing arrangements to comply with the recommendations.

One day Brian Humphreys phoned me to say that he had been told that he was going to become permanent in the position at Wimbledon. I was shocked as nobody had spoken to me about it. I asked the AM for a personal interview during which he confirmed that this was going to happen and that it was due to my poor performance at Wimbledon. This was news to me as nobody had ever complained about my work. I was hurt; I went to my brief case and took out the letter that I had written previously but not sent. The AM asked me why he had not seen it before and I told him why I had not sent it. He told me that I would not be going back to Wimbledon anyway but was to carry out a new project in preparation for another reorganisation. I was not sorry.

I went down to Wimbledon to see Brian Humphreys and put his mind at rest because he felt bad about what had happened. I was surprised to see the signs that I had asked for in position, they looked really good. Why they had suddenly appeared after my departure is anybody's guess but being cynical at the time I suspected that it was something to do with Brian coming from the right side of the Norbiton wall. I was also surprised to find the station supervisor in his new office as I had planned. Anyway, I was glad to be out of it, it had been the worst period of my career and I don't believe that it was all my fault.

Bearing in mind my intense dislike for football and its adherents, it is ironic that I should have appeared in a local paper with Gordon Banks, the famous England goalkeeper and one of my heroes before I was turned off the game. I was advised that two of my stations had won a prize in a regional energy saving competition. I have no idea how this came about because as far as I was aware no special efforts had been made, but nevertheless the prizes were awarded and were presented by Gordon Banks. Some of the staff were quite excited about this but they could claim no credit for winning the prize so it was a bit of a farce really.

The author is seen with former England International and Stoke City goalkeeper, Gordon Banks on 27th September, 1989.   *Author's Collection*

One thing which I can count as a success while in this position was saving 'Laddie'. Laddie was an Airedale terrier which used to walk about Waterloo station with a money box on his back, collecting for the Southern Railwaymen's Orphanage at Woking. When he died he was stuffed and put on display in a glass case on platforms 7 and 8 at Wimbledon station. There was a slot in the box for people to put money in so he still collected for the orphanage. I had a letter of complaint one day which said that I should be ashamed of myself, even when the dog was dead we made it work. I don't know how serious the complainant was but I took no notice. One day I was at a meeting to discuss some renovation work and a senior person told me to 'Get rid of that mangey dog'. I was upset about this as I saw Laddie as part of the Southern Railway history. I phoned the National Railway Museum at York and told them what my instructions were and they agreed to take Laddie away. I was very pleased some years later when I visited the museum and found Laddie on prominent display.

I had still heard nothing about my upgrading claim. The personnel manager at Waterloo assured me that it had been sent to Feltham when the reorganisation took place, the personnel manager at Feltham denied all knowledge of it so I went to my trade union, the Transport Salaried Staffs Association (TSSA) and asked them to find out what had happened to my claim; they agreed to investigate.

The author with Laddie at the National Railway Museum, York.   *Author*

Chapter Fourteen

Special Duties and a New Job

The new organisation which came into being in 1992 was to be called 'Organising for Quality' or O4Q for short, it encompassed the principles of 'total quality management' (TQM). The former South Western division was going to be split in two with the London area called 'South Western Lines' based at Waterloo and the country area called 'Wessex' based at Southampton. The functions were also to be divided into Operating and Retail, each with a separate management structure but sharing Personnel services. The area managers disappeared under this scheme and we were nearly back to the old divisional structure albeit in a different form. (Almost full circle in fact.)

To ensure that the safe operation was maintained I and another Manager, Dick Sharpe, were to set up a rules and regulations regime which identified precisely what each member of staff needed to know. A meeting was held at Southampton to agree the principles of the project and after that Dick and I set about creating the new format. It was not as easy as we first thought because the first idea had been that staff should be categorised by grade when deciding the rules and regulations they needed to know. However, a person in a grade at one station may have a completely different requirement to a similarly graded person at another station. For example, a leading railman at Netley on the Southampton to Portsmouth line had no operating responsibilities at all; there were no points or signals at the station and he spent most of his time in the booking office. The leading railman at Motspur Park, between Raynes Park and Epsom, was responsible for emergency operation of the points at Motspur Park Junction, the emergency crossover points at Worcester Park, the level crossings at Motspur Park and West Barnes Lane, as well as working on suburban lines with a frequent train service.

Nevertheless we felt that even the leading railman at Netley needed to know a certain amount for safety reasons. We therefore looked at every grade at every station and decided what they needed to know, then went carefully through the Rules and Regulations books and drew up a series of modules based on the levels of knowledge that we had identified. The first module was 'basic knowledge' such as how to call the emergency services, how to arrange for the traction current to be isolated in emergency, how to contact the signalman to arrange for the line to be blocked. Each module thereafter included more and more operating knowledge until the highest one, 'advanced operating knowledge' was reached. Each module stood on its own but whichever level was applicable to a post, all the modules lower than that level were also applicable.

Having created the modules, each position was examined and a list of modules shown against the position, any person working in the position must be trained to the level required by the stated modules. To simplify the system it was presented in a pyramid format with the mobile operating supervisor (MOS) at the top. Each module was given a three letter identification code, i.e. BSK for basic knowledge, ADV for advanced, etc. and each position at each station had a list of applicable codes against it. This enabled the MOS easily to identify the training requirement for each position when carrying out annual refresher training. Although it may sound complicated, it was in fact very simple to operate. We even extracted clause numbers from the rules and regulations and listed them in each module so that there was no misunderstanding and the MOS knew exactly which rule or part of a rule to test people on. If I say so myself, it was a superb system which worked well in practice and we were justly proud of it. The whole thing was entered on computer and could be easily modified if the local situation changed.

When the new organisation was set up I was placed as 'Head of Section, Operations', basically, I was the office manager in the operating department with responsibility for Safety & Systems, Rosters, Performance, Accidents & Incidents and various other bits and pieces. The former AM Feltham was to be the movements manager for the 'inner' area so he was still my boss. I was not worried about this because since the time when I showed him my letter he had been more affable towards me. David Gould was to be the audit & performance manager and I would be working closely with him again. One thing that did concern me was that my job specification said that I should be 'computer literate': I was not. I had picked up the basics in the old administration office but I had an enormous amount to learn. This was obviously a priority but there was still no formal training course so I had to find out for myself. We used a system called 'MultiMate' and it was not very 'user friendly', especially when I was using it. Luckily there were some young people among my staff who understood the system so I could call for help when I got stuck. When I did something wrong and could not put it right I would call out for Jason or Andrea to fix it, which they always did in no time at all. The problem was that they would never tell me what I had done wrong so I was unable to avoid the same mistakes again.

This position was a completely new experience for me and it took me some time to get into it. Although I only had 13 staff their functions were very diverse and I was more involved in quality control than actually doing the work. Most of the staff were fairly expert in their own field and could be relied upon to follow their remit, but I sometimes found failures when I was asked for specific information so their procedures had to be modified to encompass new requirements. My experience 'outside' was helpful when interpreting information gathered, especially with regard to accidents and incidents; the staff collated the facts but I was able to read between the lines and this proved useful at times.

After some months my boss moved away on promotion and the new movements manager was Jim Turner. I had known Jim for a short time when he came to the Waterloo area as parcels manager under Alan Futter. I did not know much about him but he had a reputation for having oddball ideas so I was not sure what was in store for me. There had been several appointments at Waterloo over the years of people from the London, Tilbury & Southend line, they were jokingly called the 'Essex Mafia' and Jim was one of them. However, once he was established I got on well with him and we developed a good working relationship. Jim, David and myself worked well together and covered each other's jobs when one or more was away. I found myself dealing with more and more of the business of the area and began to enjoy myself. I had improved my computer skills and my calls to Jason and Andrea were fewer, although I still managed to get into problems at times. Jim asked if I would cover John Jacobs, the operations manager at Woking, while he was on leave, I agreed and thoroughly enjoyed myself for two weeks, it was almost as good as a holiday for me.

The retail manager came to see me one day and told me that one of my former chief clerks had been arrested for 'cooking the books'. He had apparently been doing so for several years and in such a way that he was not detected by the checking system. He had embezzled a large amount of money and I was glad that my signature was not on his accounts. I was surprised as I had thought that he was a good person, he was certainly good at his job, (too good perhaps). However, I was not surprised that it had happened, it was the sort of thing that I suspected could happen when the LTM 2 scheme was implemented.

There were changes in the organisation and people moved to different areas. Phil Chatfield was the special projects manager and Noel Hutchinson was the performance manager who followed up all performance failures. Both of these people moved on and Jim Turner asked me if I would be prepared to take on both jobs combined. The main project which Phil had been involved in was the refurbishment of the Waterloo & City line and this project was apparently nearing completion. I agreed to take the new job and looked forward to it as it would give me the opportunity to get out and about again.

The performance side of the job was fairly easy as there were established procedures to gather any relevant information, I was involved in the follow up and report writing. The project side was more difficult for various reasons, the main one being that the Waterloo & City scheme had been running for several years and I was not aware of all that had happened until that time. It was a big scheme which involved replacing the signalling system and the rolling stock as well as many other items associated with these two. I attended regular meetings and gradually grew in confidence as I learned more about the planned work. I also found a lot of questions which did not have a satisfactory answer as far as I was concerned and I had some in-depth conversations with the various engineers, trying to get them clear in my mind.

I am not an engineer but my previous jobs had given me a wide appreciation of engineering problems, especially from an operating point of view. I could see that if the scheme went ahead as it was there were going to be problems. One thing which was a priority was the production of new operating instructions for the line. The line had always been treated separately and had specific operating instructions, with the new signalling system and new trains the existing instructions could not be applicable; the changes were so widespread that the instructions would have to be completely re-written. An expert from headquarters was brought in and I worked closely with him; he did an excellent job and the new instructions were ready in time for the training of staff before the line was opened after refurbishment. Other problems arose as the project progressed; partly they were associated with the fact that the new signalling system and trains were designed to operate automatically but, because it was planned to operate the line manually at first, the equipment would not be used in the way it was designed.

Waterloo & City unit No. 482509 during running trials for the new rolling stock and signalling system in 1993. *Author*

Consulting engineers were brought in to conduct a HAZOP exercise. The first thing established was the safe parameters of every part of the equipment and operation, then each part was examined in detail to establish the likelihood of anything exceeding the safe parameters. Several items were highlighted for further study and eventually everybody was satisfied that the scheme as planned would be safe when put into operation. The date was set for closure of the line. It was planned to carry out all the required work in six weeks which I thought was a bit ambitious, but having studied the plan I could not really fault it; the line was closed and work commenced.

The work went surprisingly well and apart for a few minor hiccoughs we were ready for staff training on schedule. I had agreed a training schedule for drivers with the training school. It was a tight programme and we had to arrange static training before the traction current was available, which we did by using a temporary 'jumper' to liven up a unit in the depot. Unfortunately this temporary supply was not available on the first day of training so the programme had to be further revised. After several minor alterations to the schedule we had enough drivers trained to start the service when the line was opened, additional drivers would be trained when the service was running. The signalmen received their training while the drivers were doing their practical driving training.

There was a problem with the traction current supply initially but this was sorted out. The trains were no problem at all, much to everybody's relief, and on opening day all the project team had their fingers crossed that all would be well. The first day went reasonably well but as the service progressed various problems arose which caused some head scratching. One of these concerned the train suspension which was designed to adjust automatically to the load being carried. This had caused no problem during testing or training and similar trains were running on London Underground's Central line without problems. Because this line had just two stations, one at each end, all the people got on and off at once and the suspension did not have time to adjust to such an immediate change of loading; the suspension was modified to overcome the problem.

There was also a problem with the traction current which was related to the operation of a current balancing system, this caused the current to be cut off from time to time until it was sorted out. Another problem concerned a computer system which monitored the signalling operation and sometimes shut things down for no apparent reason, again this had to be rectified. The biggest problem which caused the line to be closed on occasion related to the trip wire system. This system had been installed when the line was modernised in the 1940s and consisted of two wires attached to insulators on the tunnel wall. If there was a serious problem such as a breakdown, the driver attached a telephone handset to the wires using two alligator clips. When he did this the traction current was isolated automatically, the tunnel lights came on and he was in voice contact with the signalman. This system had worked perfectly prior to the shutdown but for some reason proved to be a problem with the new equipment and we were not allowed to run a service without it so there were several days without trains on the line. It was eventually sorted out but a lot of important people got very annoyed about it and eventually the Chairman of the Board, now Robert Reid, came to see the project team in order to resolve the problem. It was the first time that I had met him and I was impressed by his knowledge of the project, he knew a lot more about it than I did; anyway, the team sorted out the problem. Eventually the operation of the line settled down and I was able to concentrate on other aspects of my job which I had neglected. I had some catching up to do but I was enjoying my work again; Jim Turner had shown great faith in me and I had regained the confidence in my ability which I had lost when I was under the Feltham area.

During this period David Gould and I were actively involved with the British Transport Police in setting up table-top exercises which were to be held at regular intervals and included staff from the emergency services. They were held at various geographical locations and local staff from the Police, Fire Brigade, Ambulance service and Hospitals as well as selected railway staff attended. The aim of these exercises was to familiarise these various people with the arrangements which applied when dealing with an 'emergency railway situation', not only from their own point of view but what the other people involved would be expecting and what they would do. They were really useful exercises and I certainly learned a lot from them. I hope that the other people who attended found them as useful as I did.

The first exercise was held at an hotel in Guildford, to which we went on the previous evening and set up the room, the table-top model and made arrangements for refreshments, etc. We had a large model railway which included such features as embankments, viaducts, tunnels, etc. We jointly decided that the scenario would be based on local knowledge. Some imagination was involved in this but we were able to create a scene which reasonably reflected a location with which the participants would be familiar. We set out the model as if a railway accident had occurred and each participant was given a briefing note which described the physical conditions and other special features of the incident.

Participants were divided into groups with a member of each function in each group. Questions were asked based on the table top scenario and were discussed within the groups, each group then gave answers based on their discussion. Any answer which was considered to be in error was further discussed with the whole room and the errors pointed out. Each group member had the benefit of learning from the other members, who obviously looked at the situation from their particular viewpoint, so it was a joint learning exercise. As the day went on the scenario was expanded as the incident progressed and at the end of the exercise the whole thing was discussed. It was an excellent format and the two BTP officers, Brian Gillett and Bob Drake, who facilitated it really put a lot of work into getting it right. David and I also put in a lot of effort but it was very rewarding.

At the first meeting, as the BTP officer was outlining the fire precautions for the building, the fire alarm went off and we had to evacuate for a time until it was established as a false alarm. I thought that this was done on purpose but everybody denied responsibility. At a later meeting in an hotel in Ascot the same thing happened, but this time there was a real fire and we had to wait even longer until the local brigade had put it out. Some of the fire brigade personnel attending this exercise had also attended the devastating fire at Windsor Castle and I had a long, interesting conversation with some of them while we were waiting to get back into the hotel.

I attended the Surrey Fire Brigade headquarters at Reigate one day with a Control manager and somebody from the 'rules' section at Headquarters as part of the liaison generated by these joint exercises. While we were there an emergency was declared due to a train derailment at Bookham, between Effingham and Leatherhead. We were in the control room at the time and it was very interesting to watch the event develop from a different perspective. It was very similar to what I had learned to expect from the joint exercises, which was gratifying. One item I picked up on was that the controllers were not sure who they were speaking to at British Rail when dealing with such an emergency and were obviously ignorant of the internal working of the railway organisation. I felt that this was a problem that could be rectified, so I organised a tour of important railway installations in the area and invited senior personnel from the fire, police and ambulance control rooms to attend.

We started the day in the telephone exchange at Waterloo where all emergency calls on the Southern Region were dealt with. We then went on to Control where arrangements were co-ordinated to ensure that emergency personnel were safe on the line. After lunch we went to the electrical control room at Raynes Park and then to the Area Signalling Centre at Wimbledon. These tours were well received and I personally felt that all those attending gained from them.

Another interesting scheme which David and I got involved in was the introduction of 'Cab Secure Radio' which allowed drivers and signalmen to speak directly with each other without the driver leaving his cab to use a lineside telephone. This had been one of the recommendations of the Hidden report and was gradually being implemented. It was a complex scheme and we held joint meetings with the engineers involved, representatives of drivers and signalmen and operations managers. Most of the trains had been fitted with the new equipment and many of the problems involved areas of bad reception, later problems related to the proper use of the equipment and this became an auditable item. Although all the relevant staff received training, some of them were not very adept at using the system and it was a long time before we could have full confidence in its use.

Privatisation of the railway industry was now coming up fast and all sorts of arrangements were being made in preparation for this. I attended a meeting with senior British Rail staff and their counterparts from London Underground, to agree principles for joint operation where lines ran parallel or one's trains used the other's tracks. I highlighted the problem of LUL drivers working over lines which were operated by BR and where the BR rules applied. This had always been a problem between Wimbledon and East Putney and it was planned that LUL would take over this section of line in the new regime. Unfortunately the signalling was controlled from the new Area Signalling Centre at Wimbledon and the panel which controlled the East Putney line also controlled other lines. There was no way that a signalman could control one line using BR rules and another using LUL rules which were considerably different. The other participants at the meeting did not think it would be a problem but later events were to prove them wrong and BR rules had to be applied after LUL took over the line. It might have been resolved earlier if I had been taken seriously at the time but it was not to be so a lot of argument was caused.

Another line to be taken over was the Waterloo & City line. This was a shame because the project team had spent a lot of time getting it right and no sooner had they achieved their goal than we were to give it up. I spent a lot of time with various LUL managers arranging the handover and it was surprising to me that these people had very different ways of operating than we had on BR. Nevertheless it was interesting and I felt that I was doing something useful. On the Thursday evening before Easter 1993 I handed over the W&C keys to John Lamb, the LUL operations manager, and that was the end of a long history of the line being operated by BR and its predecessor companies.

The author presents the W&C keys to John Lamb of LUL. W&C supervisor Terry Murphy is holding the key box. *Author*

Chapter Fifteen

Railtrack South West

Things were hotting up on the privatisation front and various people were moving location in readiness for the new organisation. A company called Railtrack was to own and operate the 'railway' nationwide, and train operating companies would pay for the privilege of running trains on the tracks. That is a very simplistic outline of what was going to happen. There would be two main companies in the South Western area, namely Railtrack South West and South West Trains (SWT). I had no idea where I would finish up or even if I would have a job at the end of the day, yet more uncertainty. We were given a briefing one day on 'Franchisation'. I took the minutes for this meeting and when I typed them up and used the 'spell check' the computer did not recognise the word 'Franchisation'. When I pressed the suggestions button the only alternative offered was 'Fornication'; I was tempted to leave it in the text but thought better of it.

Early in 1994, David Gould moved to Friars Bridge Court, an office building near Blackfriars bridge to prepare for the new organisation; he was to be involved in performance monitoring in the new world. I took over his job and continued to do the other two jobs at the same time. This was not that difficult as the workload had reduced on the projects side of things and much of his performance work was related to what I had been doing. I was very busy and enjoying myself.

It was decided that I would be moved to Railtrack when the reorganisation took place and would work in the headquarters building at Waterloo. This suited me as it was easy to get to from home. My title was to be safety audit manager and I was to work with a team of people in a section of the operations office. I spent half a day in the new office getting to know the new people and finding out what the new job entailed. It was an odd set up because I was to introduce the audit system, organise and manage it but would not attend any of the area meetings. I would report my findings to my boss, who would attend the meetings and advise me of items from the meetings which concerned me. However, I was going to have my work cut out in organising it all so this was probably not a bad thing.

Unfortunately, I had been waiting to go into hospital for an operation and the appointment came on the day before I was to start my new job. I was off work for three weeks and when I returned most of the people had already set themselves up in the new organisation. This put me at a disadvantage but I soon got to know where everything was and what everybody did. My remit was quite wide ranging and I was required to visit the whole of the Railtrack 'zone' at various times to conduct audits on the safety systems. The zone reached from Waterloo to Portsmouth, Weymouth, Honiton and Reading plus everywhere in between these points. There were operations managers at Waterloo, Woking, Feltham, Eastleigh, Bournemouth and Salisbury. I concentrated on these areas first as I felt that it was important that those at the sharp end had the benefit of an organised audit first. The other departments and sections had to be included in the audit process but there was no existing audit procedure for them at the time. I decided to modify the operating audit procedure to suit each section but it would have to wait until I had perfected the operating audit.

Railtrack South West consisted of the Operations departments of the former 'inner' and 'outer' area of the 'O4Q' organisation plus technical sections related to the old Permanent Way department, the old Signal & Telegraph department, the old Electrification department and the telephone section of the S&T which became British Rail Telecommunications Ltd (BRT). The former technical departments were now considered to be contractors with a view to eventual privatisation. The related sections within Railtrack were mainly involved in planning and monitoring the work which was carried out by these contractors.

Railtrack owned the infrastructure and was responsible for operating the railway. It operated the signalling system and all the signalling staff were employed by Railtrack. The outbased operations managers and their staff were responsible for safe working of the railway in their own area, dealing with day to day problems and incidents. Each of the operations managers had a list of items which had to be checked at regular intervals and it was my job to ensure that these checks were made and recorded. There were a wide variety of items on the list including such things as level crossings which had to be tested and the associated signs checked, and the hours worked by staff; this was in response to the Hidden recommendations and was a follow on from the work that I had done when on special duties. By this time my initial work had been developed into a strict regime which controlled the amount of hours and consecutive days that staff were allowed to work. Any infringements of the guidelines had to be authorised by the local operations manager and the reason explained. Staff safety training and communications were another important item.

There were 31 sections in my audit document and all of these applied to the operations managers; for the other sections/functions items were selected from the 31 as applicable. Each question within each section was given a score and a percentage score was given for each section; the scores were totalled and a final percentage was given. Some of the managers were less than happy with the score awarded but the system was totally objective and was as fair as it could be. Basically there was a question with a 'yes' or 'no' answer; I would then ask to see something to validate a 'yes' answer. A validated 'yes' answer would gain a score, a 'no' answer or an unvalidated 'yes' did not score; it was as simple as that and it worked. I felt that the system gave a good picture of the performance of each area and highlighted any failures so that action could be taken to rectify them.

I was given the benefit of a formal course in using a computer as we were using 'Windows' in the new organisation. I attended a course on Modern Safety Management run by Det Norse Veritas, a specialist safety training company, and I learned a lot although some of the principles were the same as those I had been using in previous jobs for some years. I attended another course at the same place to become an Accredited Safety Auditor (ASA) using the International Safety Rating System (ISRS) safety auditing system; to my horror and dismay I failed. This was a shock as I had never failed anything before; I still do not know why I failed but think that I must have had a mental block because when I sat the exam again some weeks later I sailed though it with no problems.

Although I was certified as an ASA I could not conduct accredited ISRS audits without first doing so under scrutiny, so I was certified, but not qualified. However, this was not a problem because our organisation was to be inspected

Waterloo from the air on 17th January, 1984. To the left of the main station roof is the 'Windsor side' section of the station, platforms 16-21 plus the hydraulic lift for access to the Waterloo & City line for rolling stock transfers, also the north sidings, at this time used mainly for berthing locomotives and electric units.

This view dates from 17th March, 1993; where the 'Windsor side' section, hydraulic lift and north sidings used to be, the new international terminal now stands. The new terminal extends far beyond the original station and sidings which used to end about level with the hexagonal building in Westminster Bridge Road. The original brick arch structure supporting this section was completely demolished and replaced with a concrete structure; from the bottom of the picture to the hexagonal is a completely new structure built out from the side of the original viaduct.

Realistic Photo Graphics Ltd

by an outside auditor. My job was to ensure that internal audits were carried out and the business conducted according to the ISRS principles. This was not easy as the various sections of the ISRS system did not fit the various sections of our organisation, so it was difficult to make specific applications of the system. Also, being a generic system which had originally been designed for the oil industry, it was sometimes difficult to interpret in railway terms.

I spent some time out on the areas and used the information gained to modify the local checking procedures, I also carried out my own safety checks at various locations which were in addition to the regular checks. It was an interesting job but I felt rather lonely at times; although I was part of a team a lot of my work was done on my own. I made scheduled visits, conducted audits, did spot checks and when in the office I wrote reports which were then passed on for examination and further action.

One of the things which I highlighted was that, although safe walking routes were established for Railtrack staff and these were posted at suitable locations, there was no check on the walking or access routes for staff belonging to other organisations working within the zone and I was unsure who was responsible for this function. I discussed this with the Director, Jim Morgan, and he agreed that we should keep a record of all such routes even though we were not directly responsible for them under legislation. The principle was agreed that Railtrack was responsible for maintaining walking and access routes as they were part of the infrastructure, but not responsible for inspecting them to ensure that they were in a suitable condition. This was the responsibility of the various employers in relation to the safety of their staff who used them.

This was taken up at a management meeting and it was agreed that all such routes on the zone would be listed, details would include who was responsible for inspections etc. I was given the job of putting the thing together; how that happened I don't know but I suppose that as I had raised the matter it was felt that I should resolve it. I contacted all the organisations which had staff working on the zone and asked for up to date information on walking and access routes. When it came in there was a mass of information and I had to try to condense this into a document of readable proportions.

I drew a chart on a piece of paper and the format was agreed. We then hired a person to put all the information on the computer in the agreed format; after some weeks all the information was entered and I printed a copy and submitted it for approval. It came back with comments but not approved. The problem was that I had collated the information from various organisations and given each of these their own section of the document; I felt that by doing this each organisation would only need part of the document which applied to them, making it smaller and easier to refer to. The Management team disagreed and wanted all the information in one document which would be issued to all parties.

We set about a full revision; this was done by colour coding each item in the document according to the 'prime user' of the route and then listing each item alphabetically according to location. This took another couple of weeks but the end result was a user-friendly document which contained a huge amount of information in an easy to read format. I was pleased with it and have to admit that it was better in the revised form. It was accepted by the 'top team' so I was doubly pleased.

The external audit of the zone was due in the November but I was not confident of the outcome. Although there were checking procedures for all aspects of the business, they were based on historical knowledge, not on risk assessment as required by ISRS. I could see no way to change this in the time remaining, it would be too complex. In fact, although the technical departments were all part of the new organisation their attitudes were firmly fixed in their previous organisations and I encountered some really negative responses to my 'interference'. However, the performance of the zone was going to be measured using this system and that was what I had to convince people they should be aiming for. I suggested that 'champions' should be selected to answer questions in the various sections of the audit document. This was accepted by the management team but nothing was done about it. I asked to attend one of their meeting to press the point and came out of the meeting after a short time having been nominated to select the champions myself. I was angry at this as I felt that the selection should have been a careful procedure following discussion of the audit document.

Again I had opened my mouth and put my foot in it. I made my selection based on my limited knowledge of the people involved and my even more limited knowledge of the way in which the audit document would be interpreted by the auditor in relation to the organisation. I went back to the meeting, presented my selection which was accepted and left again, not very happy. A meeting was arranged to brief the 'champions' on what to expect but in the meantime I received correspondence from the audit organisation which threw the whole thing into confusion. I had been briefing the 'champions' on the questions they would have to answer and which were important in relation to scoring within the system; it now transpired that performance was to be measured not only by the ISRS system but also by the safety case, the fire regulations and other aspects relating to the new railway organisation. This was to be carried out at the same time as the ISRS audit and so I had to brief people on the additional questions, some of which were not related to their own function.

I was concerned that we would achieve a poor score in the audit and that this would reflect on the morale of the staff who had put a huge amount of work in setting up the zone as it was. There were five levels to aim for in the ISRS system and I was doubtful if we could achieve even the first level. However, I kept this to myself and continued to give advice to the champions in the hope that my fears would not be realised. I sat in on all the audit interviews and was pleased with the responses: the champions had obviously put some effort into studying the documents. However, their answers had to be verified and were open to interpretation by the auditor which was where I could see some problems arising. The champions might make a different interpretation to the auditor and, although the questions were answered well, might not be given a positive score.

This was exactly what happened and without going into detail the zone did not achieve 'level one', although it did comply fully with all the industry standards which were measured at the same time. I felt that this was a poor result but not unexpected; it was ironic that even though all industry standards were met and the zone was obviously meeting its safety requirements it did not achieve anything in the ISRS system. Still, this was a first ISRS audit and could be used as a benchmark from which to move forward and the management team decided to take the bull by the horns and ensure that a better result was achieved at the next audit.

In pursuance of this there was to be some reorganisation within the department and a new position would become responsible specifically for the audit. The person selected for this position was the operations manager at Woking. I knew him from the previous organisation and expected to get on well with him. He had taken on a difficult remit and I was obliged to support him, although I felt that I could have done the job myself given the support from the management team. However, this was not to be; although I had worked well with him in the past I found him very difficult now and I could see that I was going to become totally ineffective. He was not much good at delegation and was insistent in being personally involved in all aspects of the department and he continually interfered with what I was doing.

I could see no future in the position that I was in and when I heard that there were going to be some offers of early retirement I let it be known that I was interested. I asked for details and was pleasantly surprised at the result. I would be able to retire with a pension, have enough money to pay off my mortgage and invest some for a rainy day. I was tempted but the offer had not actually been made at that time, it was only a possibility. I discussed this at length with my wife and after a lot of soul searching we agreed that if the offer was made I would accept it. We then went away on holiday to Italy hoping that when we returned something would have been decided.

It had. When I returned from holiday I was given three days to accept or decline the offer and I could finish in three weeks time, the choice was all mine. I accepted at once and set about finding out what I had to do in the next three weeks. When I went home that evening I had mixed feelings and some trepidation. When I had started work in 1956 I expected to retire at 65 as was normal at that time. As time went on the expected age came down to 62 and I revised my 'life plan' accordingly. Now I was only 54 and had accepted early retirement a full 11 years before my original expectations. I had decided that I did not want to actually retire from work but retire from the railway industry and find a little local job to keep me in pocket money and generally take it easy and do some of the things which I wanted to do.

The next three weeks absolutely flew by, my wife and I attended a seminar for people taking retirement which was very useful. Friday 13th October, 1995, the last day, came before I knew it. I went to work on this day feeling a little despondent, but a surprise was awaiting me. As I sat at Hook station waiting for my train an announcement was made over the PA system telling everybody that this was my last day at work and wishing me well. Then a group of my regular travelling companions appeared to congratulate me. I thought that this was a nice gesture and it cheered me up somewhat. When I took my regular seat on the train one of my neighbours who travelled on the same train came in and hung bunting and union jacks all over the compartment. This caused much comment as people joined the train at following stations and the mood in our compartment was quite jovial.

Having arrived at the office in a happy mood I spent most of the morning visiting various people to say goodbye. It was strange that I would no longer be part of all this while these people would continue with their jobs and I felt a little sad that I would no longer be 'on the railway'. After lunch Jim Morgan, the Director, made a presentation to me of a limited edition print of Terence Cuneo's painting of Clapham Junction in 1966, a picture that I have always admired. I was touched and not a little embarrassed by the applause and good wishes from all those present.

Later that afternoon a 'leaving do' had been arranged in a private room at a local pub. A lot of the people from the office came as did some that I had known from my previous jobs. It was a happy occasion and I was sad when it was time to go home. I sat on the train with my wife, my daughter and her husband, and had many mixed feelings. The end of a career of 39 years during which time I had worked my way up from being an engine cleaner to an important position in middle management. The strange thing was that I had not achieved this by ambition. My original ambition was to be an engine driver in the days of steam, I achieved this but my other achievements were pure chance or based on the circumstances at the time. I moved from position to position as circumstances dictated; the only job I actually applied for was that of station supervisor at Waterloo and that was not because I particularly wanted the job, but was trying to get into a better position to get a job as motive power supervisor. It is strange how things work out, but I could not avoid the feeling that I had been 'eased out' and my elation at being released from a life of toil was balanced by the feeling that I had not completed my work and still had a lot more to give.

The last 12 years had seen a constant series of reorganisations and it was my view that after all these changes we were not very far from where we had started. Gerard Fiennes once said that when you reorganise, you bleed, and that people spend time reorganising rather than working. Although he said this many years ago, in my opinion he was spot on; I wonder if he could have foreseen the massive changes which were to take place between 1982 and 1994.

For my own part I found it frustrating. Every time a reorganisation took place we all put a lot of effort into making it work, then just as we were getting on top of it a further reorganisation was applied. It was a bit like building a sand castle on a beach and somebody knocking it down just as you finished building it. It is surprising that the industry survived intact without any major collapse of service. I think this was due to the commitment of the managers and staff rather than anything done at Board level. It is my view that the industry survived *despite* the BR Board's decisions.

Most of my career on the railway was very happy and looking back I could not have planned such a career. Of the few periods when things went wrong and I was not happy I hold no grudges. Some people did me no good at all but I imagine that they must have had their reasons for what they did. The fact that I suffered because of their actions was probably unintentional and just part of the scheme of things. All in all I have happy memories and feel that I did something worthwhile with my life. The fact that my career ended suddenly when I least expected it was just a result of the circumstances appertaining at the time. With privatisation looming it was probably a good time to depart from the scene. The generous retirement offer may not have been available from a private organisation and I know that I did the right thing at the time.

Leaving was a wrench but I took up a new position as a site manager for a cleaning company within three weeks so I did not have time to worry about it.

I find myself perfectly happy with my new life, only having to work a few hours a day. This is my choice and I prefer it to being out of the house for 12 hours a day and being under pressure for most of that time. I suppose I am semi-retired, but whatever, I am enjoying it and have a lifetime of memories of some lovely people and some very different events to sustain me.

I worked for the same organisation in various roles for 39 years and saw it transformed from the steam age to the electronic age. I like to think that I played a part in that transformation, especially in later years. I started work eight years after Nationalisation when people still remembered the 'Big Four' companies. I ended my career just before privatisation when there would be nearly as many companies as before the 'Big Four' were created. Full circle! But is it any better for it? My own view, which is probably biased, is that the British Rail organisation, especially when it was organised into sectors and run on sound business principles will take some beating (Network SouthEast was quite a dynamic organisation) and the only reason for going beyond this stage was political dogma. The Conservative Government was opposed to nationalised industries on principle and was determined to return the industry to private ownership.

The 'railway industry' has always suffered from bad publicity in the media and was rarely praised when they got things right, but the fact that the industry was transformed in the way it was should be recognised as an achievement in itself. Only time will tell if private companies can improve on what went before but the first signs are not good. Some people have invested and made a lot of money out of it and I am sure that lawyers and accountants will continue to do so for a long time, but has the travelling public gained anything? I doubt it.

A group of former Guildford enginemen pose beside Maunsell 'Q' class 0-6-0 No. 541 on an invited visit to the Bluebell Railway in June 1994. *From left to right*: not known, not known, not known, George Nurse, Clive Ingleton, Dave Cook, Dave Morton, not known, Eric Clark, George Baker, Charlie Hampshire, Dennis Osman, not known, Eddie Wells and Eddie Greaveshurd. *Author's Collection*